Covert Hypnosis

An Operator's Manual for Influential Unconscious Communication in Selling, Business, Relationships and Hypnotherapy

Kevin Hogan

Kevin Hogan
www.kevinhogan.com
Copyright 2001, 2006
Kevin Hogan
All Rights Reserved

Covert Hypnosis: An Operator's Manual for Influential Unconscious Communication in Selling, Business, Relationships and Hypnotherapy

Includes Bibliographic References

ISBN: 0-9709321-4-6

ISBN: 978-0-9709321-4-3

Psychology
Self-Help Techniques

Printed in the United States of America
Network 3000 Publishing
3432 Denmark Ave. #108
Eagan, Minnesota 55123
USA
(612) 616-0732
www.network3000publishing.com

Table of Contents

Module One
Covert Hypnosis

The title alone draws up images of the clandestine and secretive. And perhaps it should. My first goal in this manual is to show you how to utilize covert hypnosis in any setting, clinical or corporate, communication or selling.

Covert literally means, "Covered, disguised, concealed." We are going to utilize this definition.

Hypnosis literally means, "sleep." This is a poor definition and it is useless to anyone practicing hypnosis.

---

100 years ago, hypnotists would say, "sleep" when they wanted someone to go into trance. They simply misunderstood what was taking place in the subjects mind.

I am going to change the definition of hypnosis and use two different definitions often without notation throughout this text. The first definition of hypnosis I want to use is that hypnosis is "a narrowing focus of attention." We will also consider hypnosis as "dissociation" or complete "association" in this book. For example, we may have someone dissociate themselves from their current state of mind and maneuver their thinking into a different state of mind. If someone is speaking from a point of view that is dysfunctional, I may choose to covertly turn his or her thought processes towards outcomes. If someone is telling me how busy they are, I might just have them focus on the results they want and direct their attention to what is important instead of what is "busy." Sometimes they are the same and sometimes they are not.

It's not the subject of this text but hypnosis really is a lousy word, which almost needs to be re-defined as it is used in real time. Yes, it really means sleep but for the purpose of this text we are going to consider hypnosis as dissociating from one set of events or reality and associating to another experience or different reality. Then we focus in on the reality we decide we want the other person to focus on. We're going to go further than this in defining hypnosis.

Dave Elman defined hypnosis as "bypassing the critical factor of the mind." If we translate that into 21st century English, we come up with a more workable definition of hypnosis. Hypnosis is communicating with someone or some groups "mind" where the receiver of the message is using significantly less critical thought (questioning the message) to evaluate the message than they normally would.

> **Covert Hypnosis is, in part, influencing someone's (or some groups) unconscious mind(s) to change their behavior in some manner.**

In this book we are having people focus on things/events in a covert fashion. In other words, they don't know we are using covert hypnosis. It's secret. As soon as someone recognizes that they are not evaluating incoming messages the covert hypnosis is past.

For the purpose of this book, covert hypnosis is about bypassing the critical factor of the human mind without the process being known to the receiver of the message. A better way of understanding this from a social perspective is that covert hypnosis is accomplished when one person sends a message to another person and the message is received without significant critical thought or questioning on the part of the receiver.

Covert hypnosis is about state manipulation and management. The state of mind a person is experiencing at this moment may be productive or not. It might be depressed or not. It could be joyous or not. It could be scholarly or not. It could be volatile or not. When using covert hypnosis the hypnotist judiciously changes the state of mind of the individual from one state to another state.

> **If someone has lots of positive resources in their history you can utilize them. If they don't, you can point your subject(s) in the direction they need to go and take them as far as necessary using Covert Hypnosis. Most people don't have all the resources they need to make change so you will have to help create the directions and resources for new behavior.**

Imagine a six-pointed star like the Star of David. In the middle of the star you have a large area that will metaphorically represent the "core self" of the person. Each of the six points on the star represent "ego states" or part of the person that are not represented by other tips of the stars. One point could be "the volatile self." Another point could be the "scholarly self." Another point could be representative of the "gentle self." Another point could be representative of the "happy self." (Obviously we could use a 20 or 30 pointed star as a frame of reference in this metaphor but the six points make it nice and easy to understand.)

Let's imagine that a person is in the "volatile self" state. That point on the star, we'll call it point one, is pointing north. The point that is north is the state that is currently in "charge" of the entire self. If we find that dealing with the person in the state of "volatility" isn't useful at this moment, we can utilize the tools of covert hypnosis to spin the star to a more useful state. Perhaps the "scholarly self" is the third point on the star and that is the state we would like to access and maintain in our client, friend or loved one. Utilizing the tools of covert hypnosis, we help the volatile self disengage and spin the star so the third point faces north.

Covert hypnosis is, in part, the intentional manipulation of another person's ego states. This can include the intensification of a state of mind, the relaxing of a state of mind, the redirection of energies of a state of mind, the re-wiring or changing a state of mind and so on.

The volatile self, noted above, will not easily disengage, however. Generally speaking the more intense a state is, the more difficult it is to disengage.

Covert Hypnosis, among other things, includes shifting and maintaining specific ego states within another person or group of people.

Now, before we go any further, let's make sure we understand what covert hypnosis is and is not.

Examples of Successful Covert Hypnosis

1) A hypnotist tells a client to imagine the future clearly without formal trance induction and the client does so without saying, "I just can't see it..." IS using covert hypnosis.

2) A parent telling her children to stay away from the highway without the children significantly questioning the message IS using covert hypnosis.

3) A commercial on television that you receive without significantly questioning the claims IS covert hypnosis.

4) An ad in the newspaper that you read without significantly questioning the claims IS covert hypnosis.

5) A preacher who preaches a message and you accept it without significantly questioning the messages IS using covert hypnosis.

6) A salesperson that tells you about a product without you significantly questioning the message IS using covert hypnosis.

All of these experiences meet the criteria of covert hypnosis.

Examples of what is Failed Covert Hypnosis

1) A hypnotist who tells his client to see the future, but the client says, "I just don't know where I'm going…" is NOT covert hypnosis.

2) A parent who tells her children to do something and a fight ensues is NOT covert hypnosis.

3) A commercial on television that you receive and say, "I don't think that is even remotely true," is NOT covert hypnosis.

4) A weight loss ad in the newspaper that you read and say, "There is no way you can lose 10 pounds per week…" is NOT covert hypnosis.

5) A preacher who preaches a message and you like the preacher but you disagree with the message is NOT an example of covert hypnosis.

6) A salesperson that tells you about a product and you do not believe the salesperson is NOT an example of covert hypnosis.

You might wonder why in the case of the salesperson I didn't say that the person had to buy the product or service. Actually buying is not a sign of covert hypnosis. A person without the money could easily have been in "state" but they simply didn't have the money to buy. It should also be noted that you cannot always measure how much in "state" a person is.

Can a person be in a state of "fear" and be in trance? A state of "anger?" A state of "depression?" A state of "frustration?" A state of "annoyance?" You bet. All these are common everyday trance states, and it can be the desire of the person utilizing covert hypnosis to ethically or unethically access these states in someone. You might be wondering how someone who is being encouraged to access a state of "fear" could possibly be in waking trance. I can understand that, so let's look at some examples.

Imagine that someone tells you that if you don't pay your taxes you will go to jail. You may not like the person. You may not be in rapport with the person. But you probably trust them and believe them and you access the feelings of fear instantly. That is trance, and the person used covert hypnosis very effectively to get you into the state of mind that they wanted you to be in.

Imagine that someone asks another person what it would be like to have cancer and die a slow, agonizing, painful death because of smoking cigarettes. The person doing the imaging may not like the person, they may not trust the person, but if the person puts those pictures in their mind and follows the suggestions of the communicator, that is covert hypnosis because the listener did what the communicator asked without question.

As you can see, trust and belief are critical to hypnosis. Liking and rapport lead to trust and belief but they are not necessarily the same thing. Generally speaking, liking and rapport are necessary for belief and trust.

It's not necessary for you to like someone to be covertly hypnotized by them. Imagine someone puts a gun to someone else's head. That person's state shifts very quickly. Fear instantly takes over the body and a laser beam focus of attention to the exclusion of all other stimuli begins. Certainly there is nothing about "liking" the person holding the gun necessary for this trance.

That said, I believe it is very important for liking and affinity to play a role in almost all forms of Covert Hypnosis.

The Ethics of Covert Hypnosis

This book is not about walking up to people, performing the ritual of an induction and having someone fall into a deep eye-closed state of relaxation. That would serve no purpose in real life and could be very inconvenient in most all cases. This book is about utilizing the tools of hypnosis in a very "wide awake," often intense, and wide aware state. Before we go any further, let's look at the ethics of this.

Is it ethical to do this or to actually "change someone's mind?" Is it ethical to influence someone without his or her awareness? Is it ethical to influence someone with his or her awareness?

I certainly believe that it is not only ethical but also necessary for survival in the 21st century. I also know that the tools of covert hypnosis can be used for ill and that will never change.

Generally speaking, if you are utilizing the tools of covert hypnosis and you are doing so because of, and for, the best interests of another person you are probably utilizing covert hypnosis ethically. If you are utilizing the tools of covert hypnosis to promote the behavior of another person to do something that is not in their best interest, that is not ethical.

This conversation wouldn't be complete without asking, "Who are you to say what is in someone else's best interest." I completely understand. Please do remember that every day people are making hundreds of decisions for you on your behalf. These decisions are ethical and unethical. The Congress and the President tax your money and spend it. Some of those things are for ethical purposes and others are not. You did not have a say in the matter, however. If you are a parent, you make hundreds of decisions for and on behalf of your children. You tell them what they can and cannot do. You tell other people what they will do. If you are a teacher you are constantly making decisions for and on behalf of your students. One of the most common behaviors we take place in every day is making decisions for and on the behalf of other people.

The Power of Suggestion Changes Perception

Covert hypnosis is, in part, about creating change in the mind of your client without the client necessarily being aware of the changes that are occurring. The client has come to you and asked you to help them make the changes necessary in their lives. As will become obvious, a person's eyes don't have to be closed to covertly generate images in a person's mind, which become new memory.

What is the foundation of covert hypnosis? Dozens of elements seem to be involved in suggestibility. As we look at each of them throughout this book, you will discover what changes people's minds and you will see what is impotent. You'll see why a script is normally ineffective... but at the right time with the right words and the right conditions, your words will change minds and lives.

Suggestion Changes Perception…and can easily create false memories.

Elizabeth Loftus (one of the world's leading memory researchers) performed a fascinating experiment. She showed a film to a group of people. The film was about a traffic accident. After the film she asked the group, "How fast was the white sports car going when it passed the barn while traveling along the country road?" Several days later when witnesses to the film were quizzed about what they'd seen, 17 percent were sure they'd spied a barn, though there weren't any buildings in the film at all. In a related experiment, subjects were shown a collision between a bicycle and an auto driven by a brunette, then afterward were peppered with questions about the "blond" at the steering wheel. Not only did they remember the nonexistent blond vividly, but also when they were shown the video a second time they could hardly believe what they were seeing. It was nothing like they remembered it. Loftus concluded that hints leaked to us by our fellow humans over-ride the scene we're sure we've seen with our own eyes.

In another Loftus experiment done in the 1970's, the film is different. The people view slides of a pedestrian-auto accident. They also see a slide of a red Datsun at a yellow Yield sign. The group was asked, "Did you see the other car pass the Datsun while it was stopped at the Yield sign?" The biased recall group however was asked an even more biased question: "Did you see another car pass the Datsun at the stop sign?" Later most of the biased group remembered a Stop sign instead of a Yield sign! The verbal information again leaked into the visual recall. Suggestion changes perception….and can easily create false memories.

> **Suggestion from an *authority figure* can often over-ride a person's visual memory to create a new memory.**

How do we utilize this information in the clinical setting?

Most of this book is not dedicated to the clinical setting. Frankly, the clinical setting is the least common place that I use covert hypnosis every day. I'm going to start with the clinical setting then as the book progresses discuss more and more about how to use covert hypnosis in business and especially, selling.

Our objective is to use covert hypnosis to create images in the person's mind (see simple strategies for utilizing covert strategies earlier in this manual.) that target the behavior the client wants changed and paint pictures on the landscape of the mind that vividly show that the changes are going to be taking place. The brain will begin to see/remember what you tell it to, if you meet the other fundamental pillars of covert hypnosis which we will discuss in detail in the coming pages of this manual. To simply read off of a script and say, "The pain has gone, how do you feel?" is impotent. Once you have utilized the tools of covert hypnosis something quite different happens. The person will begin to feel less pain. There is no power in a script. There is enormous power (or not) in the hypnotist, the client, and the alliance of the therapist and the client. Once the fundamental power structure is in place in the hypnotist, the client and the alliance of the two then change can begin to take place and covert hypnosis becomes effective.

> **Covert Hypnosis allows you to paint pictures on the landscape of another person's mind.**

When Resistance is Likely, Distraction Creates a Receptive...and Easily Persuaded Mind.

Festinger and Maccoby conducted an experiment in which they attempted to prevent members of their audience from inventing arguments to refute messages being presented to them. (AKA resistance in hypnosis) This was accomplished by simply distracting the audience somewhat while the communication was being presented. Two groups of students were required to listen to a tape about the evils of college fraternities. The argument was powerful and was obviously not going to be well received by the audiences. During the presentation to one of the groups, the audience was also distracted by a highly entertaining silent film. (That group is engaged in TWO tasks simultaneously.) The other group was not disturbed by a film. They simply listened to the tape. What were the results of the experiment? The students who were distracted by watching the film underwent substantially more opinion change against fraternities than did the students who were not distracted.

The distracted mind is easier to manipulate and create change in than the undistracted mind.

How do you utilize this in the clinical setting?

Erickson said there was no such thing as resistance. Erickson was wrong. We now know that there is resistance. *There is resistance in the mind of every human being to that which the individual does not believe to be true. There is resistance in the mind of each person to that which creates fear within the individual.*

There is resistance in the mind of every human being to that which the individual does not believe to be true. There is resistance in the mind of each person to that which creates fear within the individual.

If any ego state is not in alignment with what messages are being shared between client and therapist, resistance will be met. Be aware of this now. The resistant client more often than not needs to experience pictures he creates in his mind not pictures created by the therapist. (See: *The Hypnotherapy Handbook, Hogan*)

1. **When Resistance is Unlikely, Affirm Present Beliefs.**

Numerous studies have been done that reveal that people are receptive to information and attitudes that agree with their point of view. People will formulate arguments on the spot against any point of view that disagrees with their currently held belief. Therefore: Always discover current beliefs and attitudes so you can affirm them. On the other hand, do not have your client verbally state anything that you will want them to change later. Once an attitude is communicated (verbally or in writing) it will be maintained, even in the face of overwhelming evidence to the contrary.

Key Point: Resistance is unlikely when people agree with the presented point of view. In these cases powerfully affirm the individuals point of view.

---

2. When Ego States Battle for the State of Mind Utilize Ambiguity.

Ambiguity allows ego states on both sides of a viewpoint to be equally accepted. By allowing different elements in the unconscious mind to be accepted, we validate the whole person and not just one part of a person's unconscious feelings, beliefs and attitudes. Erickson, for all his inconsistencies, was a master of ambiguity. Barton said that ambiguity is the vehicle for expressing conflicting feelings simultaneously. "Part" of the client wants to experience trance and another part doesn't. You say, "Please don't go into trance until you close your eyes." Both ego states are satisfied and trance is experienced. The suggestion is a bit confusing and distracting in itself. In some cases indirect suggestions can be helpful in facilitating trance or even creating a direction. "You may or may not find yourself wanting to be more productive in your everyday life." The obvious suggestion is to "be more productive" but because there is permission offered, "You may or may not...," there is no pressure on the unconscious parts that do not want to be productive. This permission for ambiguity is non-judgmental and can be useful when it is obvious there are internal battles brewing in any situation (clinical or non-clinical.)

Key Point: Be ambiguous when building rapport with someone who has battling ego states. This ensures that both (all) ego states will be honored and will enhance affinity with the hypnotist.

Critical vs. Uncritical Thinking

I remember speaking for a group of 30 or so one time about the subject of critical thinking. I had brought several Bibles and a baseball. One half of the baseball looked like every other baseball you see. The other half I painted black. I stood at the front and in the middle of this group. I held the baseball up in such a way that almost everyone saw either a black or a white baseball.

"What color is the baseball?"
Half said white and half said black.
"How sure are you that this baseball is the color you said it was?"
Most said they were sure or positive.
I rolled the ball onto the table. I threw it up in the air. I spun it. It was black **and** white. I remember thinking how important it was that people view the same thing or idea from many different vantage points before taking a stance on something in a definitive fashion.

I took out the Bible and I told a story about how David was told to take a census of all Israel because a war was about to take place. David would need to know how many men he had to fight his upcoming war. I explained how the books of Kings and the books of Chronicles were roughly the same story told by different writers. I had one group look up in several different Bibles one verse in Kings that cited this request of David to take a census. I had the other group look up the same module and verse in Chronicles. Here's what I did next.

"OK, loud and clear. Say it out loud. Even shout it: who told David to take a census?"
Half the people said, Satan and half said The Lord.
"How sure are you that you are right?"
"Positively sure. It says so right here."
It took a while to sort out but all of my participants soon came to realize the story was recorded very differently in the two books. (Kings and Chronicles) The group was dumbfounded.

"What's the point?" I asked.
Many responded that something was wrong, mistranslated, they compared all the translations. Some were angry! I let things cool down then I took over to cool the savage beasts I had just created.

"We become emotionally attached to things like Bibles. We have beliefs about these books. We expect this to be THE source. We expect it to be correct and without error. Someone told us that and some of us believed it. The fact is that when you look at something, anything, you must look at it from many different angles before drawing a conclusion as to what is true or real or right or wrong."

All of this is to teach us that perception is 9/10 of the law. What we believe we see to be true is what we consider to be true. We don't test our perceptions to see if they are true. We just perceive and assume stuff is real. That's what hypnosis is all about.

The baseball is black on one half and white on the other. Tools of covert hypnosis can be used to get people to see a black ball, a white ball or a ball that is half and half. The Bible (1 Chronicles 20:4) says that Satan moved David to take the census in one place and it also says it was The Lord in another passage (2 Samuel 24:1) referring to the exact same event. Two writers often yield two very different stories. With tools of covert hypnosis I could have had someone focus on one part of the Bible, ignore the rest and have the person come up with any conclusion I wanted. I could have told a story about the relationship of David and The Lord or David and The Devil **and** I could have proven the interest in the census of Israel with the Bible. To this day, I believe that David was working for the guy in the white hat...but I can't prove it.

Reframing: What it really means to reframe.

Here is what most people think of when they think of reframing.

"So can you see how having this problem has really helped you in your life?"

"Aren't you thankful now that you have had this experience so you can help others with the same problem?"

These are not reframes, they are things parents say to children that didn't faze the child and they still don't work 20 years later. A reframe **helps** the other person see the same situation or thing in a different light. A reframe does not create resistance because the person designing the frame is the person asking the questions. The person responding is actually building the reframe from the design questions offered by the re-framer.

Here is an example of a master re-frame, which is only borderline ethical in my opinion. A salesperson is selling to a customer.

Cr.: I can't afford this car. It's just too expensive.
SP: What can you afford?
Cr.: I can afford $300 per month. This is $330 per month.
SP: Can I ask you a question?
Cr.: Sure.
SP: Would you be happy driving this car?
Cr.: Of course. It's great.
SP: Is it worth $30 each month…one dollar per day to be happy?
Cr.: Yeah. It really is.

This is an old-fashioned sales closing that uses flawed logic on the part of the salesperson which creates the illusion (hypnosis) in the mind of the customer that one-dollar per day is going to make the customer happy. That of course isn't really what is happening. In reality it's $11 per day for this car. (330/30) This type of communication is what is considered borderline ethical. The customer is being asked to believe that happiness is costing $1 per day. The customer is also being unconsciously directed to not consider the actual cost of the vehicle. The salesperson could have said, "Isn't it worth one more dollar per day to have a car that will really make you happy?" That would be ethical.

The argumentative client is not a bad person. They simply are frustrated. They don't have answers and they want them. When people don't have answers and everyone thinks they are crazy they are backed into a corner. Here is a conversation where I used covert hypnosis to reframe the mindset of my client. I was explaining how sometimes our problems and health issues are not a result of a virus or a disease that comes into the body from without but from within. This raised the defenses within my client. Here is how I handled this woman. Watch closely what I do to defuse her frustration. Notice how I magically zap her defensiveness and then lay the foundation for healing.

Covert Magic

Ct.: But I don't think Fibromyalgia is not psychosomatic.

KH: When someone has cancer, do you believe that it's possible that their frame of mind and their environment could influence how long they will live?

Ct.: Of course.

KH: And influence the quality of their life?

Ct: Sure.

KH: Is cancer psychosomatic?

Ct.: Of course not.

KH: So the mind body connection is important for someone who has cancer.

Ct.: Yes. I agree.

KH: We know that some people have miraculous recoveries from cancer.

Ct.: I guess.

KH: You've heard about people who tell them that their doctor said their tumors had shrunk.

Ct.: Not very often, but yes, I've heard cases.

KH: Me too. And I wonder what it is that causes tumors to shrink. It certainly isn't the cancer. Cancer's natural track is to spread.

Ct.: That's true.

KH: So something aside from the disease is causing the cancer to remit in some cases.

Ct.: Yes.

KH: So my question is what is that?

Ct.: The mind?

KH: Yes. The mind's effect on the body. Exactly. Now think about your day-to-day life.

Ct.: I hurt.

KH: I know.

Ct.: Kevin it's hard when you hurt.

KH: I understand. Now, we know that cancer isn't psychosomatic, whatever that means.

Ct.: Right.

KH: Let's say that fibromyalgia isn't psychosomatic either.

Ct.: OK

KH: Let's just say that we don't know what causes firbromyalgia, because we don't.

Ct.: Right.

KH: Is it possible that the same mind that can shrink a deadly cancerous tumor that is programmed to kill can help reduce the pain of fibromyalgia?

Ct.: I think so.

KH: When a person experiences a miraculous healing from cancer do they think the cancer was psychosomatic?
Ct.: Of course not.
KH: When you start to feel better, how will you feel?
Ct.: I will feel great.
KH: And when you feel great, will you be thankful to have a mind that had the power to help you heal your body?
Ct.: (Smiles)
KH: Ready to go to work?
Ct.: Yes. Let's do it!

The resistant client comes in different packages. This next situation was truly a challenge. A 48-year old woman was my client. She lived with her father because she was partially blind and had poor hearing. She also had a severe case of tinnitus. Her father had called on her behalf and I accepted her as a client. She was dropped off for a 10AM appointment. I greeted her and watched her father drive away.

More Covert Magic

KH: Come in. Nice to meet you.
Ct.: Thank you. Nice to meet you too.

Those were the last nice things she would have to say to me for a long time. I took a 60-minute case analysis then began this conversation.

KH: Now, what I want to do is just give you an idea of what trance is like.
Ct.: I'm not doing any hypnosis.
KH: Pardon?
Ct.: I'm not doing any hypnosis.
KH: Oh. Then why did you make the appointment to see me?
Ct.: I didn't. My father did. I told him the tinnitus wasn't in my head and that hypnosis would not help. He made me come today.
KH: Do you believe that hypnosis is only useful for people who have problems that are in the head?
Ct.: I think hypnosis is a joke.
KH: I have to confess to you, that a lot of people who do hypnosis **are** a joke and that a lot of the things that some people do in hypnosis are a **real** joke.
Ct.: What are you talking about.
KH: It's like financial advisors. Most advisors don't make money in advising their clients. In fact, an interesting study actually showed that throwing darts at a newspaper, children selecting stocks and chimpanzees pointing to stocks in the Journal actually did better than most of the biggest selection firms. So, when you say that hypnosis is a joke, I know how you feel.
Ct.: What's that got to do with hypnosis?

KH: I have no idea but when I think of something being a joke, that's where my head goes.

Ct.: Well hypnosis is a joke.

KH: There's this one woman who picks stocks. Her name is Elaine Garzarelli and she has this amazing record of selecting stocks. She is like a goddess. Everything she says is going to go up, goes up. She is a piece of gold among piles of fool's gold.

Ct.: And you are saying you are a piece of gold among the fools!

KH: Not at all. In fact, I don't do what most people call hypnosis. I find it to be largely useless.

Ct.: But my Father says you are a hypnotist.

KH: I have to confess that I am only a fair hypnotherapist but I am an excellent therapist.

Ct.: What are you saying?

KH: Well, a lot of people who do hypnosis make people cluck like chickens and I think the whole thing is kind of goofy. It embarrasses me like most of the investment firms embarrass Elaine Garzarelli.

Ct.: The goddess.

KH: You got it.

Ct.: Well I'm still not doing hypnosis.

KH: Don't blame you. I wouldn't either.

Ct.: Now what are you saying?

KH: If I didn't know that Elaine Garzarelli was the smartest person on Wall Street I wouldn't invest with her because she said she was the best. They **all** say they are the best.

Ct.: So you are saying that you are the best hypnotist in the world?

KH: Not at all. I think I'm average. I am a good therapist though.

Ct.: So what are you saying?

KH: I'm saying I'd have to see Elaine Garzarelli at work before I'd put a penny of my money on the stocks that she picks.

Ct.: What does all this have to do with stocks?

KH: I don't know. I'm very conservative. I go with proven winners. I like to surround myself with the best of everything, especially when it comes to money.

Ct.: Yeah...

KH: And I think that you shouldn't do anything without having some evidence it's going to be the best and the best way to do something.

Ct.: So...I don't get it.

KH: So, if I had tinnitus, and I did for two and a half years, I wouldn't listen to anyone except for someone who had it and got rid of it.

Ct.: And that's you?

KH: That's me.

Ct.: How did you get rid of it?

KH: You really want to know?

Ct.: Hypnosis?

KH: That was a small part of it.

Ct.: I thought that was how you got rid of your tinnitus.

KH: Who told you that?

Ct.: I don't know, I guess I just thought.

KH: Never just think. Keep that critical mind of yours working all the time. You were doing better when you were a skeptic.

Ct.: OK then how did you get better?

KH: I used medications, did auditory habituation, psychotherapy and hypnosis. All were necessary to getting well. At first I listened to all the wannabee's then I figured it out. I needed to seek out what really worked. I needed evidence. Proof of what worked and I wanted to be darn sure.

Ct.: And what did you find out?

KH: I found out most people didn't know squat about tinnitus and most people who knew anything about hypnosis or therapy didn't know anything about tinnitus. It was a joke.

Ct.: So what did you do.

KH: I researched what worked. I did hundreds of hours of research as to why people **really** get tinnitus and how they really get well and I developed a unique program to get rid of my tinnitus.

Ct.: And now you are telling me I should do hypnosis.

KH: Nope. I think it is a waste of your time.

Ct.: Why?

KH.: Because you haven't seen the evidence and a skeptic is an idiot if he doesn't get the evidence before doing something. It's a survival mechanism programmed into people like you and I. We know that there is a parachute before we jump. It's called simple brilliance.

Ct.: So what do you want to do for the rest of the session?

KH: Not hypnosis.

Ct.: Well we have to do something.

KH: I'm not so sure.

Ct.: Well I don't want to sit and look at you until my Father gets here.

KH: Don't blame you one bit.

Ct.: Well?

KH: Well what?

Ct.: You are getting paid almost $200 for this session.

KH: That's true.

Ct.: So you should do something for that money.

KH: I already did an extensive case analysis.

Ct.: That was only an hour though.

KH: Yeah. I think we need to look at the evidence.

Ct.: Such as?

KH: I have a number of papers from all over the world describing the efficacy of hypnotherapy in regard to tinnitus.

Ct.: And you want to read papers to me.

KH: No. I want you to do whatever you want. I'm going to grab them. I'll be right back. Can I get you a glass of water while I'm out?

Ct.: Please.

(I go to my office outside of the work area and grab my "big book" which has my tinnitus and hypnosis research in it. This is the material that helped me write my book about tinnitus.)

Ct.: Thank you.

KH: No problem.

(I open the three ring binder and hand her one of the papers that is heavily underscored with my notes and exclamation points that I use on research that makes me go, "Wow!")

KH: This one might be interesting.

Ct.: What do you want me to look at?

KH: Anything that looks interesting.

(I grab a paper and sit back. I recline!)

Ct.: It says here that 69% of people who use this protocol improve with hypnosis.

KH: I remember that was a pillar of the work that I developed.

Ct.: What's the difference between this protocol and what you do?

KH: I found that we could improve that number quite a bit by making some adjustments in the therapeutic process. Here's another paper. (I hand her the one I'm reading.)

(She looks it over while I take another paper for my own edification.)

Ct.: This one says 74% improve with this protocol.

KH: Right, that was really important in developing my program.

Ct.: It says that people get some positive results in less than 3 months.

KH: Beats having to "live with it," doesn't it?

Ct.: That's what the ENT said.

KH: I know. That's what they all say.

Ct.: Why don't they read this? (She waves it at me.)

KH: I guess they don't have time. They are busy people.

Ct.: That's no excuse for not staying on top of what's going on in your field.

KH: Well in their defense, it isn't their field. They are specialist in ears, nose and throat.

Ct.: Tinnitus is in the ear.

KH: Sometimes it is but only about half the time.

Ct.: Then they should be up on this.

KH: I guess you are right. (I hand her another paper)

(She reads the abstract.)

Ct.: This one says 62% improvement with hypnosis.

KH: That was a good study too. I found it particularly helpful in creating my protocol.

Ct.: So you used all of these studies to make up your protocol.

KH: Right. I remember when someone first told me hypnosis could be helpful in tinnitus reduction. I laughed.

Ct.: You didn't think it could help?

KH: Nope. I had been working on my doctorate in clinical hypnosis and I had never read a thing about hypnotherapy of any kind being useful for tinnitus. I thought I had read it all.

Ct.: And you were wrong.

KH: Absolutely.

Ct.: Did you start to use hypnosis when you read this stuff?

KH: Immediately.

Ct.: And what happened.

KH: I was already getting improvement from medications and seeing my osteopath. Then I started the therapeutic methods I learned about and pretty soon it was December 1995 and I woke up one morning and my tinnitus was gone. It was the most amazing day of my life.

Ct.: What do we have to do?

KH: About what. (I hand her another paper.)

Ct.: To start hypnosis.

KH: Well, the next time you come we start what's called regression hypnotherapy.

Ct.: OK.

KH: I can see you next week at the same time as today.

Ct.: That works for me.

KH: You want to take the papers home?

Ct.: Can I?

KH: Just bring them back with you. Those are my only copies.

Ct.: OK.

Now that's a lot of covert work to get a client to be willing to work with me! The result was positive and long term it was important for her to become comfortable with me and the concept of hypnotherapy in a way that she would be open to therapy.

Selling Yourself with Covert Magic

A few years ago the telephone rang in my office. The voice on the other end said they wanted me to speak for their group. They asked me for my price. I said, $5,000 for the keynote. They said they just didn't have it. Of course, when it's local like this you are comfortable negotiating to some degree. Sometimes you can bring your books and audio programs, sell them at the back and then take a lower fee from the event. Here is the conversation with the (then future) customer once she heard, "$5,000."

Cr.: $5,000? I don't care if you are Oprah, no one is worth $5,000.

KH: Oprah is probably charging $100,000- $500,000 for a one hour keynote and I doubt she's actually booking any dates.

Cr.: Well, nevertheless, $5,000 for an hour is a lot of money.

KH: It really is. I mean I know people who have to work two months for that kind of money.

Cr.: There ya' go.

KH: That's why I insist I earn $5,000.

Cr.: I'm sorry?

KH: Money paid to speakers only reflects two things. First those dollars might represent the celebrity status of the speaker. That's why Oprah can ask for $500,000. She's a celebrity and people like the idea of having **her** there. They don't care if they learn anything or make more sales. They are simply ecstatic to have Oprah there. The other thing people make money from is value. Some people simply provide so much value that you have to pay them. If I agreed to come for $1,000 what would you think about me?

Cr.: I'd think you were reasonable and that you didn't have this overly inflated ego.

KH: Right. And do you want to bring in someone who is an "average speaker" to this event or do you want someone who is exciting and informative as Tony Robbins at 5% of his price?

Cr.: Good sales line but we just can't afford $5,000. If you were as good as Tony Robbins why aren't you charging 20 times as much as you are?

KH: Because Robbins is both celebrity and value. You pay for both and you get both. I'm simply an enormous value. Remember, that's how Robbins got to be **Robbins**. He charged nothing for his first couple of years of guest events, then all of a sudden he became a celebrity and could charge the $1,000,000 that he does. That's how the business works. You can get paid because people recognize your name or because you can help increase sales. If you have both you pay a much bigger price. So my question for you is what do you want in a speaker?

Cr.: We want someone who will come in and inspire and motivate our people to get out there and sell.

KH: And how will you know when you have selected the right speaker?

Cr.: Hmmm…well, I guess because of their track record.

KH: Would you want to bring in someone who is so influential that he has been recognized by two President's for getting kids off drugs and creating massive drug prevention efforts that largely succeeded?

Cr.: You were recognized by two Presidents?

KH: Clinton and Daddy Bush. Yes. I created an event that was so intensely motivational that we watched drug usage drop in the school districts I spoke in.

Cr.: That's impressive.

KH: It's not the same as selling more cards but it's the exact same process. Few speakers know how to put the two together. So my question is, are you willing to pay a little more for the absolute best value?

Cr.: OK, I'm ready.

Covert hypnosis has been used for millennia but only in the last 60 years has it been refined. During these last six decades covert hypnosis has been used to help athletes run faster, hit more homeruns and catch more touchdown passes. Covert hypnosis has been utilized to create conformity thinking in everyone from military personnel to corporate employees to churchgoers. Covert hypnosis is a powerful skill in the therapist's office as well.

(25 minutes after my client first walked in the door, it became apparent that a little covert hypnosis should precede our case analysis and trance-work. This conversation recently took place in a slightly more expanded form.)

KH: What will happen if you continue to yell at your husband?
Client: I suppose he will leave me.
KH: What would that be like?
Client: It wouldn't be any fun.
KH: What would that look like?
Client: Well, I suppose I would be alone with the kids and there would be no one there to help out.
KH: What else would it look like?
Client: I think I'd be pretty depressed.
KH: What do you feel like?
Client: I think... I feel sad...I cry a lot...I'm really very sad.

{As you can see, the client has gone into trance as she talks with me. Her eyes were wide open...in apparent every day conversation. Notice that I suggested almost nothing to the client. The client suggests to me what it will look and feel like. (My predictions of what her life will be like are not important at this time.) What she visualizes as the continuation of this particular target behavior is very important. By the way, the client was seeing me for anxiety and depression. The anger she was experiencing with her husband was significant and probably relevant to her long-term improvement. Notice what we do next.}

KH: I understand. (Pause) And if you stopped yelling at your husband, what would that look like?
Client: (She looks away.) I think that he would want to spend more time with me.
KH: And what does that look like?
Client: We'd have more time to talk and be with the kids...more cuddle time.
KH: And are those all things you want to see in your life?
Client: Yeah.
KH: And how do you feel?
Client: I feel good.
KH: Do you see any bad things about not yelling at your husband anymore?
Client: (Pause) No. I don't think so.
KH: Are you certain?
Client: Yes. I really have to stop screaming at him.
KH: OK. So the next time you feel like you are going to scream at your husband are you going to go inside and say to yourself, "STOP! Do something else?"
Client: Yes, I can do that.
KH: What will you do instead of screaming at your husband?
Client: I can just shut up.
KH: What else can you do instead of screaming at your husband?
Client: I could just go do something else.

KH: What else can you see yourself doing instead of screaming at your husband?
Client: (she looks away) Take a breath and tell him what I feel instead of yelling at him.
KH: Are you sure that is a good thing?
Client: Yes. (she looks back at me) I can take a breath and quietly tell him what I'm feeling and what I need him to do.
KH: Let's just pause for a minute here. See what that look like. Pause, take a breath and quietly tell him what you need him to do.
Client: (Long pause as she looks away) OK
KH: How does that look?
Client: He listens.
KH: Do you like that?
Client: (grins) Yes. I like that.
KH: And how do you feel as you say to yourself, "STOP! Do something else?"
Client: (smile) I feel good.

{As you can see, several things happen here covertly. First we find the target behavior (screaming at her husband) and we have the client ultimately identify what they would prefer to do instead of the behavior we are targeting to extinguish. We do this before regression hypnosis and before parts therapy. A critical element is to have the client tell you in this light trance state what they want to experience instead of the target behavior. They must see this behavior not just verbalize it. They must see the consequences of this new behavior just like they did of the actual target behavior.}

Covert techniques of hypnosis are among the most useful in trance if you utilize them correctly.

Here is what we have learned so far:

1) Identify a target behavior. This is a behavior they no longer want to experience. It could be anxiety, hair pulling, swearing, anything.
2) Have the client see what the continuation of the behavior will ultimately mean.
3) Have the client identify a preferred behavior.
4) Have the client identify the consequences of this new behavior.
5) Be certain that the behavior is REALLY the behavior they want to experience. (Sometimes a client will tell you what they think you want to hear instead of what they want to do.)
6) You as the therapist need to be certain the behavior is ecological. (That means that it is going to be good for the client and others in the environment.
7) Do not judge what you perceive to be inappropriate responses by the client.
8) Never tell a client they are wrong.

Everyone knows you are a hypnotherapist.

They know you get paid to help people change their frame of mind!

Therefore you can assume that people are going to be more sensitive and aware of your communications than that of the average person. This means that to create change in apparently resistant clients you will need to utilize this awareness in effective ways. What is the difference between covert hypnosis and covert conversational hypnosis then? The distinction is a fine but specific one. Covert hypnosis is the act of directing a person's mind to outcomes when they are seeing you as a professional. Covert conversational hypnosis is utilizing hypnosis covertly in everyday conversation. In other words, you are not acting in a professional capacity.

Immediately a flag should be raised.

Is this ethical?

My answer: Absolutely. Millions of communication messages are wittingly or unwittingly exchanged every single day. These messages often contain trance inductions and persuade people to take some action, or not. The difference between covert conversational hypnosis and conversation is that of intention. In everyday conversation we tend to communicate without conscious awareness of our unconscious intentions. In covert conversational hypnosis we tend to operate with full awareness of our intention and that of the person we are communicating with.

Imagine (note the hypnotic word induction) that you are a parent and you don't know how the unconscious mind acts and reacts.

"Don't put your fingers into the outlet son!"

The son immediately moves to the outlet and places his fingers in the outlet. Why? The parent clearly ordered the child NOT to do that behavior. The reason is multi-fold. First, the child (in all probability) didn't know it was an outlet. It is a child's (people's) innate programming to be curious and explore that which is novel. Second, there is no unconscious or conscious representation of the word "don't." In fact, the word "don't" is what I call a "directive." This word is useful because we tend to have a polarity response to this word. In fact, in most people, the polarity response is quite strong.

The unwitting child was put into trance and told to place his fingers in the outlet. That was not the intention of the loving parent of course. This was a trance-inducing conversation where the result was negative...and examples of these in conversational hypnosis are endless.

Covert hypnosis is not only powerful it is very real. We accomplished getting the son to put his fingers into the outlet with hypnosis. Now that we know what we are doing we can use covert conversational hypnosis appropriately and make sure his fingers stay occupied with more appropriate behaviors!

Covert Hypnosis for Sports Enhancement

Specific types of self-talk and imagery have been scientifically shown to improve sports performance. Other strategies fail to help individuals perform optimally. Covert hypnosis can be used in many effective ways. What follows is an abridged and edited dialogue of a client I saw this summer. The dialogue takes place in the first of three meeting we had together.

Client: ...it just always seems that I blow it. I shoot five holes perfectly then I go to pieces on one hole. Then I shoot perfectly for a while. Then blow it again.
KH: What would you like to see happen?
Client: I'd like to shoot like Tiger Woods.
KH: What would have to happen for that to occur?

Whenever someone wants to have the same results as the one professional at the top of their profession a bit of re-direction is critical. People like Michael Jordan, Tiger Woods, Mark McGuire, Sammy Sosa, Chris Carter, etc. spent their entire lives on developing a set of very specific skills which they practiced for tens of thousands of hours. Therefore the client must see that while possible to replicate such a set of skills, it is unlikely to occur if the same recipe of success is not followed. In other words, if the client is willing to quit their job, leave their family and friends, yes it is possible that if they are young enough and in the proper physical shape, that they possibly could accomplish the success of Tiger Woods. They will have bout the same chances as winning a lottery. It is never ecological for a therapist to assist the client in the decision making process of making such a move.

Client: I'd have to play a lot.
KH: And how many years did Tiger play before he achieved his results?
Client: 20 or so I guess.

KH: And are you willing to dedicate 5-7 hours every day for the next 20 years to achieve the same results?
Client: Well of course not.

(Had the client answered this question with a "yes" response, we would have had some problems!)

KH: So what would you like to see happen in your golf game?
Client: I'd like to shoot my best on all the holes on any given day, not just 15 of them.
KH: If you shot that well on every hole would you be a par golfer?
Client: Just about.
KH: What does that look like?
Client: (Laughs) That looks good.
KH: Tell me, what does it look like to you?
Client: Well, I see myself finishing a round happy for a change and not all pissed off because I blew it again.
KH: And what does it feel like to be happy?
Client: It feels good. It just never happens.
KH: Does Tiger Woods know that visualizing his shots before he makes them helps him be a superstar?
Client: No question.
KH: He still occasionally shoots a bad hole.
Client: Of course. Everyone does.
KH: So you would be happy about what?
Client: Shooting my best on each hole.
KH: And what if you blow the 4th hole at Valley Wood. You shoot the next six well. Do you need to blow the 11th as well?
Client: (Looks at me) Of course.
KH: What usually happens when you blow a hole?
Client: I get too excited that I'm doing well. I say to myself that "this can't last" and I'm always right. It doesn't. (laughs)
KH: (laughs) I understand. Now, when you hear yourself say, "this can't last" can you say to yourself, "STOP! It can last...and it will this time because it can last."
Client: (looking a bit confused) I suppose.
KH: OK, let's look at that. Hear that. Walk up to a familiar tee thinking that "this can't last" and then say to yourself, "STOP! It can last...and it will this time because it can last."
Client: (Pause) OK. I did it.
KH: How does that feel?
Client: Good I guess.

(Good I guess, is not a response I settle for.)

KH: Great, now in your mind, tee off and tell me what happens.
Client: (Looks away) OK, I'm on the fairway.

KH: Is that good?
Client: Yeah, absolutely.
KH: Great, now what happens next?
Client: (pause) I walk up to the ball and I hit it perfectly. Right onto the green.
KH: Excellent. Now what happens.
Client: (pause) I sink a long putt.
KH: Fantastic. How do you feel inside?
Client: I feel great. (Big smile)

The client has no idea he has been in trance for five minutes. He is totally unaware but he perfectly visualized the experience and a very positive emotional response. That sets us up perfectly for the balance of our work. There will be no resistance because he now has a wonderful goal in mind. He feels good inside! The client is ready to begin more formal trance work.

Covert Hypnosis with Children

I was working in a school a few years ago and was asked to create behavioral change in the teens that were most "at risk." It was clear that this "at risk" group were really "troublemakers." The school officials were paying me to get these kids off drugs and straighten up their behavior.

At my suggestion, my hour with these kids was to be called Leaders on the Edge. Here's how the videotape recorded the events…after all of the teachers were dismissed at my request.

KH: You gotta give the teachers some slack. Can you imagine putting up with you guys all day long? You'd have to go home and kick the cat, shoot the dog and bury your head in the snow. I figure we should let them go get their blood pressure down so they don't blow up or something… It's a funny thing…you guys are the guys who are going to lead America into the next century. I don't mean that you have to lead American into the next century if you don't want to, I'm just saying that history shows that those who are rebellious and spirited when they are in their teens are the ones who really get rich and change the world.

(Now, have we started the rapport process here? You bet. These kids are now caught a little off guard and are listening. The group of 60 was noisy when the teachers were here…now they are silent…they still aren't "buying into me" but they are open…)

KH: Ever hear of yahoo.com? The guys who started Yahoo! went to a few years of college then said, "Screw it." Now they have this multi-million dollar corporation. They were rebels. They finally looked at their college professors and realized that they had learned enough to get rich. They had a plan, took their brainpower and created Yahoo! Now they have servants waiting on their every wish, drive Porsche's and essentially live like you and I want to live. They were rebels. As soon as they had a plan and the brainpower, they hit the road. That's what it takes. Brainpower and a plan.

(Rebel story number one creates a positive image in their minds.)

KH: Now, the funny thing is that there are a lot of people working at Mc Donald's. In my opinion, everyone should work at Mc Donald's so you realize how much you DON'T want to work their for more than a couple of years. I worked at Mc Donald's for two years and I realized that this was the best motivation for me to be a successful rebel. There was no way I was going to work for McDonald's more than those two years. I hated it. The only things I learned were that I hated it when people were jerks to me. Sometimes the customers would lip off and I had to take it. I hated that and promised myself that I would never lip off to other people and that when people lipped off to me when I was older, I'd realize that I was a successful rebel and that they worked at Mc Donald's.

(Now they have covertly been taught not to "lip off" to people. Behavior counts.)

KH: I hated school. It totally sucked. I was the smallest kid in my class and I used to get hammered on by all the big jerks in the class. I hated that so much. I hated going to school. The teachers didn't care. The principal didn't care. It was then that I promised myself, "I will be rich and I will pay you minimum wage someday you morons." But I knew that I had to learn enough to get me to the point where I could be a successful rebel.

(These kids hate school too. I am now in massive rapport with them. Now, I can completely blow the whole thing or I can hit a home run.)

KH: So, I figured out what I had to do. I had to learn as much as I could about what I wanted to do in life and then get out of this place. Now here I am in a school today and it makes me want to get out. You guys want to skip the rest of the day and go to the Mall? (laughter and lots of verbal comments)

(Response to humor is a good gauge of rapport.)

KH: So, here's the story: You guys are where it's at. You are the next successful rebels. Clinton isn't some wimpy guy who does what everyone tells him to do but he does have a staff of advisers who tell him what to do and he listens to them. Why? Because he knows they want him to succeed. I don't care if you are a Republican or a Democrat, Clinton has succeeded and that dude is a rebel. Thing is, he's smart enough to know which rules to break and which to follow. That's why he's President.

(Now, more than half of these kids are from Democratic families and we just won some brownie points there. The picture is getting painted isn't it? Rebels that follow SOME rules succeed.)

KH: Look at Dennis Rodman. Now this is one weird dude. He has more tattoos than Pamela Anderson and he isn't half as good looking but he makes $8,000,000 per year. How would you like to make $8,000,000 per year? You know what Dennis did right? He became an expert at basketball. He is the most amazing guard in the NBA. No one is better than he is at his position because he practiced every day as a kid, through high school, through college. Every day. Never quit. Then his talent paid off. The contract. Then the Bulls decided to take a chance on his BS and look what happened. What happened?

Male Student: They won the championship three years in a row.

KH: That's the story. Rodman was a key. He was a successful rebel. But he had to become an expert. The best at his position. If Rodman can do it, ANYONE can do it. Now what did Pamela Anderson do right.

Male Student: She posed for Playboy.

KH: And that was great but what did she do that was so great?

Female Student: She starred in Baywatch.

KH: Right. She realized when she was a goofy looking teen that she was going to lose a few pounds and take advantage of her appearance. Did she succeed? Come on? She did $3,000,000 last year. She succeeded big time. She will for the next 20 years. Because she has a plan. This girl is going to be producing TV and movies someday. Probably when you guys are sitting drinking beers in college she will be producing…you know what producing means? It means PAYING for the TV shows to be made. She will OWN all the guys around who were going, "what a bod!" She will be paying their salaries and having them fetch her hamburgers…If you ever watch her on Howard Stern or on Jay Leno, she's not all that well spoken. She isn't a genius ….But she has a plan. She has a dream. If you have a dream and a plan you can do anything. No kidding. Even you and me.

(Now we have even more rapport. These guys and girls are with me.)

KH: I had a dream. I grew up poor in Chicago. My main form of entertainment was watching a black and white TV that got its reception from a piece of aluminum foil strung from the antenna to the ceiling. It looked like a signaling mechanism for aliens…I dreamt that I wanted to be a writer and a public speaker. Today I have three books in print and I do public speaking about once per week. I'm doing pretty well. Not like Dennis Rodman or anything, but I followed some of the rules, broke some of the rules, had a dream…had a dream and devised a plan to get rich…and if I can do it, anyone here can do it. I'm just like you. I didn't want to be in school, but I needed to get the expertise I needed so I could make my dream come true. THERE WAS NO FRICKING WAY I WAS GOING TO GO TO SCHOOL FOR 16 YEARS AND BE A LOSER. THAT SINGLE PICTURE KEPT ME GOING.

(There is the covert negative image to the downside of rebelliousness.)

KH: Princess Dianna. I like her. She is awesome.

(Now I have the girls complete attention for the first time.)

KH: What Princess Dianna does right is she breaks some rules and follows some others. She wasn't ALWAYS a princess you know. She was just a nice girl in England until about 15 years ago when she got married to the Prince. The Royal Family in England was never to hot on her but I was. She was a rebel. She constantly would piss off the Royal Family but she is SO MUCH OF A REAL PERSON that she is now the most popular person in England. She doesn't do everything she is told. But she listens to her advisers and does what they tell her to do. Ever notice that her husband isn't one of them! What I like about this girl is that she is the successful rebel. She snagged a Prince because SHE was charming and kind and had all the good traits a person needs…and then she said "screw the BS." She knows all that royal stuff was a lot of crap. She never plays that game. She goes to India and helps kids. She is always doing something good instead of getting her nose stuck in a chandelier at Buckingham Palace. Everyone always wants to talk to her because SHE IS JUST LIKE THEM. This girl is going to be the best-known person in the world next to Michael Jordan, for a long time.

(Now, everyone is on my side. Now it's time to unleash the pain.)

KH: So what is the difference between these people and the people that live on the street? The people who are the losers. The people who don't have a life. The difference is the people who don't have a life don't care about other people enough to follow SOME of the rules. They don't have a dream and they don't have a plan. Everyone wants you to follow ALL the rules. Those people end up in mental institutions. Hey, follow most of the rules. Everyone who succeeds does. Ya' gotta stop at the red light. BUT you don't have to get a "real job." You can if you want to, but you can be the next Princess, or the next Arnold or the next Pam Anderson or the next Jordan or Rodman. You can pretty much do anything you want to. No kidding. There is no difference between Rodman or the Princess and you. None. All of these people were in the same place as you are. They all created a dream. They all created a plan. That's it. You gotta have a dream then you have to make a plan. It's not rocket science unless you want to be an astronaut…then it is. But that's a different story. So, I want to know, if you could be anything you wanted to be, anything at all what would it be.

Male Student: I'd be a porn star. (everyone laughs)

KH: Great choice. Sex all day. Can't beat the work. Money's decent. Who else?

Male Student: Wrestler. (more laughter)

KH: Excellent. Fun job. Lots of money. Media Exposure. Who else?

Male Student: Pilot

KH: Great choice. Not only can no one tell you what to do, you shut the door and don't have to listen to everyone's whining. Good bucks. What do you have to do to be a pilot anyway?

Male Student: College and get your license.

KH: Can you handle college?

Male Student: No problem. It's just school.

KH: Good point. Who has a HUGE dream?

Female Student: I want to be a singer but ….

KH: Great choice. Singing is fun, pays good money. You could do music school or do it with mentors. The recording industry has success stories in both ways. Who is your idol?

Female Student: Janet Jackson.

KH: Excellent. Smart girl. Janet did it right. She does music people want to hear. Follows most rules…breaks a few rules. You want to do music like she does?

Female Student: No, I sing country.

KH: There ya' go. Who else has an ENORMOUS dream.

Male Student: I want to be an actor.

KH: TV, movies or theater?

Male Student: Movies

KH: Cool. What's the plan?

Male Student: Finish High School, go to Acting School, try out for every part I can and …

KH: And never give up. Keep going until you fall on your ass. That's what Samuel Jackson and Tom Hanks did. That's what they all do. They all have a huge dream and they all work their asses off. The biggest dreams are the hardest work and are the most fun.

(nice complex equivalences, huh?)

Module Two
Gaining Compliance

Covert Hypnosis will help you gain compliance whether you are performing therapy, talking with your children, your date, your spouse or making sales.

I want your clients and client to beg you to hire you, your company, buy your, ideas products and services. My objective is to focus on what really drives the process of unconscious communication and persuasion. Closing sales is a result of asking someone for an agreement. As you will see, closing sales will take on an entirely new meaning after reading this book. It becomes easy. Instead of the ancient warrior mentality of selling where you have to beat your client over the head 6.7 times before she says "yes," you now have the science and psychology of covert hypnosis at your fingertips to make the process a pleasure instead of a contest.

You will see the phrase "Mind Access" sprinkled throughout the text. Therefore you really should know what mind access is and what a mind access "point" is. I coined the phrase "Mind Access" in 1996. It is a phrase that encompasses unconscious communication and the instinctual drives that move us in one direction instead of another.

A Mind Access Point (MAP) is any stimulus-response "mechanism" that has been conditioned in a person's mind either genetically or through life experience.

A Mind Access Point (MAP) is any stimulus-response "mechanism" that has been conditioned in a person's mind either genetically or through life experience. This book shows you how to avoid setting off negative stimulus-response "mechanisms" while carefully and ethically pulling the strings that encourage your client or client to say "yes." The whole point of pushing buttons and pulling strings is to gain ethical and rapid compliance.

Mind Access is much more than a number of powerful techniques for making money and gaining compliance through the selling process. Mind Access is also a philosophy of success that encompasses your whole life. People who read this book will easily improve their sales and gain compliance in non-monetary exchanges quickly. If you apply what you learn here, your life will literally change. You will double, triple or quadruple your income. You will be happier. You will be more excited about life. Therefore, before you help other people get what they want, you want to make a commitment to yourself. You want to commit to yourself and those you love that you will take good care of yourself and those around you. Turn the page and commit now!

After decades of studying psychology you learn that commitment is NOT just a mental process. We know that people who commit to something, to anything, in writing are far more likely to fulfill their commitment than those who verbally say they will do something. Because this is true, we want you to participate in the simple act of signing your name below as a commitment to your success.

Commitment

Whether you are influencing yourself or others, the power of commitment is critical. Promise yourself now that you will be great and live your dreams. You probably have heard or read about a decades long Harvard study that revealed that **3% of students who wrote their life goals down in college out-earned the remaining 97% of all Harvard students.** The power of written goals and signing your name to your promise of your future is absolutely essential in your success plan. What follows are the keys to long-term success.

1) Becoming a black belt in persuasion requires committing yourself to mastery and the cessation of dabbling. Only people who are experts in communication truly become successful in covet hypnosis, in sales and life. Today, you commit to becoming an expert in communication. Conscious and unconscious, verbal and nonverbal. Interpersonal and textual skills are all necessities to long-term success.

2) Commit to find a coach, a mentor and a model. Who are people who can assist you in your quest for excellence in persuasion? Who are people who can assist you in your quest for excellence in life? If you don't know of anyone, you can call the International Institute of Coaching at 1-800-398-4642. People and therapists are all too often try to be go-it-aloners. I want you to have someone to keep you going to the next level…and the next after that one!

3) In a notebook, write down everything you will tell your coach about what motivates you. What are you moving toward in life? What are you moving away from in life? What things do you want to experience more of. What are you tired of? What don't you want in life anymore? Write down everything and we mean EVERYTHING. Write down everything that relates to your family, friends, values, beliefs, attitudes, your lifestyle, everything.

4) Develop a mastermind group. The success philosopher Napoleon Hill popularized the word "mastermind". A mastermind is a group of people that are focused on creating and directing the success of themselves and others in the group. Once you decide upon who will be in your mastermind (your coach, your mentor, your motivators), give your coach your, e-mail, your fax number and phone number.

5) Ask your coach or mentor to call you twice each month to keep you inspired and keep you on course for sales excellence and happiness in life. Give your mentor to fire you up and give your mentor permission to help you when you miss your mark.

6) Your coach or mentor should sign the Commitment to Achievement below, which you can copy on a separate sheet of paper. If you don't have a coach yet, sign anyway and begin the process now! Remember: The 3% earned more money than the 97%. Do you think commitment matters? Here's your chance.

Commitment to Achievement

1. I am 100% committed to taking action on the information I learn in this book in my everyday life. I know that my success or failures in using the skills I learn in this book are based solely on my effort and practice.

2. I am 100% committed to be completely responsible to and for myself. No one but me can take responsibility for what I learn from this program and its applications in my life. If I don't apply the material I learn from this program I know I am destined for mediocrity. I know that my emotions drive my behavior and I will begin taking charge of my emotions today.

3. I am 100% committed to becoming a flexible communicator and flexible in my behavior. I know and understand that I am the key to my own success by being the most flexible person in every communication I enter into. I have the widest variety of possible behavioral choices of any person I meet. I know what exactly what result I want at the beginning of each encounter. I always take appropriate action. I constantly monitor feedback and change my approach when necessary.

I am 100% committed to becoming part of the top 3%.

Signature_____

Coach_____

Here is the first key question of this book:

Question: What is the difference between the top 20% of people who earn 80% of the money and the 80% of people who earn 20% of the money?

> *Answers:*
>
> *The top 20% of people are expert communicators. They know how to ask questions and discover the needs and desires of others.*
>
> *Those who dwell in mediocrity do so until they have powerful reasons to move in a different direction...or any direction.*
>
> *People who don't live up to their potential have not set and planned for powerful goals.*
>
> *Outstanding people are experts in two fields. One is the field in which they are communicating in, and the other is in communicating at the unconscious level.*

Most people who are currently involved in the therapy or sales professions are influence-impotent because they do not have compelling reasons and goals to take advantage of their potential knowledge. They do not understand how other people think and they do not know how to motivate themselves so they can catch fire to act on knowledge.

Why are you going to be different? What benefits and reasons do you have to become an expert?

WHY?

...is the most important question in the journey of success.

1) Find the BIG WHY your client needs your products and services and you will be influential, you will be successful, and you will become wealthy.

2) Find the BIG WHY you must be successful and you will be.

> *When you know what motivates a person you can influence them. When you know what motivates yourself you can change your own behavior.*

Mind Access Points (MAP) : Become an Expert

Recent research revealed that a waitress who touches a client as she gives him the bill is more likely to get a larger tip on average according to research than a waitress who doesn't touch her client. That is a MAP. The waitress purposefully and ethically "pulls the string" (or pushes the clients button, if you will) and because she does so, she gets a larger tip. She knows either consciously or unconsciously that her tips are larger if she makes contact with her client. There are thousands of MAPs installed in the minds of your clients. Knowing which strings to pull and when to pull them will determine how many sales per contact you have and the volume of sale per contact will go up as well if it applies in your business.

With all of the knowledge you are about to discover how will you actually utilize this information? What is the process to use to go from being in awe of what you are going to learn to mastering it?

Mastery

There are five basic steps to becoming a master using covert hypnosis. You must do these five things if you are going to be in the top 20% who earn 80% of the money.

1. Find an excellent model. A model is someone who has done what you want to do. You must discover how they do what they do. This book in many ways includes an ideal model of sales success. The authors are revealing not only their secrets of success but also the secrets that have been scientifically tested and proven by the best people in the world.

2. Repeat and duplicate the work of your model. As you learn the skills, attitudes, thought processes and actions of your model, you duplicate what they do.

3. Regularly utilize the skills that you are practicing. This book contains hundreds of MAPs that you will want to practice. Practice is the mother of skill.

4. Integrate the skills you are learning into your behavior. Always choose people to model who have the highest values and beliefs that you are comfortable with. As you begin to experience success, you want to be happy with your new patterns of behavior.

5. Reinforce the skills you are learning into your behavior. Each day notice where you are on Maslow's learning curve, which you will find below.

The Sales Learning Curve

Abraham Maslow, one of the leading psychologists of the twentieth century, discovered that we all go through a four-step process in self-mastery. (He used slightly different terminology as you may remember from your psychology classes in school!)

1. Unconscious Incompetence. Stage one in learning is where you don't even know that you are ignorant of what is effective in selling.

2. Conscious Incompetence. Stage two in learning how to sell is where you become aware that you do not know how or why people buy in each specific situation.

3. Conscious Competence. Stage three in learning how to sell occurs when you become an effective salesperson at the conscious level. In other words, you are able to pay attention to the communication styles, MAPs, decision strategies, buying profiles, etc. of your client, *and* discuss your products and services at the same time.

4. Unconscious Competence. Mastery is the fourth and final stage in learning how to unconsciously influence others. Once you have reached the level of unconscious competence you are no longer consciously aware of what you are effectively doing in the sales process. At this point you have become a master and you sell as naturally as you drive or walk. At this stage you sell your products and services to the vast majority of people you interact with.

Thought Exercise: How these four elements occur in all learning and not simply using MAPs. Are there any exceptions?

Mind Access Point (MAP) Knowing when and where to touch someone can dramatically increase your income.

Dozens of the world's largest corporations in America have *some* of the research you are about to learn. No one has all of what you are about to learn because much of this research in selling at the unconscious level is unique. Some of it is so cutting edge that it has been released only in the prior 18 months of writing this book!

Obviously, not all covert hypnosis can be taught in a book. Hundreds of strategies and techniques relate to vocal intonation, vocal pacing, tone of voice, tiny facial expressions and specific body postures and motion that are simply impossible to capture in the printed word. Don't worry, you can learn them too either through my audio and videocassette programs or at live seminars. (See the resource guide/bibliography at the back of this book.) We promise you that we will hold nothing back. You will learn the complete lexicon of unconscious persuasive communication.

Becoming a black belt in covert hypnosis gives you the ability to pull mental strings to get the predictable responses that have been programmed into your client, often since childhood or before. MAPs all occur below the level of conscious awareness. In other words, few if any people are aware of why they are making a decision if a MAP is being pulled. This puts an immense power and responsibility into the hands of the expert with the techniques you are about to learn.

When you bought this book you really hired me to teach you the MAPs that are the most applicable to you as a person who sells products or services. If you are in the field of sales, you have hired me to show you specifically what to do to increase your sales per call ratio. You have hired me to show you how to simplify the sales process for you. You have hired me to show you how to communicate with another person's unconscious mind in a simple easy to understand manner. *If you carefully utilize the strategies and tools in this book* **we promise that you will make more "sales per call" from this moment on, for the rest of your life. We guarantee it.**

Most books you have read about influence have focused on selling your idea, product or service to someone or some group at the conscious level of thinking. On a random chance basis that is nothing more than a numbers game. 10 cold calls might get you an appointment in the old system of thinking. 10 appointments might earn you a sale using the old school methodologies. If you want to be able to decide whom you are going to allow to buy from you, and whom you are going to pass by, then you can begin incorporating the concepts and techniques in this book immediately.

Why would anyone release this powerful technology to the public? Wouldn't it be better to just keep this information closely guarded and use them only for one person's or corporations benefit?

No.

I have an ulterior motive. As I write this confession, I need you to know that we have made some predictions. First of all, you are learning new information, new strategies and techniques. Some of this information has never appeared in text before. We know by the unconscious law of reciprocity (see the module on the 10 Unconscious laws of persuasion and selling) once I give you this information you will almost certainly be appreciative and want to do something nice for me. Question: If I show you how to earn $10,000 more money next year than you did last year, would you tell 10 friends about this book? Of course you would! That's what reciprocity is all about!

People make the world go around. The more people who get help in therapy and the more sales that are made, the better the economy. The better the economy the more expendable income there is. The more expendable income there is, the more people can afford to own a copy of this book or utilize my programs. This is the ultimate win-win technology.

For years only the largest corporations in the world had many of these strategies and techniques available to them. In recent years, I have discovered many nuances in successful selling. Many more have been discovered by social psychologists and have NEVER been talked about until now! Even more techniques have been leaked from the major corporate advertising firms. The problem that faces the salesperson is finding out what works and what doesn't. This book solves the problem for you. Everything in this book is tested, tried and true. Everything in this book works.

Everything you read in this book has been thoroughly studied and researched. The tools, techniques, skills and patterns you are about to read about work in real life and regardless of what you sell. There can be no doubt that much of what you are about to learn about the science of covert hypnosis is new to you and unknown by everyone else in your office.

---

*There can be no doubt that much of what you are about to learn about the science of **covert hypnosis** is new to you and unknown by everyone else in your office.*

You will not be bored with the scientific jargon that has helped me discover this information but you will be given an extensive bibliography that will help you do further research into selling and specifically selling to the unconscious mind. Why all the attention on the unconscious mind?

---

*The unconscious mind is where **covert hypnosis** is experienced.*

The unconscious mind is the storehouse of memory and emotion. It makes up 99.999% of all of your experience. Your conscious mind is the part of you that is aware of what you are reading at this moment. It is engaged in some "critical thinking" and learning processes and that is about it. Most people try to influence the conscious mind and that is why most people fail in covert hypnosis and persuasion in general.

Influence is much more fun when *you* decide whether the other person is going to agree to with you instead of the other way around. The difference between talking to the conscious mind and the unconscious mind is the difference between random success in effectively persuading almost everyone you want to.

In *The Psychology of Persuasion: How to Persuade Others to Your Way of Thinking*, (Kevin Hogan, 1996, Pelican Publishing), I showed you how to be more influential, make more money and improve your personal relationships by utilizing the powerful techniques of persuasion. From the many letters and e-mails I received (and continue to receive) it became clear you wanted more...much more. I know you are already making more money and that is exciting news. The cry was heard and here is the beginning of the answer to the voices that yelled, "more, more, MORE!"

The difference between this book and *The Psychology of Persuasion* is very simple. This book goes beyond altering someone's behavior. As you learn the material in this book you will discover that many MAPs were "programmed" into you and your clients before birth. That means many of your behaviors are shaped in your genes, in your DNA. Better? We make it simple to understand, easy to apply and *we promise that you will learn how to change people's minds by simply appealing to them at an instinctual level!* Nothing is more compelling. Nothing.

I guess what I'm saying is that this book takes you straight to the double helix, the DNA and you don't even have to know how DNA works or even what it is to use the techniques in this book. We did the research, applied the techniques in real selling experiences and have simplified them into easy to master themes and concepts. All you have to do is push the right buttons.

The Microsoft Approach

I want you to be the dominant force in selling what you sell. Your name will become equated with your practice, product or service. What was Microsoft's goal? To make good software? Nope. To sell lots of software? Nope. Microsoft's goal was to dominate the market by becoming the operating system in every computer on earth. Did they succeed? No. They only are in 97% of the computers on earth. I guess they will have to suffer the embarrassment of knowing that all of their competitors combined only have 3% of the market. Microsoft really did it right didn't they? They produced the friendliest software on earth and decided they wanted everyone to use it. This is what we want you to do. We want you to be the sales person this side of Tokyo and we want you to decide who will be buying your products and services.

There is one important point we should discuss. *If you use covert hypnosis to convince someone to do something that cannot benefit from your idea, therapy, product or service, you will not develop the long-term relationships that are necessary for success in business or life*

---

*If you use **covert hypnosis** to convince someone to do something that cannot benefit from your idea, therapy, product or service, you will not develop the long-term relationships that are necessary for success in business or life*

A black belt in the martial arts doesn't prove his skills by harming the helpless. He proves his skills by defeating the competition. This book shows you how to virtually eliminate the competition if necessary. Never use covert hypnosis with anyone who doesn't benefit far more from participating in your therapy or purchasing your product than the money they pay you! With this one cautionary note, you can know that the edge you have over your competition is literally in your hands...and it is enormous.

This extraordinary technology picks up where *The Psychology of Persuasion* leaves off and comes very close to what would be the ultimate in unconscious communication: psi abilities. We haven't broken that barrier yet, but you don't need to be any closer. You're knocking on the door!

Using the tools you learn in this book, you will eventually be able to almost "read" people's minds. You will be able to know what program is running at each given moment and easily "see" what strings are "in play" and ready to be pulled. *You will be in control of each communication you participate in.* Your confidence will soar. People will literally beg you to sell them your products.

Mastering covert hypnosis means that you will be able to move people to the point where they seemingly cannot control themselves. They will demand to be with you, to want your input or buy from you. You will never "sell" anything again.

Mastering covert hypnosis means that you will be able to move people to the point where they seemingly cannot control themselves. They will demand to be with you, to want your input or buy from you. You will never "sell" anything again.

I want to share with people a tremendous value in return for their buying the book. What I do is provide huge value to the reader and in return you always remember where you got the information and tools that changed your life. Zig Ziglar once said, "They don't care about how much you know until they know how much you care." That is a Mind Access Point, and that is our philosophy in teaching you.

If you truly care about your customers and clients, they will demand your services and they will be loyal to you for a lifetime.

Napoleon Hill, the great success philosopher, said to "go the extra mile" for people.

Are You READY?

*Say "Yes," or **"YES!"***

What will you learn as you turn the pages in this book?

- You will learn how to predict human behavior with accuracy.

- You will learn specifically what to do to create demand for your products or services.

- You will learn exactly what the motivating forces are within each individual and among groups as wholes.

- Discover how to alter your products or services so people insist that you allow them to buy from you, NOW.

- Learn how genes influence your client's behavior, so you can pull their genetic-strings.

- Find out all the keys to writing powerful copy that backs up verbal claims and makes for great personal presentations.

- Realize the limitless potential of unconscious communication.

Unconscious Communication:
Reaching The Only Decision Maker
You Will Ever Need To Talk To

What is unconscious communication? Before we define it, let's see if we can give you two vivid examples to prime your mind to understand the concept before putting it into words.

1) Have you ever met someone who you had instant chemistry with?

2) Have you ever met someone who you knew you didn't like, before they ever uttered a word?

In both cases, unconscious communication was occurring long before anyone spoke.

Unconscious communication includes the sending and receiving of verbal and non-verbal communication as it is perceived by the unconscious mind. The unconscious mind is that part of our thinking that we are not aware of at any one moment. It's always there and it's always paying attention. In fact, it's always communicating.

What are some other examples of unconscious communication?

- The way a person smells may or may not register at the conscious level of thought but it "speaks volumes" at the unconscious level. The scent you wear or whether you wear none at all alters the entire perception of any selling situation you enter into.

- The exact body posture and gestures you have can trigger positive or negative emotions in anyone you meet. People aren't aware of these triggers at the conscious level but the unconscious mind immediately detects them.

For example: If your buyer (your client) was physically struck by a parent as a child, just viewing a hand raised above the head can create fear. At the conscious level the buyer doesn't know that he rejected you on the basis of something that happened to him as a child, but the unconscious mind knew instantly that it didn't like the salesperson.

- Where you sit at a table will increase or decrease your chances of making the sale depending on what chair you select and how you sit in that chair.

- When making a presentation, whether you use a podium, and/or how you use a podium can make or break a successful communication attempt before you utter a word.

- Wearing contact lenses will make some attempts at using covert hypnosis more likely to succeed and others less likely. This book will teach you how to know whether to wear glasses or contacts.

- Jewelry sends messages at both the conscious and unconscious level. You'll learn all of the correct types of jewelry to wear and when to wear jewelry. Each person you meet will be different and you will need to make adjustments.

- Your physical appearance will make and break communication. This book will show you when casual is a must, when an expensive coat and tie are demanded, what skirt lengths a female should wear and how the unconscious mind perceives differences in dress.

- The unconscious mind processes the tonality of words and phrases while the conscious mind processes the language. The tonality will normally overcome the actual words and phrases. Do you know when to change your tonality?

- There are words that the unconscious mind almost always says "yes" to. The conscious mind finds them irrelevant but the unconscious mind makes the decisions. Read on and you will learn what they are.

- How close you stand to a person will determine whether or not he is instantly turned off to you and your products and services.

This book brings to your fingertips, (which by the way also send unconscious signals to everyone you meet) the secrets of MAPs . We all have coded into our brains thousands of stimulus-response experiences. Any person can knowingly or unknowingly pull your strings and you react immediately without conscious thought. Each of these is a Mind Access Point. If you master only 20 of the hundreds of techniques to gently touch other people's MAPs, you will increase your sales volume without ever needing to increase the number of contacts and persons you see.

Every presentation you make from this day forward is going to be much easier. As you find yourself becoming more skilled at unconscious communication you will find that you rarely ask for a sale. "Closing the sale" will quickly become a thing of the past or at worst a mere formality. Your clients will literally *demand* that you sell them your products and then they will develop loyalty to you in a such a way that makes future selling a mere formality. *That isn't a promise, it is a guarantee.* Utilizing unconscious communication is a skill that takes some time to master.

As you practice one technique each day, you will find yourself in control of every sales situation you enter into. You're on your way to being in charge from this day on.

Turn the pages and learn how these MAPs developed in each of us. Then learn how to pull the right strings and push the right buttons with each of your clients. Enjoy!

Module Three
Covert Hypnosis Using Story

Each of us sells something if we are to be successful in life. We all exchange our time and energy for dollars. The more assertive and successful we are the better we are paid. This module is not only dedicated to the field of selling but it is written in such a fashion as to carry numerous key cover messages with you to the end of the module. Read on and we will discuss what the specific covert elements were at the end of the module.

Every person on earth owes an eternal debt of gratitude to people because without people there would be no jobs for anyone.

The Birth of A Salesman

Autumn 1972
Selling: My Only Hope

I (KH) started selling when I was 10 years old. I had to. I was the oldest of five children and we had no money. My stepfather was going to die in less than 18 months and Mom's time was divided between her job and taking care of Dad who was confined to a hospital bed in our home. It was a heck of a way to live... We lived in a "lower-middle class" suburb of Chicago. If I wanted to have money for anything (and I did) I would have to sell something.

I sold my services in the wintertime as the kid on the street who would shovel your driveway. $1 per hour... The Chicago winds would blow out of the North and off the lake with a bitter coldness that I'll never forget. Sometimes I'd take the $3 I would earn and give it to Mom. Sometimes I'd keep the money and buy Pepsi and Reese's peanut butter cups. In the summer, I would sell my services cutting people's lawns or pulling weeds. (I hated pulling weeds.)

Realizing that there was no hope for me in the lawn and garden services, I knew at age 10 I would have to do something where I could utilize my time in a far more efficient manner. I saw an ad in a Sunday newspaper for Cheerful House

Greeting Cards. I read that I could earn from fifty cents to two dollars for each box of cards sold. I immediately sent the company my $10 for a sample kit. ($10 was a lot of money in those days.) In return Cheerful House sent me five boxes of Christmas cards. Some quick math calculations revealed that if I just sold the five boxes I'd make one dollar per box sold! The sales literature said that there would only be four "selling seasons" per year, so whatever money was going to be earned would have to last a LONG time.

I got home from school the next day and as soon as my paper route was done I was ready to go make some real money! I knocked on my neighbor's door. It was Mrs. Gossard. I showed her my cards and she bought a box. My first dollar was earned! Then I went to Mrs. Singer. (She couldn't buy a box.) Mrs. Hendricks bought two boxes, Mrs. Serdar bought a box. Mrs. Makela bought a box. Lots of other people didn't. I was gone until 8:00 and had knocked on 30 doors and sold about 18 boxes of cards. I looked at my watch as the sun was setting. I knew I had to go home and help put the kids to bed. I had checks totaling about $60, of which my math whiz brain figured, $20 was mine...

Mom was so excited when she saw the order sheet. I told her that I'd give her all the money I earned. She said, "No. You earned it, you are going to keep it." Wow! The next day I left the neighborhood to start selling in a neighborhood I never went to. I was out from the time my paper route was done until sunset. I sold only four boxes of cards. Some of the people's houses were...scary looking and being a skinny little kid...I decided that I wouldn't go back there again! Nevertheless, I made about $4. I showed Mom when I got home and she told me that it was mine to keep.

The problem was that I knocked on about 50 doors to earn that $4. I couldn't believe that more people didn't buy my Christmas cards. They obviously weren't as smart as the people in my neighborhood. The next day was Saturday and I remember getting up, delivering the Saturday Morning Waukegan New-Sun (They had to be delivered by 7 A.M.!) cutting the lawn, and then at noon off I went on my bicycle. I went into neighborhoods I had never been to and knocked on over 100 doors that day. I didn't stop to eat lunch...or dinner. I sold 6 boxes of cards. I got home to find that there was no Hamburger Helper left. (I was eternally grateful.) I told Mom that I didn't have a very good day. I made $6 but I was driving across highways and I was kind of scared of the neighborhoods I was going into. She suggested I stick with the neighborhoods where people knew me and that I wouldn't be crossing the highways anymore. (She would later tell me she was scared to death that her son was going into some of the neighborhoods!)

We totaled the order sheet. I had sold 28 boxes of cards. My total earnings would be about $30. I would get paid after I delivered all of the cards to my clients. I couldn't wait!

I learned a lot that week.

I learned that people were more likely to buy from me if they knew me. I realized that if people had the money, I could talk them into buying an extra box for someone else as a gift.

I learned that selling cards was a lot better than cutting the lawn, pulling weeds, shoveling the snow or delivering the newspaper.

I learned I could only work four weeks per year selling cards. Selling cards was going to make me $100 per year next year but I'd need to think of something else to sell if I was going to make more money.

More importantly, after delivering the cards to the people a few weeks earlier, I realized how much fun it was to see people smile and say "Thanks, Kevin." "They're beautiful." "You got those to me faster than I expected."

Most importantly, I made $30 for about 20 hours of work that was not physically killing my scrawny 10-year old body!

I sold greeting cards for the next four years as a source of income. I sold flower seeds and vegetable seeds. (I also continued to sell my body shoveling snow, pulling weeds, cutting lawns, and doing anything I could.) The most fun was selling cards though. The women were (for the most part) fun to talk with, the work was all sitting down in their living room and some of them even gave me cookies and milk those few days per year when I was selling. I was actually having fun working at something.

The ad from Cheerful House Greeting Cards changed my life. Not because it made me rich. It didn't. It gave me hope that I could escape living in poverty. The Boy Scouts wouldn't need to bring me clothes and turkey dinners on Thanksgiving anymore. (The Boy Scouts delivered clothing and food to our home on Thanksgiving on a couple of occasions. I remember appreciating the clothes and food...and hating being needy.) I knew whatever I was going to do when I was older, it would be selling.

I was right.

I discovered as a 10-year old that the ability to think quickly and talk with people could give me a chance to escape being poor and maybe...just maybe...be rich. Selling was hard work in some ways, but it was fun. It certainly beat "physical work!"

Selling would give me security, freedom, independence and the ability to be productive...to be valuable to other people. It was something I could do well.

Fast forward to1998.

Autumn 1998

I've been earning a six-figure income for a few years. I've owned my own business, consulted or sold for other people since 1987. The idea of receiving an hourly wage and punching a time clock is almost a phobia. Business is good. I have several books in print including one, The Psychology of Persuasion, that is doing pretty darned well in the bookstores…But…

I've stalled. I've stagnated. I've been earning $1,000- $2,000 per speech I give. Nothing wrong with that but I've been there and did that. What is going on? No one is offering me more than that. I am baffled. People compare my speaking style to Anthony Robbins and my physical and offstage presence to Kelsey Grammar, David Letterman and Drew Carey. Now, what more could a guy want? That's enough talent to feed off of for FOUR lifetimes.

Enter Dottie Walters, the author of "Speak and Grow Rich" (Dottie owns the world's most prestigious speakers bureau and publishes Sharing Ideas magazine for national speakers.)

I see her "Speak and Grow Rich" course listed next to mine in the Open U catalog. I have no time to take a full day off and learn what I already know regardless of whom it is with. But for years I have been wanting to meet Dottie. She would now be about 70 or maybe older…and it was her book, Speak and Grow Rich that helped me focus my world into teaching and speaking in public for a significant portion of my current living.

I decided to take the Saturday off and go see Dottie. If nothing else, I should thank her for being inspirational in my life!

I experienced her class with about 20 other students. I enjoyed watching the woman speak for 5 hours. She was able to keep the group enthralled with stories she had no doubt told for decades. Her approach was simple and somewhat "grandmotherly." She was kind and direct. I was in love. (Not to mention watching her do back of the room sales was inspiring!)

I didn't get what I came for though. I hadn't really learned anything "new." But I was in love. I approached her after everyone had left the class and her grandson had finished packing the few books and video's that hadn't been snatched up by the audience.

"Dottie, I'm Kevin Hogan. I want you to know you have been an inspiration in my career."

"Thank you Kevin." She looked up into my eyes. She was tired. I've been here before. The last person wants to keep you forever. You (I) have been on stage for six hours and you want to find the bed in the hotel and fall flat on your face and have them wake you in 15 hours for breakfast...

"Dottie, I want you to have this." (I hand her my book, The Psychology of Persuasion.)

"Thank you dear."

O.K. Kevin, her brain is fading. Either ask or get the hell out of here. She has a date with a hotel pillow and you are being as charming as a bottle of mental Drano.

"Dottie, I have one question for you. I have been doing about $1500 per speech for the last couple of years. It doesn't change. They don't offer more than $2,000. What do you suggest? You tell me, I'll do it. Anything. What is going to take me to the next ($5,000+) level?"

"Have you asked Kevin?"

"Pardon me?"

"Have you asked for $5,000?"

"Well, not really. I mean...no...you know, I haven't."

She put her hand on my arm and patted me like I was a little child.

"Well honey, just ask." (She looked at my book and smiled.) "Just ask."

"Thanks Dottie, I will."

As I walked out of the door on that brisk Minneapolis afternoon I wondered just how stupid I must have looked. Successful author towers over sweet woman asking the dumbest question on the face of the earth. Thank God no one would ever know about this moment.

Fast Forward: One Month.

Early Winter 1998

I have a sore throat and a terrible cold. My nose is stuffier than it ever has been in its life. I feel terrible. CNBC is on in the background. The market is not doing well and I'm not making money today.

(ring)

"Who could that be?" I talk to CNBC when no one else is around.

"Kevin Hogan, can I help you?" (It didn't sound like that...maybe they bought it on the other end."

"Is this Dr. Hogan?"

"Yes it is." (Dr. Hogan has actually left the building for dead. This is his associate who has not yet succumbed to the flu...)

"Oh...you sound terrible...this is Richard Marks (Not his real name) with the Sales Association (Not their real name either)."

"How can I help you?"

"Well we were at your website and are looking for a speaker for our winter meeting in Minneapolis. What are you charging nowadays."

Here it is, Kevin. You spent the last month finishing, Talk Your Way to the Top. It's over. The book is at Pelican. What are you going to tell this guy? Your voice sounds like hell. You've just yelled at CNBC. You...just ask, honey. Just ask....

"$5,000 is my fee but I'd sure like to know more about your group and what you are looking for."

Richard tells me about his group, tells me they want me to talk about "body language" and asks if I will settle on $4,000, which is what his budget is approved for. What's the difference between 4K and 5K anyway? You're working for ONE HOUR Kevin? You moron. It's an hour drive and you are working for an hour....Just ask honey...just ask.

"No, My fee is $5,000 and I think I can give you exactly what you are looking for. An hour of massive entertainment combined with an hour of data all happening simultaneously."

"I'll have to check for approval on $5,000. I'll call you back. Thanks Kevin, we'll talk soon."

I thought to myself, "You stupid moron." (CNBC was running a commercial with Ringo Starr in it...I could use a little help from my friends...Ringo...) "What the heck are you thinking? Guaranteed $4,000. Been paid that once for a full day, never for an hour and you say, $5,000. Idiot. Idiot. Idiot." Sue Herrara talks with Ron Insana about how the market is taking a hit today and I'm feeling like a bigger idiot by the microsecond. The phone doesn't ring for the rest of the day.

Fast Forward: Next day.

(Ring)

"Kevin Hogan."

"That really you?"

"Who's this?"

"Richard Marks."

"Hi Richard, good to hear your voice." (I'll take the $4,000. Just offer it again, now, and I'm yours.)

"Kevin we got the $5,000 approved and would like you to....blah blah blah blah...(Get out of here. DOTTIE, I LOVE YOU... Just ask honey....I never doubted you Dottie, I swear to...just ask...and I wrote THE PSYCHOLOGY OF PERSUASION. I mean, how long does it take to realize that you are unable to follow your own advice...just ask honey...DOTTIE, YOU ARE THE GREATESET...)

"How does that sound Kevin?"

"Yes, absolutely, let's run through the details again. My head is foggy from this flu."

Deal closed. Check received in 6 business days. That was the last time I doubted that still small sweet voice in my head. Dottie is with me always...

Have you ever suffered from low self-esteem? We all do. I tell you this story because every time I think of it I remember that I'm worth an enormous amount to people, to society, to my self. I also think of my childhood because it reminds me that no matter how tough things get, they aren't going to be that bad ever again.

> When you sell, **you** determine your outcomes.

Whether you are 10 years old or 70 years old you are going to determine your own fate in selling. You are a free agent and can choose to sell almost any product or service you want. Once you have the product or service picked out that you want to sell remember this fact:

> **People don't buy your products they buy you.**

You must represent a great product or service. What you sell is critical to your self-image and your self-esteem. It needs to be the best and if it isn't dump it and go get on the team that is the best. Every product has problems. Every service has its weaknesses. My question is, did you pick the best of the group? If not, go sign up with the best. Because, once you do, the rest of the story is about YOU!

Selling is an inside job. It all takes place inside of people's minds. Selling is a simple science that encompasses beliefs, values, attitudes, lifestyles, emotions, feelings and psychological shifts. Selling is the most wonderful profession on earth because it gives you what you want:

- ✓ Freedom
- ✓ Security
- ✓ Productivity
- ✓ Independence
- ✓ Sense of Accomplishment

No longer are you a slave to anyone. You are your own boss and you are the master of your life. You'll never work 40 hours again. You'll work 50 or 60 because they are for YOU and the people you love. Selling is the solution to the destructive "dollars per hour" mentality that exists everywhere. You'll never get paid an hourly wage again. You'll be "unemployed" every day for the rest of your life and you will never feel more in charge of your own life!

Covert Hypnosis Lesson 1. Through the stories in this module you I was able to teach you about my dedication to my family when I was a child. You learned that I cared about my family. You learned that I wanted to take care of them.

Covert Hypnosis Lesson 2. Through the stories in this module you learned my exact process of finally asking to be paid what I am worth. You saw my struggle with my own self-esteem and discovered that you are a lot like me. If I can do it you can do it. That message was critical to get through from my conscious mind to your unconscious mind.

Covert Hypnosis Lesson 3. You now know that I have been successful in the field of influence and are therefore more likely to accept what I tell you as factual and therefore you are more likely to act upon those messages.

Covert Hypnosis Lesson 4. I have disclosed personal weaknesses to you so you know that I am not a superman...nor do I think I am. If you want people to like you and respect you, you must let them know that you are not arrogant. You are just like they are.

Module Four
21st Century Persuasion:
The Ultimate Covert Hypnosis

WIN/WIN Relationships
Create Near Term Wealth and Long Term Happiness

There is a special energy that is exciting about communicating with the intent of influencing others. Occasionally the experience is seen as a chess game where there are two opponents who must "buy" and "sell" from each other and only one will ultimately win and one will ultimately lose. Far more often **the persuasion setting is one where both sides MUST win**. In some situations, you will never see the other person again. Selling your house, a timeshare, or a car is typically a one-time interaction between the salesperson and the client. The pressure experienced by both salesperson and client is far greater in each of these settings because it is a "one shot deal." The necessity of a win/win scenario is still critical to the long-term success of the client's finances and the salesperson's reputation. The "feel" of these kinds of transactions is very different from long term relationship selling though. Insurance people, have a slightly different kind of pressure on them. People who sell to a client every week or month (pharmaceuticals for example) have an even different type of pressure. One thing is certain: Engaging in Win/Win deals will make you sleep at right and be proud of the work you are in.

My personal insurance agent is Denis Dunker of Cannon Falls, Minnesota. In all but two years of my adult life he has served as my casualty insurance agent. He has never had to close a sale with me. He has always utilized MAPs effectively and ethically in working with me. On many occasions in the past I have "demanded" that my coverage be improved. That is one of the tell tale signs of someone who is a master at walking on someone else's mind map! When the client demands the salesperson sell them more and more, the salesperson has become a master.

Every couple of years Denis makes it a point to drive the 45 minutes that are necessary to get to my home in the Twin Cities. He drives past several other State Farm Insurance agencies on the way up here for a visit or a luncheon date. In theory, I should have had my business with one of those agents he drives past, but Denis has built a long-term relationship, a friendship and has always shown great respect and interest in my work. Those are all important to me and they are all related to many of the 16 basic desires you will learn about in the next two modules.

All people, need respect and friendship.

Denis probably didn't know that being a friend and respecting someone's work is part of my instinctual drive...he simply likes people and works hard to do what is in his client's best interests. Today Denis is a wealthy man and has a substantial client base that will take care of him and his family for the rest of his life. He never has asked me buy an insurance product I didn't want. In fact, he has never "closed" a sale with me. He has always allowed me to "close myself." He utilized my personality, which includes analyzing data, being in charge, being a decision maker, and has acted as my advisor instead of what other less astute individuals may have done...and lost my business. Here is Denis's key to success:

Build rapport and ask questions!

Denis has taken care of me for over 20 years and hopefully will do the same for the next 20 years. He is an unconscious master of selling and I don't think he is fully aware of it. On his next island vacation trip, I'm sure he'll not be too concerned...as he sits on the beach with his wife sipping from the tall glasses...That's what happens when you care about people...they demand you sell to them...because they know you care...just like Zig said.

When I think of Win/Win on a different level I think of the great expense and the great fun involved in a trip to Disneyland.

 When was the last time you went to Disneyworld or Disneyland? Remember how much everyone had? The rides were great. The shows were great. Meeting the cartoon and fantasy characters was a thrill for the children. The day or weekend at Disney may have been the focal point of the vacation. You look at your pictures from Disney and think of how thrilled the kids were to get there.

In between the parking lot and the park was a ticket booth where you paid over $100 for your day of fun. You may have been shocked at how much the price had gone up since the last time you had been there. Was it worth it? Looking back, was it worth it? You bet. You paid a lot of money to allow your family to have a great deal of fun. It was definitely worth it. It was a win-win deal. Disney's tradition is to continually generate enormous revenues from the masses of the world populace in exchange for an experience of great fun and enjoyment.

Win-Win thinking is not a platitude with a wink attached to it.
Win-Win is at the core of every long term successful business venture and sales meeting in the free world. Win-Win Thinking is the foundation for every technique utilized in this book.

Two Levels of Awareness

Decisions to comply or not are made and lost on two levels of awareness and communication. One level is called the conscious level of awareness and the other is the unconscious level of awareness. After you read this book, there will no longer be anything mysterious about the unconscious level of awareness. The unconscious level of awareness is that which you are not consciously aware of but are still responding to in your mind and body. Communication is ongoing at both levels of awareness all of the time during the sales setting and no one is ever *fully* aware of what is happening at both levels of awareness.

Here is what is even more fascinating. **Before two people see each other in the sales setting many sales are made and broken**. Even before a client and a person ever meet or know they will meet sales are made and broken. You will shortly learn how to prepare for what used to be largely unknown in the sales process: the beliefs and attitudes of yourself and those of your client.

The Four Features on the Covert Hypnosis Map

The 21st Century Covert Hypnosis Model begins with an understanding of the beliefs, values, attitudes and lifestyles of both the person who will influence and the person who will comply.

What do these four words mean and why are they important to your success?

Beliefs are what people know to be true, with or without enough evidence to have made a rational determination that the belief itself is actually true.

Beliefs are what someone else knows to be true. This doesn't mean that the client is right or wrong. It's their belief. It's foolish to argue about beliefs. It's foolish to debate beliefs. People's lives are supported by their beliefs and people are normally slow to change them.

Values are what people hold in esteem or significance in their life. Some people consider love, happiness, peace of mind, money, security, freedom, justice and companionship among the highest values in life. There are hundreds of values. Values arise from the core desires and drives that unconsciously motivate us. Values are normally more difficult to change than beliefs. Therefore, don't try.

Better: Utilize the values of another person. Acknowledge them and appreciate them.

Attitudes *are people's states of mind or feeling as they pertain to specific issues.* Unlike values, which are over-riding themes in a person's life, attitudes are specific. They relate to specific things in life.

Lifestyles *are how people live considering the means, values, beliefs and attitudes they currently have.* Lifestyles are all about how we behaviorally respond to our beliefs, attitudes, and lifestyles.

Beliefs, values, and attitudes are unconscious "filters" of our experience. We see everything in life through the glasses of our beliefs, values and attitudes. Once we open our eyes to our own beliefs, attitudes and values, it makes it easier to understand other people's values, attitudes and beliefs. In the course of an average day, we don't discuss our attitudes, values and beliefs but we do perceive and experience life based upon these filters. Once you know a person's beliefs, values, attitudes and lifestyles you can ask them for anything in an appropriate fashion and they will in all but the rarest instances say, "Yes!"

Understanding your own beliefs, values, attitudes and lifestyle comes first in the persuasion process. Long before your client meets you, you spend time with your belief systems, values, your attitudes about life and your work, and live within a certain lifestyle that often make or break a communication before you meet the woman who will say "Yes!" to you today. Take a few moments to learn about yourself first and understanding others will be easy.

Values: Opening The Doors of the Mind

Take twenty minutes and write down the answer to each of these questions.

A) What are the 10 most important things to you in life?

_____

_____

_____

_____

_____

_____

_____

_____

_____

_____

B) Rank the above ten values in order by placing the numbers one through ten by the value.

C) Write down the 10 values in the spaces provided below and to the immediate right, write down specifically how you know when you have that value. (If you wrote love, for example, then write down, exactly how you know when you have love next to the word love.) Take your time this isn't as easy as you might think!

My Top Ten Values and Evidence of Them

1)_____

_____

2)_____

_____

3)_____

_____

4)_____

_____

5)_____

_____

6)_____

_____

7)_____

_____

8)_____

_____

9)_____

_____

10)_____

_____

Understanding your values is the beginning of mastering covert hypnosis. Your values are what you move toward. These are the states of mind and "things" that you want most in life. One element that separates great people from those who are mediocre is the ability to discover what is important to others in business, relationships and life. As you learn what is important to others you work hard to meet their values and needs and find that what you hold in highest esteem, while wonderful for you, is not what you are selling. You must sell your products and services to meet the values, beliefs, attitudes and lifestyles of others around you.

Magical Questions...
...that Open the Doors to the Mind

There are three key magical questions that allow you to uncover another person's values instantly. They are very simple to learn and once you can utilize them in any context, your personal power as a communicator is enhanced dramatically.

The reason you want to know another person's values is that once you know what is most important to another person in the persuasion process you are virtually guaranteed to gain compliance.

Generally speaking, you want three pieces of information. I am using selling situations in most cases in this book. You can obviously adjust this for the therapy, dating, and relationship setting.

1) What is most important to you in X?

(X is in "buying" or "considering the purchase of your products or services.")

"What's most important to you in deciding how much life insurance to buy?"

"What is most important to you in deciding what computer system to use?

"What is most important to you in buying a new home?"

"What is most important to you in deciding what to invest in for your retirement?"

Your counterpart or client will respond with whatever is important. He may respond with one word like "quality" or "service" or he may respond with a 20-

minute monologue that you will recap into one or two sentences. Regardless of how your person responds, his response and your summary of his response now become "Y."

2) How do you know when you have Y?

(P) Person: I want a car that is a good value.
(M.S.) Master salesperson "How do you know when you have a good value in an automobile."

(P) I want enough life insurance to protect my family when I die.
(M.S.) "How do you know when you have enough life insurance to protect your family?"

(P) I want a house that is big enough for my whole family to live comfortably in.
(M.S.) "How do you know when a home is big enough so your family is comfortable?"

[Once the client responds to your inquiry, they do so by stating something that is often ambiguous. For example, they may say, "We like quality." Therefore, the master salesperson wants to know, "How do you know when you have a quality X (house, automobile, mutual fund, insurance company)?" This is called, "evidence" in this book.]

3) If I could give you Y, would you Z?

If you can meet their highest value, quality, using the example above, will they work with you?, or hire you?, or buy your product? It is very difficult to say, "no" at this point because of the framing of questions one and two. Consider the following examples.

"If you can be certain that this is an A+ rated insurance company will you feel comfortable?"

"If you can be certain that this is the best value in automobiles will you feel comfortable owning it?"

"If you feel sure that this is a quality home, will you feel comfortable living here?"

The Fourth Magical Question

On occasion the client will say no to a "stage three question." If that ever occurs you have one more magical incantation that will turn the key.

4) What else is most important to you in buying/owning an X?

At this point you merely cycle back through the value elicitation process noted above. There are times when the client does not know what is most important to him in the purchase of your product. Question four eliminates the concern and continues the magic cycle to a positive solution!

You now know the magic formula for eliciting values. This is one of the single most important factors on the journey of success that you will learn in this book.

Two charts appear below. The first chart is an assessment of what men and women value the most in life as far as their "ends values" are concerned. Ends values are states of mind like happiness, freedom and love. This chart was compiled from a study where a number of values were shown to participants. The participants then created a hierarchy of those values. This first chart will help you have a basic understanding of what you will discover in the marketplace when you begin eliciting values from your clients.

The value you can gain from this important ranking is two-fold. First, you see the values that shape America. Second, you can observe the difference between men and women and their hierarchies.

The second chart reveals the personality traits that Americans value most. If you can mirror the American values you will appeal to the greatest number of people.

<u>Ends Values and Composite Rank Orders</u>
for
American Men and Women

(adapted from *The Nature of Human Values* by Rokeach)

Terminal Values	Men (665)	Women (744)
Comfortable Life	4	13
Exciting Life	18	18
Sense of Accomplishment	7	10
World at Peace	1	1
World of Beauty	15	15
Equality	9	8
Family Security	2	2
Freedom	3	3
Happiness	5	5
Inner Harmony	13	12
Mature Love	14	14
National Security	14	14
Pleasure	17	16
Salvation	12	4
Self Respect	6	6
Social Recognition	16	17
True Friendship	11	9
Wisdom	8	7

Instrumental Values and Composite Rank Orders
for
American Men and Women

Instrumental Value	Men	Women
Ambitious	2	4
Broadminded	4	5
Capable	8	12
Cheerful	12	10
Clean	9	8
Courageous	5	6
Forgiving	6	2
Helpful	7	7
Honest	1	1
Imaginative	18	18
Independent	11	14
Intellectual	15	16
Logical	16	17
Loving	14	9
Obedient	17	15
Polite	13	13
Responsible	3	3
Self-controlled	10	11

Changing Values in America

American values are not remaining static however. Each year we re-shape our society and the individuals within the society re-shape themselves. It is a slow process but there are definite changes that have been evidenced. Notice how many values and attitudes have been re-shaped in just the last two decades.

Changing Values in America
(adapted from: The Futurist)

Old	New
Self-denial ethic	Self Fulfillment ethic
Higher standard of living	Better quality of life
Traditional sex roles	Blurring of sex roles
Accepted definition of success	Individualized definition of success
Faith in industry/institutions	Self Reliance
Traditional family life	Alternative families
Live to work	Work to live
Hero Worship	Love of ideas
Expansionism	Pluralism
Patriotism	Less patriotism
Unparalleled growth	Growing sense of limits
Industrial growth	Technology/Info Age
Receptivity to technology	Technology Orientation

The United States and Canada are changing countries. Values and beliefs are shifting with time and growth. You become an expert in Mind Access by having the foundational knowledge necessary for sales success as detailed in this book. You become a sales success by applying the strategies and techniques you learn in this book in your everyday life.

The 21st Century Covert Hypnosis Model

There are hundreds of ways to present information to clients, clients, persons, and buyers. The 21st century model of covert hypnosis is really just one of my top ten favorite models of persuasion.

When we are making our presentations and proposals to others in the sales process we should note the following key elements are occurring whether it is a one on one lunch date or a public speaker before a group of 1,000. This model has been proven effective and I recommend you utilize it in your business.

Specific strategies for each of the elements below are detailed elsewhere in the book. For now, we want you to have a useful framework for persuasion. Some of this will be very familiar to you. A few of the points will be new distinctions that you had forgot about or perhaps they are brand new to you!

1) Establish and Maintain Rapport

Rapport can be defined as being "in synch" with another person. Generally people are more likely to be in rapport with someone else if they like that person. How do you know if you are in rapport with someone? Answer this question:

Does the person respond to you in a positive manner?

If so, you are in some degree of rapport. Remember what Ziglar said, "They don't care what you know until they know that you really care." Therefore, you will want to begin to develop a sense of empathy and sincere curiosity about others. Rapport occurs on different levels of communication. You can be technically skilled at acting and appear to be in rapport, but if you don't sincerely care about your client and the people you are working with, what is the point? There are several methods of developing rapport.

2) Use Content to Build Rapport

Discover what their interests are and if you are already not in tune with the interest, learn about it. *People love to talk about what they love and what they know about!* When I (KH) lead sales training seminars one of my favorite stories about building rapport is the "learning about fishing" story.

Living in Minnesota, many of my clients are avid fisherman. How would I connect with my clients knowing absolutely nothing about fishing? I grew up a Chicago Cubs fan, a child prodigy in mathematics, and even though I lived very close to Lake Michigan, unlike most kids, I never enjoyed fishing. In Minnesota, a big deal is made every year when it is time for the "opener." To my mind, "opener" means opening day at Wrigley Field. To the mind of many of my clients the only Wrigley they know about is the chewing gum. It seems I am doomed at meeting many of my clients at more than a superficial level...until one day...

...I decided to learn about fishing by asking all of my clients that love fishing to tell me their favorite fishing stories. I began asking questions that to them must have seemed absolutely ridiculous. Over the last few years, I have built an array of knowledge and stories about fishing. I can direct you to all of the best lakes for fishing and I can tell you what to fish for at these lakes...and I've never been fishing in the state, not once.

You can build a great deal of rapport and long term friendships by showing and experiencing sincere interest in what is important to other people. Sharing the experiences of your client's hobbies, lifestyle, and interests is called "using content to build rapport."

3) Use Processes to Build Rapport

There is more to building rapport than swapping fishing stories. Becoming in synch with another person or a group can take a great deal of skill, in addition to the sincere interest that is necessary in building relationships. Many people will not feel comfortable discussing their families, hobbies and lifestyles with you, a perfectly nice, perfect stranger. How does the ice get broken when stories are very uncomfortable for the client? Many of your contacts were taught as children to not talk to strangers. Many of your contacts were taught to keep private matters, private. How do you help these people become comfortable with you?

4) Pacing

When in doubt, an effective way to begin building rapport with anyone is by pacing. Pacing is essentially synonymous with the term "matching" or "mirroring." In other words, be like your client, because he likes people who are like him. There are a number of techniques that can be used to effectively pace your client, to begin building rapport. An entire module will go into much greater detail about building and enhancing rapport. Rapport is one of the pillars to success in sales and in life.

5) Use Your Voice

Imagine that the person you are communicating with is in an upset mood. He has a sharp edge to his voice and you get to make your presentation. Many people attempt to get him out of his mood with enthusiasm or a cheery story. In fact, the rule of thumb is, *"when in doubt, pace your client."* If your client has an edge in his voice, let your voice have an edge. If he sounds angry, let yourself be angry, however briefly about something that occurred today as well. This vocal pacing will help put you in synch with your client. Eventually you will lead your client out of the negative frame of mind, if you choose to. (There are many times when a negative frame of mind is necessary to making a sale.)

There is more that you can do with your voice than match the tone of your client. We all speak with a measurable average number of words per minutes. Many people drawn to the sales profession happen to speak quickly. Part of this experience is due to the nature of the business where we are obligated to be quick and to the point. Unfortunately, if your client speaks slowly and you are speaking quickly to meet a time constraint, you probably will lose the sale. People tend to speak at a rate that is consistent with how they process their thoughts and internal representations. if people tend to think in pictures (movies), they tend to speak very quickly. People who tend to speak very slowly process information through their feelings and emotions. In between are what we call the radio announcers. These people are those who speak with a more rich and resonant voice. They normally think in words.

. Building rapport is fundamental to covert hypnosis. One specific strategy is to speak in the same rate and pitch of voice as your client.

6) Why Pace Breathing?

Admittedly, one of the more difficult pacing techniques is that of pacing your client's breathing. Breathing is one of the most unconscious of all body functions and pacing of breathing is one of the great rhythm generators of all time. Two people in the heat of sexual passion often are breathing at the exact same pace. Two people sitting side by side in deep meditation often experience the same exhale and inhale points.

When leading a group in hypnosis, hypnotherapists find that having the group breathe together actually creates a wonderful bonding rapport in the room.

It is this Mind Access Point that you will now enter.

As you watch your client breathe, begin to breathe in when she does. When she exhales, begin to exhale when she does. It is best to practice this pacing technique when you are not in verbal communication with people. For example, if you are waiting in line somewhere, and someone is talking to someone else, begin to pace their breathing. You can practice this at home by pacing someone who is unaware that you are doing it. Our research shows that by pacing another person's breathing, the liking between the two people rises!

7) Physiology and Posture

Unlike pacing someone's breathing, pacing someone's posture and physiology is much easier. If you sit erect and stiff and your client is seated in a comfortable, slightly bent over manner, you are not likely to develop the rapport you hope for.

Pacing physiology too closely can be a mistake. If every move your client makes is mirrored immediately back at him, he will begin to feel uncomfortable. The most effective manner of pacing physiology is to match the posture and general body position of the other person. When we discuss "leading," below, you will learn how to appropriately test your pacing skills with your client and be certain you have established rapport.

8) Leading

Developing a sincere interest in relationships and friendships with others is the first step in the sales process. Pacing your client is the second step. Leading comes third. A lead is successful when the person follows you. If you are sitting across from your client and you both have similar physiology and you are both enjoying each other's company you have an opportunity to now begin leading, which is the beginning of the active process in selling.

Will the client now follow you into the sales presentation? You have been following him for minutes and minutes. You've matched his vocal pacing and his physiology. You have shared mutual interests. Now it is time to take a non-verbal break from pacing and start leading. If your client follows your lead you have successfully built rapport at the unconscious level and you can begin your sales presentation momentarily. There are a few key methods of determining if you are in rapport with your client and we will move on to them now.

9) Lead with the Tone, Rate or Pitch of Your Voice

If you have been successfully matching your client, you have an opportunity to lead by altering one of your vocal qualities. You may, for example, increase your speaking rate a little bit and induce a more enthusiastic attitude in the tone of your voice to help you bridge the conversation to your product. The context of your discussion will help determine when and if this is appropriate.

When you notice that the client follows your lead with a more enthusiastic voice, an increased rate of speech, a higher or lower tone of voice, you can feel assured you have successfully developed rapport.

10) Leading with Physiology, Posture, Movement

A client that is in rapport with you will often mirror the simplest movements you make identically. Imagine that both you and your clients have been sitting with a hand to your chin for several minutes. Now, imagine that you believe you are ready to "test" to be certain you are in rapport. If you are sitting at a restaurant, you can take your hand to pick up a glass of water and watch to see what your client does. If he follows you by also picking up his glass of water, or, even picking up a pen or a napkin, you have successfully led your client to the next stage of the selling process.

> *If your client does not follow your lead, you need to begin the process of building rapport again.*

11) Induce Reciprocity

Building rapport begins within you. The entire process of building rapport is built upon the foundation of concern, caring, compassion, interest and a desire for the well-being of your client. Pacing and leading is a process that creates comfort for you and the client to know that you are moving along at a pace that is appropriate for the client. The entire process of building rapport, pacing, and leading could be as little as one minute and as much as an hour or more. After rapport has been established you can enter into the body of your presentation. There are many ways to begin the sales presentation, but, my favorite is to give my client something. I regularly give a book that I (KH) wrote, called *The Gift: A Discovery of Love, Happiness and Fulfillment,* to my clients. You may not have a book to give, so here are some ideas to consider when deciding how you will induce reciprocity.

What you will give to your client to induce reciprocity will be, in part based upon the average profit per sale and the significance of your gift. You should know that gifts tend to be reciprocated with sales in direct correlation to the dollar value of the gift that is given. Specialty items, like pens, date books and calendars are perceived as advertising items and do not induce reciprocity. You must think of something appropriate that you can give to your client that will be appreciated. Inducing reciprocity is not just a sales technique, it is a way of life. There is almost a metaphysical energy that seems to emanate from the giving of gifts. Expect nothing in return when you induce reciprocity. The simple act of giving helps you develop a caring and compassionate personality. *That* is what people are buying when they buy from you....*YOU!*

People don't really buy into ideas, products or services....
they buy YOU!

---

12) Share Part of You, With Them

Show your confidence in your client by helping them with one of their potential clients (or problems). In other words, offer to help them in any way you can. Can you make a phone call for them as a referral? Can you help them bring more business to their store by taking 50 of her business cards? What can you do to freely help them with their business that is above and beyond the scope of your sales call. *OFFER TO HELP.* I've done this for years in selling and marketing and you can't believe how many times my kindness has been returned a thousand times over, over the years. Would you be willing to write them a testimonial on your letterhead for your client to show *HIS* clients? That is the kind of treatment you would like from your clients, so why not offer it out first!

13) The Common Enemy

Nothing binds two people, groups, or nations like a common enemy. Find their enemy and align yourself with their viewpoint. Do they hate the IRS? Do the same people try to hurt your mutual businesses? Jibe with them. Once someone shares with you who his enemies are, you have built a relationship for life. Drugs? Gangs? Taxes? Unemployment Compensation Insurance? Lawsuits? Government? Criminals? What are the common threats to business and society that you both dislike and you both know hurts your business.

You won't find a common enemy in every sales interview, but if you are thinking of the theme, the opportunity to put both of you on the same side of the table will occur during 50% of your interviews. Once you have a common enemy you have rapport and a lifetime relationship.

14) Tell a Short Story About Someone Like Them

If you can build a reservoir of stories *(short stories)* about people who have become your clients you can utilize this covert persuasion tool. Tell today's client about another client who recently bought from you. This client should be someone they remind you of. You can build an entrancing sales presentation around such stories and they make great lead ins to the core of your presentation.

15) Respect

Sincerely show respect for the person via a compliment. Always be looking for things to like about other people. Compliment them. A little respect goes a long way and you cannot under estimate the value of a sincere compliment of respect in the environment of influence.

16) Knock Their Socks Off

The shortest amount of time we spend with any client is normally that of the actual communication itself. When you do actually begin the process, the very first thing you do is this: *Blow them away with an astonishing claim, an amazing fact, something that few would know. Show them something amazing that no one else has shown them.* Make the biggest claim that you can substantiate. The client will always remember and consider this introduction. Start strong, finish strong. Your claim for your product or your service should be colossal and it must be true. Knock their socks off.

17) Always Give More Than You Promised

Napoleon Hill always made sure his audiences knew the principle of going the extra mile. Follow the example of those who sell who become millionaires. If you promise something make sure that your client gets exactly what you promise and then some. Remember that phrase: *...and then some!*

18) The Power of Understatement

After making your big fat claim you can quickly work your way into your sales presentation. This is the time to make sure you don't over-inflate your product or service. You made your big fat claim, now support it with the power of understatement. In other words, if your mutual fund portfolio has a track record of 12% return per year over the last 10 years, then understate that by saying, "Now, if you average 10% per year..." For 10 years you have earned a 12% return, but you are being conservative for your client and he knows it and *appreciates it.*

19) Be Precise: Then Beat Your Precision

If you know that this automobile is going to get your client 19 miles per gallon, tell him that. Then tell him a secret. "...but, if you use Mobil One oil, you can literally add an extra 3 miles per gallon of gas and that translates to an extra $100 of gasoline savings per year." Be precise, then be better than being precise.

20) Get It Done Faster, Easier, Better

You live in an age where your client wants everything to be better, cheaper, faster, quicker, smarter, easier, and more luxurious. So promise what you can, and then deliver...and then some. If they tell you that your competitor will get them X, then if you can really do it, you tell your client that you are going to get them X+2. Never be beaten because of the lack of going the extra mile. What can you do for your client that no other agent will do for them? What can you do for him or her that no one else in the business does? Answer these questions then do it.

21) Be On the Edge of Your Seat

Pay attention with baited breath to every word your client has to say. It should be clear that what your client has to say is the most important thing in either of your worlds at that moment...and it is. If these were the last words you would hear while you were alive you would want to know what your client has to say. Live your sales presentation as if the significance of each word will change your very life. Relationships are cemented when you do this. With the attitude of respect, going the extra mile and intense excitement about your client and his life, you won't need to use a multiplicity of closing tactics "on your client." He will demand that you sell him your product...*now.*

22) Asking for Compliance

As you begin to experience this kind of a relationship in the communication setting, the idea of gaining compliance is literally just that of consummating the relationship. Your client knows you care, they know you have their best interests at heart. You know their values and what is important to them in life and in the process of this sale. They know that you are going to help them solve their problems and they know that you will be there for them when you need them. It's the same as a friendship. Specifically how you want to do your paperwork is up to you. Simply ask a question or make a statement.

Your client is your friend. You are now involved in a relationship that will be long in duration and loyal in nature. Aside from leading the client to take action now, you don't have to "close" in the traditional sense of the word.

"OK John, we can wrap this up and do lunch again next week on me. I'm thinking a half million life insurance, level term 20 years. By then you are likely to be self-insured. Agreed?"

"Janet. Can I make a suggestion? You have $80,000 ready for retirement. You still have 30 years until you are going to need the money. I know you are averse to risk and I know that bonds and money market funds aren't going to do it for your retirement. Are you ready to divide the money evenly between Small Cap Growth and Large Cap Growth funds?"

"Bill. In my mind you need to be careful not to overextend yourself on your payments. I think you should finance for four years. If you go six years, most of the extra money is interest and that's a waste of money. In addition to that it will be forever before you own equity in the car. On the other hand, if you find yourself in a bind you can always refinance later on. Most banks will look at this as a new or virtually new car for the first year. Take it home now and pay it off faster and then you own it. OK?"

"Christina, as I look at this your company will be able to save thousands of dollars with our new system F90. You could spend a lot more on other systems I sell but this is the one that will optimize your return on investment. But, it's up to you. What do you want to do?"

Now, I know what you are thinking.

"They can say no!"

"These aren't alternative choice closes!"

Nonsense.

People don't buy because they don't need a product, they don't trust you, you haven't shown benefit to having the product, they don't like you, they don't have the money and perhaps a few other stray reasons.

The 21st Century Model of Covert Hypnosis is one that is based upon the foundation of trust and liking. It demands Win/Win or No Deal scenarios. If the client can't benefit from your product you wouldn't ask them to buy it and if they don't have the money they can finance it or simply not buy it. If financing is a reasonable and ethical option, and it normally is, then you can make the product affordable for the client in payments. Your client is your friend. No longer are they enemies that people have to outwit.

The client is your friend. They are someone to be cared about and nurtured. When they see that in you, you won't need to worry about hundreds of closing lines and techniques. It turns out in real life, that closing is actually the easiest part of selling.

Building rapport, identifying the driving needs (those that they see and do not see) and wants of your client and understanding how and why your client buys is really where the time in the selling process needs to be focused. That's what the next several modules will cover in detail.

Module Five
The Core of Covert Hypnosis
Your Client's 16 Human Desires

A boss, seeking desperately to motivate his low-morale employees, decided to give everyone in his company a generous raise. He expected the extra money to make his employees happy and increase their productivity. Instead, employees were resentful. "He's just throwing money at us" was a common response. "He doesn't care about what's really important to us." It wasn't that he didn't care, but rather that he had no clue what motivated his employees—what drove them.

According to the latest academic research, there here are sixteen core desires found in human nature. These are the desires that motivate us to move in one direction or another in our lives. The desires all take place at the unconscious level though on occasion we may actually become aware of our desires, our instinctual drives.

People, on average, have a very high desire for competition. That's one of the 16 basic desires and without that desire you probably couldn't be successful in selling. Lots of people have a very low desire for competition. These are people who should not be in sales! The basic desires include the desire to have power, the desire for tranquility, the desire for having a family and the desire to belong. There are numerous others that round out the 16. In the next two modules we will catalog them all and have you learn how to enter into the MAPs that trigger the desires.

Each of these desires can be objectively measured, which is nice for you and me because then we know that someone didn't just dream these 16 up one night and write a book. The 16 core desires have been thoroughly researched at Ohio State and I'm convinced that:

Understanding the 16 desires that humans experience makes motivating others and getting them to want to buy from us not only easy but also virtually instantaneous.

Where did these 16 desires come from? They came from our evolutionary drive to reproduce, locate and eat food and from the fight-or-flight response. All 16 desires stem from these basic drives. The remaining desires all come into play because they assist the core desires or attempt to "control" or squelch them in some fashion. The interplay between genetic predisposition and environmental factors is obvious in the 16 desires and it is something you will not only become proficient at identifying but also something you will learn to utilize.

Your client is nothing more or less than a human being. (We know you have often wondered it this were really true, but rest assured...) Your client is alive and here today (in part) because she is a carrier for her genes and more specifically for her DNA. DNA is something that replicates over millennia and you and your client are both alive today because your genes "found a way to replicate."

Before we go any further, I know you probably believe in God and that God made you in his image. You are probably right. If you are right and he did, then the DNA that has replicated is probably going to have some staying power! Let's do a mini-lesson in evolution to see just who and what you are so you can see what MAPs will trigger strong responses in your client. You don't have to believe that your ancestors are apes to utilize this information! In fact, understanding the theory of evolution allows you to understand just how unique you are and how many things had to go right for you to be here. Nothing you are about to read will even ask you to set aside your belief in God or your religion. What you are about to read is what happens after God puts your great-great-great-great-great grandparents on earth and they begin to have children and reproduce. Enjoy!!

In every cell of your client's body there is DNA. On this DNA there are genes for which we now finally have a complete roll call. We don't know what they all "do," but we "know" them all. (The census has been taken, their "jobs" will be discovered later.)

Because the material in this module is so vital to the science of selling, I want you to get a free mini-lesson about evolution and genetics from the inventor (author) of *Microsoft Word* and author of *Virus of the Mind*, my friend Richard Brodie. Richard has one of the brightest minds on earth. I've had the privilege of his friendship and have been his travel companion on many occasions where we discuss the significance of what he will now share with you. Richard's ability to explain the complexities of evolution and genetics in an easy to understand fashion is something that always leaves me awestruck.

"... the theory of evolution by natural selection -explained the facts well enough that it held on for a long time. But Darwin had never heard of DNA.

"The selfish-gene theory shifted the evolutionary spotlight from the fittest individuals onto the fittest DNA. After all, it is the DNA that carries the information passed from one generation to the next. The individuals of a species don't, strictly speaking, replicate copies of themselves. Parents don't clone themselves to produce children who are exact copies. Instead they cause copies of pieces of DNA to be reproduced in a new individual. The pieces of DNA that are best at causing themselves to get replicated become most numerous, and it is they that participate in the survival of the fittest, not whole individuals.

"Those pieces of DNA that play this game, causing themselves to be replicated by whatever means, are called genes. The fact that evolution seems to revolve around their well being rather than ours makes them selfish genes.

"Paradoxically, one way that scientists confirm the selfish-gene theory is by noticing unselfish behavior in animals. Female worker bees have evolved to labor all their lives to support their mother, the queen, and have no children themselves, because by a genetic quirk their mother's offspring share more DNA with them then their own offspring would. It serves their selfish genes better to behave that way than to go off on their own."
(Virus of the Mind: The New Science of the Meme, Richard Brodie, 1996)

Four "drives" are critical to the survival of genes. (Yours, your clients, your children, your friends, all of your "relatives" who live in every nation on earth) Each of these drives or programs is running all the time but they are running at the unconscious level in your mind. You probably don't ever think about these drives in the course of the day. They are simply part of you and every living creature on earth...understanding and appealing to these drives is what will double your sales...or triple them...or more.

1) The first is food. *We all need to have food to keep the body alive that allows the genes to live in your body.* You are hosting your genes and your genes "want" your body to eat. They don't much "care" what you eat but they "want" you to eat until you reproduce and copy them into other little clients. (Genes don't think by the way, they simply have instructions for influencing your physical appearance and behavior.)

2) *The second experience necessary to the survival of genes is the ability to flee in the face of danger.* If it makes more sense to the survival of your genes to run from danger than fight you will instinctively do so. Now, remember that YOUR genes are not only in your body. Many of them are also in the bodies of YOUR children!

3) *The third experience necessary to the survival of genes is the ability to fight in the face of danger.* If it makes more sense to the survival of your genes to fight than flee you will instinctively do so. Now, once again, remember that your genes are not only in your body. They are also in the bodies of YOUR children! In addition, also

remember that some of the same genes are in the bodies of other humans as well. As Richard points out in *Virus of the Mind*, if your family is together and you all come into danger at the same time, it may be in your genes best interest for you to intervene between the threat of danger and your children. Sacrificing your life for your children is selfish on the part of your genes. It's all part of how genes get replicated...

4) ***The final experience necessary to the survival of genes is that of reproduction. You must reproduce or your genes will not be copied.*** The desire to have sex is the key "moving toward" program that is running your life. Your genes are "telling you" to make as many babies as you possibly can. Your genes don't care if you just got laid off from work. Your genes aren't interested in your financial situation or changing diapers...they simply "want you" to reproduce. To your genes there is no distinction between reproduction and having sex. Therefore, anything that you can do that appeals to the desire to have sex is going to appeal to the unconscious minds of the majority of people on earth. We will have a lot to say about this later!

Each human being is driven instinctively by these four needs. In fact, these four needs form the foundation of what are known as the 16 basic desires. Before we arrive at the core desires of human experience let's take a careful look at the four programs that are running our life:

1) The desire to eat.
2) The desire to flee from danger.
3) The desire to fight when in danger.
4) The desire to have sex/reproduce.

Remember this key point:

You don't fulfill these desires to keep you alive, you fulfill these desires to allow your genes to survive.

Question: If you only knew these four astonishing facts about your genes (and we might as well say your "self"), how would you sell your products and services?

Answer: You sell your products and services so that they appear to meet the needs and desires of each of these four key drives. In general any sales message that meets your instinctual needs is likelier to be acted upon than messages directed at other desires.

This may seem obvious (or not!) but how do we apply this immediately into our careers as people?

Look at some specific examples:

Life Insurance: If your client buys life insurance his genes are protected. His children will survive until they are old enough to reproduce. His children will be able to eat and his children will be able to have the resources to ward off danger. Now you don't say that when you are selling life insurance, you frame your presentation in such a manner that these points become clear.

Real Estate: If your client buys a home from you, she has a place to cook her food. She has a place that is safe from the dangers of the world for her and her children (her genes). She also has a place where it is safe to reproduce and nest.

Clothing: If your client buys clothing from you, she has (hopefully) improved her appearance so that she looks more attractive thus increasing her chances for reproducing her genes. Buying new clothes will (hopefully) also help her stay more attractive so she is more likely to be viewed in a positive light by others for mating, continued mating or so she can earn more money to protect her genes.

Almost every product or service has a connection with at least one of our instinctual drives and by highlighting these drives we make our products and services far easier to sell and far more attractive to the buyer.

If you sell clothes at Macy's you probably won't find your sales going up if you say, "Oh, and if you buy this skirt, you will ultimately have lots of sex and marry a guy who has lots of money to take care of your biological need to reproduce." Framing your communication so that it is artistically grounded in science is going to be the key. The woman you are selling clothes to already knows at the unconscious level that clothes that enhance her appearance will improve her "face value." Your job as the sales person is to reinforce the fact that, "you look absolutely stunning in that dress."

Emerging from the core desires and needs to have sex, avoid or ward off danger and eat, come 13 other desires. Dr. Steven Reiss of Ohio State is the first individual I know of to successfully catalog each of the 16 basic desires. Others (William James, for example) have recorded most of the human desires, but Reiss, in my opinion is the first to scientifically categorize and distill them all. The balance of this module will discuss the 16 basic desires and how they relate to selling. (For further reading about the 16 basic desires, I recommend, *Who Am I? The 16 Basic Desires that Motivate our Actions and Define our Personalities* by Stephen Reiss.)

The 16 Core Desires

Perhaps the responses we show under stress are those that are most telling about our motivations. We will do a great deal to avoid pain but what specifically will we do? As noted earlier we are going to be protecting our genes survival and those responses may indeed be "calculated" but what response protects the genes the best. Over time however, people may miscalculate and develop tendencies to respond to a majority of fearful situations in a flight *or* fight mode.

When you become afraid do you tend to respond to fear by fighting or fleeing? Most people don't really know themselves very well so let me give you a few examples to consider.

1) You see a police officer on the highway while you are speeding. Do you challenge him to come and get you (fight) or slow down (flight)?
2) The IRS sends you a notice that you are going to be audited. Do you go in and fight like hell or do you start making up receipts and reconstructing records (flight)?
3) A tall stranger approaches you (you are alone) on the street late at night. Are you prepared to run or fight?
4) Your boss yells at you about something. Do you scream back at him? Do you quietly apologize?

As you can see there are many situations that can represent danger to an individual. Now that you have thought of a few of them, you can look at the continuum of behaviors below and how people see themselves and others along the continuum. Which side of the spectrum do you tend to be on? Notice that timid people, (people who consider themselves wise enough to flee from danger see themselves as cautious, prudent and careful. They see other people who may consider themselves to be brave, as foolhardy and reckless. Where do you see yourself?

With this thumbnail sketch of evolution we now turn to the first three (four) core instincts and desires.

Desire for Tranquility and The Flight Fight Response

Many people move toward tranquility as a basic human desire. When this is thwarted, people respond with the flight-fight response. Show people danger and they go into preparation mode. They prepare to fight or flee. In order to do so they may need your product or service!

What is the danger if your client doesn't buy your product or service from you, now?

    You sell new automobiles.
- ✓ What is the danger if your client doesn't have a new car?
- ✓ What is the danger if they have one of the other type of cars?
- ✓ What is the danger if they own one of those SUV's that tip over?
- ✓ What is the danger of not having the best for your family?
- ✓ What is the danger of waiting for a different day to buy from you?

You sell skin care products.
- ✓ What is the danger to your client's skin if they don't buy your lotions?
- ✓ What is the danger to their appearance if they don't buy from you?
- ✓ What is the danger of using the competitor's products?
- ✓ What is the danger of waiting for another day to buy?
- ✓ What is the danger to your "face value" if you don't protect your skin?

You sell yourself as a personal coach.
- ✓ What is the danger to your client if he doesn't hire you?
- ✓ What is the danger to your client if he doesn't utilize you regularly?
- ✓ What is the danger to your client if he uses a less qualified coach?
- ✓ What is the danger to your client if they wait to hire you?

I will answer one question for each of the above examples for you then you respond to the rest.

1) If your client doesn't buy a new car from you they put their family at risk. They are running the most important things (their loved ones) on earth in a ten or twenty year old vehicle. The brakes could fail, the car could stall at an intersection, and the tires might not give you the 10 extra feet you need to prevent a serious accident. Question: Is it worth it? I didn't think so.

2) If your client doesn't buy skin care products from you they put themselves at risk on many levels. First, the fact that they are considering skin care shows they care about themselves. Do you know how many people don't care about themselves? Do you know what this does to people's self esteem? Do you know how this affects every day life for the person? Their level of happiness or depression? On another level, the skin is the largest organ in the human body. It needs to be cared for. Skin care products will keep it looking better for a lot longer and that makes your clients not only feel better about themselves but let's other people see them in their best light. Other people will respond better to your client who will look more attractive because of your products. That isn't fair, that's just the way life works.

3) You are a personal coach. If your client doesn't hire you then you have possibly created harm for them. You charge $200 per hour but let me ask you this. If your client could have saved or earned $10,000 in exchange for that time isn't it worth it? If you could have coached them to save their marriage are you willing to put a dollar figure on that? If you could have shown them five ways to draw more interesting people in their lives do you really believe that isn't worth $500? A person's daily life is all they have. Are you going to let your shyness about your personal income stand in the way of another human's rich experiences?

As you can see, a big part of your job as a salesperson is to highlight the risks inherent of not buying your services from you, now. That's the big picture of danger. Now let's fine-tune utilizing your clients instinctive responses to dangers so they become buyers.

You will notice that throughout the rest of the books you will find many continuums of behavioral experience. On one side will be one desire, say, "timid." On the other side will be the other end of the continuum, in this case it's "brave." Now at some times in your life you are brave and others you are timid. However, research clearly shows that you will respond typically from one point on the continuum. I want you to find where you are on these continuums. Then look at how you perceive yourself to be by reading, "Believe themselves to be." Next look on the other side and see how the other think of themselves. Finally, go back to the next set of descriptions under your side. It says, "Others believe to be." This means that other people perceive you in this fashion! (What is THIS information worth to you?!?!?!) On the other side you will be shocked at how accurate the phrases are that describe how you feel about others. That's how these charts work. (For more details about each of the desires, see Reiss's *Who Am I?*)

Desire for Tranquility

Timid ←--→ **Brave**

Believe themselves to be:

Shy	*Fearless*
Cautious	*Courageous*
Wary	*Bold*
Prudent	*Daring*
Careful	**Confident**
Mindful	*Valiant*

Believe others to be:

Imprudent	*Fainthearted*
Reckless	*Cowardly*
Foolhardy	*Neurotic*
Unaware	*Worrier*
Daredevil	**Overprotective**

Imagine a tax accountant is attempting to sell their services to a fairly timid person when it comes to their own personal safety. When it comes to the rest of their genes (their children) they are quite the opposite as might be predicted from our previous discussion. Perhaps part of the conversation might go like this.

"Mr. Johnson, when you give me your tax information I want you to be as careful and prudent as you can. I don't want you to get into any trouble. But your kids deserve to live as well or better than they are and not have all of this extra money going to the government, which is going to blow it on pork projects. Let me shoulder the responsibility for going to war with the IRS. I'll be up there on the front lines fighting for every dollar you deserve."

Wow! Mr. Johnson gets to be prudent and the tax accountant is going to be courageous on Mr. Johnson's behalf. She's going to fight the war for Mr. Johnson. He can live with that! She will shoulder the responsibility and fight for Mr. Johnson. She has closed the sale!

This is just one example of being aware of people's response to dangerous situations and then utilizing that information into a communication for the purpose of making the sale.

The following exercise can help you double your income. But there is a danger. If you don't do it, you will probably stay in the same income bracket you are in for eons. Do the risks of skipping this exercise outweigh racing through this text, which you bought to change your life?

Exercise:

Write down all of the possible dangers your client could face by not buying your services/products from you, now. Write down the possible dangers to your client if she waits, even one day. Write down all of the dangers in light of the evolutionary needs we have discussed. Do this now. (If you don't you will fail to see the value of this information and are unlikely to utilize this material. That means no increased sales. Please do this exercise!)

The Drive to Eat

People have an instant response when presented with food. If they like the food that is presented (in thought, on television, on radio or set on a plate in front of you) a MAP is about to be entered. If you show people food (that they like) and you associate it to your product or service you are on the right track.

Do you sell groceries, fast food, own a gourmet restaurant, or have anything to do with the multi-billion dollar food (or dieting for that matter) industry? If so, you have an obvious MAP you can enter into. The need for food consumption is one of the core desires. Utilize that fact!

Are you in that multi-billion-dollar multi-level marketing business that sells herbs and vitamins? Nutritional supplements you call them right? It's a terrifying thought to consider that *all* the food you are currently eating isn't giving you enough or the right nutrition isn't it? *It could threaten your very survival*!

It's funny though. Every time someone approaches me to buy their supplements they tell me how much better I will feel, how healthy I will feel. Those are fine reasons to use such a product, but wouldn't it be more effective to simply tell me, "Kevin you're 40 years old. If you want to make it to 90 on your current diet, well, you are hallucinating. Supplement Q810ZX is going to keep you out of the nursing home and on the beach frolicking…if you know what I mean…"

Now, I don't know about you…but there's something there that appeals to me. There is food, there is danger, there is frolicking. (What is frolicking anyway? I don't know but my genes seem to be responding to the notion…)

You can tell people you sell herbs and vitamins or you can tell them that they will still be frolicking when they are 90. Are we on the same page?

BUT! Maybe you don't sell Reese's or own a McDonalds. What can we do for you? How could your product or service possibly relate to food consumption? (Food consumption is an obvious survival need for both your client and his genes, but so what?!)

Question: If you sell Mary Kay cosmetics what does that have to do with food?

Answer: Maybe nothing...maybe everything. If you sell Mary Kay and you know that cosmetics help a woman appear more attractive to men then that brings certain benefits to the woman. She appears more attractive and therefore she attracts a wider range of men. She has more choices as to whom she can be with. Her genes have a better chance of being replicated and her genes have a better chance of being passed on in further generations if she can locate men that will help her provide a safe environment to raise children in. It sounds so simplistic. It sounds very old fashioned. Here's the reality: It's (the DNA, the genes) millions of years old and it isn't interested in the feminist ideology or much of anything except getting the genes replicated. Finally, the fact that the genes are more likely to get copied...they will be cared for... means that food consumption will not be a problem.

Appealing to the evolutionary need of food consumption is absolutely critical in the selling process. (Have you ever wondered why successful people close a lot of deals at lunch? Even they don't know...and now you do.)

- ✓ After all, we all have to eat.
- ✓ It puts the food on the table you know.
- ✓ You don't work – you don't eat.
- ✓ An apple a day keeps the doctor away.

(By the way do you see how "danger" is threaded into the last two common phrases. Welcome to the world of scientific selling.)

What subtle implication of easy access to food can you link to your product or service? What implication of limited access to food can you link to your product or service if your client doesn't buy from you?

You sell automobiles.
- ✓ Who will be the first person your client takes to their favorite restaurant in their new car?
- ✓ How will having this new vehicle make their access to their basic needs easier?
- ✓ How will having this new vehicle make your client more aware of his or her own physical body?
- ✓ How will having a new vehicle help your client feel going shopping?

Desire to Eat

Hearty Eaters←---→ **Light Eaters**

Believe themselves to be:
Connoisseur   *Physically Fit*
Happy   *Slender*
Sensual   *Healthy*
Gourmand   *Sensible*

Believe other half to be:
Self Denying   *Lack willpower*
Unhealthy   *Unhealthy*

The desire to eat, to be nourished, is something we always consider as important in the science of selling. I find it useful to close deals over lunch and dinner and so do others. Research shows that people are more likely to say, "Yes" when dining than when doing business in an office setting. Certain foods have certain effects on brain chemistry of course and this is part of the reason. We also have many traditions about sharing food and "breaking bread" as way of bonding and celebrating.

Many people in the United States do try to control the instinctual need to locate and eat food. It is extremely difficult for most people who are overweight, for example to actually lose weight and keep it off. Whether food is abundant or not people look and consume as much as they can. It's prepared into the nature of who you are. 90% of all people who diet gain their weight back in less than two years.

So how will we utilize the evolutionary urge to find and eat food in the sales process?

First, it's very important to place the implications of having no food or too much food in the clients mind. Second, on a cautionary note, you should know that people who are extremely overweight or underweight have serious problems and this becomes an area that people should steer clear. Entering minds through MAPs is necessary to increase sales but we don't need to encourage anorexia, bulimia or obesity!

The Icing on the Cake

It's obvious from the chart that people who are light eaters perceive themselves to be sensible, slender and healthy. So, when they go out to eat with us, doesn't it make sense to have something that will be healthy for us both? Wouldn't it also make sense to eat something along the same lines that our client does to show our wisdom as far as being healthy goes?

It's also obvious from the distinctions in the chart that people who are heavy eaters consider themselves to be happy and sensual in nature. I'm sure that we will be able to model this behavior for one lunch ourselves and not raise a fuss about the amount of food they consume. Hearty eaters love to talk about food and I'm certain that you will find ways to weave their favorite restaurants and meals into conversation.

Sex, Romance and Sensuality

Here is the key to your sales success. Here is the key to most people's buying pattern. The drive to reproduce (the behavior for which is romance, flirting, and the act of sex) is virtually unparalleled in humans. We could write a book about how this single drive is what life is all about.

Because this drive has been suppressed for over 3,000 years by many world cultures and religions there are many tricky nuances about specifically how to utilize this drive in the process of selling. The genetic urge for reproduction runs squarely up against many society's moral values that make it wrong to want to reproduce. Therefore when using the Sex MAP you have to be very careful indeed.

Men and women both want to be perceived as attractive. Men are hardwired to spread their seed everywhere and do so as often as they can. Women are hardwired to find a secure location for their offspring and fill it with as many babies as possible with one mate who will provide for that brood. That's at the unconscious level of course.

These very specific instinctual needs then meet society. For the most part in the 21st century, the evolutionary urges are regulated by laws. You're generally permitted one wife if you are a man and there is a limit to the number of children that is considered "reasonable." To be sure there are some religions that encourage the birth of many children. These organizations even make rules that make it almost impossible to not have kids. However, almost all of these organizations see the folly of having multiple wives and set ground rules so it can't happen.

All of this is very interesting and it makes you want to talk about it all day, but what does sex have to do with selling?

Just about everything.

There are several reasons people enter into the selling profession and most of them relate to three of the four core instinctual drives…and one of the other 13 basic desires plays a very strong wild card in the mix.

People as a group tend to be fighters. They are aggressive and face challenges daily that they overcome, get around, move beyond and they love to win. Everyday for a salesperson has an element of danger in it. People wake up unemployed every morning. If they sell they live another day, if they don't they…must return to working for someone else. (You may work for a big company as a salesperson and think that you work for the big company. You don't. They work for you. You are paying the salaries of the rest of the employees with all of the net profits from your salaries after you are paid. Only when you become a liability to you actually work for the company. This happens when your net profits do not pay for your salary and commissions.) There is something incredibly attractive about people who are in control of their own destiny to people of the opposite sex. Women in particular are attracted to providers and what are people? They provide for everyone.

People work to eat first. This doesn't mean they are overweight or even hearty eaters. Not in the least. But people work to eat. People who have jobs that pay the same amount every week don't work to eat. They work for their total sustenance. They have no control over their lives in any meaningful sense of the word. No one eats until the salesperson eats. No one. If no sales are made no other employee gets their paycheck. Once again the salesperson is the provider. They work to eat first and nothing is more attractive (to women in particular) than someone who can provide food for the group. Most people don't know this but now you do!

People have intense sex drives. (At least driven people do.) Selling is one of the few professions that require proactive action on the part of the individual. Look at these professions: Carpenter, attorney, medical doctor, chiropractor, psychologist, social worker, teacher, priest, etc. Almost every profession or job that is not a sales position requires people to come to them. In selling it's the opposite. You have to go to other people. People therefore must have an enormous set of strengths to overcome everything from rejection to the fears of interpersonal communication with every type of human being. People are generally speaking fearless in the communication setting. They are the ultimate adaptors. They have the ability to communicate with every type of person and therefore they are the most interesting people to communicate with. They have adventures to tell that are unparalleled by other professions. People are ultimately attractive to others. The drive to reproduce keeps the salesperson successful. The salesperson is someone who channels his intense evolutionary desires into profits. The sex drive, coupled with the desire to eat and the flight/fight response come together to create a lean, mean fighting machine known as a salesperson.

Now that you know that you are driven by your instincts in such a fashion, let's look at our clients.

Your client has the urge to reproduce to. You aren't the only person that "feels this way."

Your client will buy your products and services if at the unconscious level they know this will improve their ability to reproduce.

Please remember that genes don't think. They just replicate and have their orders to replicate. Those orders are causing drives in your client.

Question: How does your product appeal to your clients instinctual drive to reproduce?

Answer: Almost all products and services will help this desire or can be linked to this desire if you think about it in the right fashion.

You sell mutual funds and stocks.
✓ Who is buying your product? (Men) Who is attracted to men with resources?
✓ How might your client benefit sexually from having more money?
✓ How might your client be perceived more attractive if they are successful?
✓ How does owning stocks and mutual funds NOW, make your client more attractive in contrast to waiting?

You sell real estate.
✓ How might your client benefit sexually from buying property or homes?
✓ How might your client be perceived as more attractive if they own a beautiful and elegantly decorated home?
✓ How does owning real estate NOW, make your client more attractive in contrast to waiting to buy later?

You sell automobiles.
✓ How might your client perceived as more attractive if they own a new car?
✓ How does buying a new car now make your client more attractive in contrast to waiting?

"So you know Charlie, if you buy a home, own Cisco and IBM and get a new Lexus you're going to have some amazing sex this week."

While that might be true, we aren't going to quite frame things this way in the sales process.

"Can you imagine how you will look flying down the highway in that new Lexus? Man, I'm telling you, you will be unbelievable." (His unconscious mind fills in all the blanks.)

"Isn't owning your own place what it's all about? (For a man, the unconscious mind fills in the blanks.)

"When you two own this home you will be able to finally settle down." (For women, "settle down" = "make babies" at the unconscious level.)

"Won't your wife feel more secure if you go ahead and invest in stocks that will ensure your long term security?" (The woman is nodding her head. It's biologically wired in!)

Appealing to the needs of reproduction, sex and desire for sensual experience is a powerful motivator. Every man's magazine (Maxim, FHM, Details, Arena, Loaded, Playboy, Penthouse) is sold with a cover that features a beautiful woman on the cover. Every woman's magazine (Cosmopolitan, Mademoiselle, Ladies Home Journal, People, Entertainment Weekly) is sold with a cover that features a beautiful woman on the cover. Attraction and desire sell. Period.

Appealing to the nesting instinct sells to. Better Homes and Garden, Country Living, American Home, all are sold to women who want to nest and "settle down." They want to stay put and make their surroundings safe, secure and attractive. These desires are hard wired in to the woman's genes and they are exhibited in her behavior. What are you doing to sell to these unconscious urges and needs?

Have you ever gone into the Romance section at Barnes and Noble? There are thousands of books there with the same cover, same theme and same story. Women devour this material like men devour pornography. Women want to be romanced and they can't get enough of it. How are you linking your product or service to these needs?

Here is the continuum of the urge to reproduce in human beings. Find where you are on the continuum then see if how you perceive others matches the chart. It should. Then see how people on the other side of the spectrum perceive you. This will help you sell more efficiently both people who are like you and people who are very different.

Sexual Desire

Pleasure Seeker ←--→ **Ascetics**

Believe they are:

Flirtatious	*Conservative*
Romantic	*Virtuous*
Sensitive	*Saintly*
Carnal	*Spiritual*
Lustful	*Cerebral*

High Sex Drive   # Self Controlled

Believe other half to be:

Puritanical	*Wild*
Prudish	*Hedonistic*
Hung up	*Lacking in Control*
Impotent	*Superficial*

There are also large numbers of people who have successfully suppressed their sex drive. These people are sold by tapping into the MAPs of self-control and virtuosity. As you listen to what people say when they talk to you, discovering their most powerful drives will be simple. As with all skills, it just takes practice!

In the next module we will look at the balance of the drives that all emerge from the three core drives that we have discussed. By now, I think you are starting to see how your instincts drive your behavior and you are now probably starting to see an emerging picture of others around you that may have been foggy, until now.

Module Six

The Next Pillar of Covert Hypnosis:

Your Clients' Second Tier Desires

Each drive in this module emerges from the core drives in module five. However, they are definitely distinct from them and are important in developing a complete picture of yourself and more importantly, your client. After reading this module, your client will essentially be an open book.

People tend to be very competitive. They have to be to survive. They certainly have a strong tendency to cooperate with their clients but they are definitely competitive with others in their profession.

However, let there be no question that some people are juiced by being part of a team. Competing as part of a team energizes other people. Still others love to compete one on one. Who are you? (Remember you may fall in the middle of the continuum!) You may also find that you are on one end of the spectrum at home and another at work.

Desire to Compete or seek Vengeance

Competitive ←---→ Cooperative

Believe themselves to be:
Go Getter
Winner   *Conflict-avoidant*
Competitive   *Kind*
Aggressive   *Forgiving*
Will get even if necessary   *Turn other cheek*

Believe others to be:
Failure   *Bent out of shape*
Loser   *Aggressive*
Non-assertive   *Competitive*
Passive   Angry
Always wants to win   Always need to win.

Vengeful behavior probably began as a way to punish aggressors who stole possessions from the individual or the group. Those who would take revenge upon others may have been the protectors of the community. Perhaps 10,000 years ago they were higher on the totem pole in the society and had to protect the group from outsiders. These vengeful people became leaders because of their drive for "justice" and need to be "the best." Vengeance of course has its downside in behavior. Men still kill out of jealousy in our civilized society. The need to get even can be very intense, especially in men.

Individuals that have a difficult time controlling their anger, those who compete, and those who seek revenge fall on the competitive side of the spectrum. People who tend to avoid competitive situations definitely fall on the other side. These critical distinctions help us sell our client. Imagine that your client falls on the competitive side of the spectrum. Here is how we want to enter his MAPs.

> You sell securities. (Stocks and mutual funds)
> ✓ What matters most is what you end up with at the end.
> ✓ "Don't you deserve more because you've worked harder?"
> ✓ "Aren't you as good as the rest of them?"
> ✓ "Don't you deserve as much as anyone else?"

> You sell real estate.
> ✓ "Would you like to own the nicest house in the neighborhood?"
> ✓ "Is it important that you get the best price possible?"
> ✓ I know you. You just want the best.
> ✓ What it all comes down to is are you getting the best deal.

You sell advertising.
- ✓ "Whose image do you want to pop into people's heads first?"
- ✓ Don't YOU want to be known as the go to guy?"
- ✓ "Do you want a bigger ad than (your competitor?)"
- ✓ "What do you think the best long term strategy is to knock them out?"

Drive to Nest

Research continues to show that better educated and higher IQ people are having fewer and fewer babies. (How's that for an evolving mess?!) What is going on here? I'm not certain but understanding a person's drive to have a family is very important indeed. Obviously this drive emerges from the instinct to reproduce but it is not the same thing. Wanting to have lots of sex is not to be confused with wanting to have lots of children. Your genes don't know the difference but your 21st century brain sure does.

I often look around the office of my clients to see if they have several pictures of the wife and kids or if they have the one obligatory picture of the family...probably several years old. That helps me understand this most important desire.

Stephen Reiss notes that if raising children is essential to your happiness then you fall on one side of the spectrum. If having kids is mostly difficult you fall on the other side of the spectrum. There seems to be no difference between men and women on average with the desire to raise children so be careful of stereotyping!

When I listen to people talk about their children I want to know how much affection for those kids is resonating in the person. (I am not interested in how people view other people's children in most cases.) If they say, "my kids are great," I haven't heard anything to MAP into. If they say, "My kids are my reason for living. They make me thank God every day." That I can MAP into and here's how I do that:

You sell cars.
- ✓ "Won't your kids love having this new car?"
- ✓ "Doesn't it make you a proud Dad to be able to bring this home?"
- ✓ "What have your kids been asking you to get?"
- ✓ "How important are your kids in your decision to buy a safe car like this?"

You sell securities. (Stocks and other Financial Investments)
- ✓ "Do you factor in your kid's future when you make your investments?"

- ✓ "What's it feel like to be a responsible parent in an age where no one cares?"
- ✓ "What weight do you assign to your kids when making these decisions?"
- ✓ "Are you looking for enough to put the kids through college?"

As you consider the continuum below, where do you fall on it? Are you responsible and domestic? Do you just relish every moment with your children? Are they the center of your universe? You're on one side of the spectrum. Do you sense kids are more work than they are worth? Do you feel that children conflict with your desire for freedom? Are kids going to just tie you down for 20 years? You are on the other side of center.

The Nesting Instinct

Family←---→ Non-Family

Believe themselves to be:

Cocooner	*Out and about*
Domestic	*Independent*
Responsible	**Free**

Believe other half to be:

Selfish	*Burdened*
Irresponsible	*Tied Down*
Immature	*Imprisoned*
Unaccountable	*Obligated*

Exercise: The desire to nest and raise children is common and dominates the decision making process of most parents. How does your product or service MAP into both groups? Answer now before going on!

The Desire to Connect with Others

It is an interesting fact that people who have many friends and rich relationships tend to be healthier, live longer and heal faster when they are sick. There is an inborn drive to connect with other people that serves an important purpose in ensuring the replication of those little genes. In ancient times it was very important to gather together in groups so you could survive everything from attacks by enemies to animals. The same instinct can be seen in the modern world. People tend to live in cities. The cities are expanding to where there was once just farmland. People may not like everything about being in close proximity to others but for the most part it is how we feel comfortable.

To be sure, there is a significant percentage of the population that feels the need to live in rural areas or lead very private lives, tucked away from others. This is not the norm however and it is not the drive that has perpetuated the safety that is found within a group.

Social connections for the individual can be very important. Each week many people take time out of their everyday lives to congregate at their local church. They renew friendships and make new ones with like-minded individuals. The same experience is true of people who go to Rotary, Lions, Kiwanis and other fraternal organizations. Similarly, most people tend to find more security in working for a BIG company in contrast to a small company. The drive to connect with others is powerful and there is a price that may have to be paid for those who don't connect with others. Everything from the safety the large group provides to the healthier life one experiences with lots of connections makes it clear this instinct pays dividends.

Not everyone prefers the group though. They've fought the desire to be one of "the group." They've "gotten over" the need for acceptance. They might just want to be left alone and appreciate the solitude of peace and quiet. The stress and hustle and bustle…just aren't worth the effort for these people.

Wouldn't it be useful to MAP into the specific thinking that is driving your client?

Where do you fall on the continuum of connectivity? Do you feel happiest when you are in a group? Do you feel like there are groups to which you "belong?" Do you like to have fun with others?" Do you consider yourself a very friendly person? If so you are on the side of the instinctual drive to connect with others. On the other hand, do you tend to be serious and studious? Do you find time alone preferable to time with others? Do you find the group repulsive? Do you find yourself lonely or alone (in either a positive or negative sense)? If so you are on the other side of the fence.

Now as you think about your clients think about where some of them fall on the spectrum.

Desire to Connect with Others

Sociable ←--→ Private

Believe themselves to be:

Warm	*Intimate*
Approachable	*Secret*
Friendly	*Serious*
Fun	*Unhappy*
Lively	**Lonely**

Believe other half to be:

Cold	*Out There*
Reclusive	*Loud*
Aloof	*Lack Depth*
Private	*Superficial*
Serious	*Shallow*
Shy	*Boisterous*

You sell cars.
- ✓ "Won't it be fun to go out in your new car?"
- ✓ "Traveling becomes fun again with this car doesn't it?"
- ✓ "Won't it be nice to drive up to the office in this one?"

You sell real estate.
- ✓ "Won't it be nice to throw a party in your beautiful new home?"
- ✓ "Isn't it going to be fun entertaining here?"
- ✓ "Isn't it nice to have a neighborhood with so many nice people?"

You are a travel agent.
- ✓ "Won't it be fun to take spring break in Orlando with all the people?"
- ✓ "Won't it be great to take a cruise and meet people just like you?"
- ✓ "Can you imagine Las Vegas at Halloween and all the people you will see?"

Exercise: Write key questions and sentences that will help you enter your client's Mind Access Points. Include sentence and questions for people on both ends of the spectrum, not just the side of the instinctual drive!

Seeking Power

Power is the ability to influence the behavior of others.

Poland's leading magazine is called *wProst*. It's as influential in Poland as *Time* in the United States. *WProst* did an extensive interview with me in 2000. They printed the interview and a nice photo to boot. The caption read something like, Kevin Hogan, "The Guru of Business Psychology." *WProst* lent power to my work for the people of Poland who didn't know me from your brother in law. On my next trip to Poland I received the royal treatment. Everyone from the people in the hotel to the people who came to the Sales Conference I spoke at in 2001 wanted autographs and pictures. Why? Because *wProst* said I was the Guru of Business Psychology.

Particularly interesting about this specific experience is that the millions of people who read this magazine believe what they read. The magazine, like magazines in all countries, shapes opinions about who or what is important. It creates perceptions in people's minds that may or not be accurate. In my case, the stamp of approval was important to my message being well received. I used that instant rapport in many ways that were useful for the audiences I spoke to.

Power is a two way street. People have to be willing to give someone power and someone has to desire the power for the power to be utilized on a long-term basis. Power is a fascinating subject but let's see how to tap the drive for power with your client.

The word alone creates images in your mind. The drive to reach the top of some pecking order (to become a big fish in a small pond) is common among men. They seek power in different ways. Some strive to political power. Do you know how many multi-millionaires there are in the House of Representatives?! Why would a man who is a multi-millionaire spend millions of dollars of his own money to get a job that pays $110,000 per year?

Power.

Other men seek power in different ways and on different levels. The evangelist who is enlightened seeks the followers to listen to his message. The author wants people to read his book and the judge wants to be the representative of justice. The police officer wants the power to control behavior and the mayor wants the reigns of the city. They want to have the biggest burger joint, the biggest airline, the prettiest wife, the most fans, the most clients, the most money and on and on. They all want power and to some degree or more they get some power.

Unfortunately the drive for power can get ugly. The striving and acquisition of power can cause wars and literally cost millions of people their lives. Power is a powerful drive that can help individuals to ascend to do great good or ill. This deep desire of human nature is chiefly a drive of male behavior in contrast to female behavior. (Understand that both men and women want power, the point is to what degree the genders want power. There is no question that great power is sought and acquired by far more men than women.

Whether your client is male or female isn't that important. Everyone (almost everyone) wants to influence human behavior. We all want our children to obey. We want the neighbors to change some of their behaviors. We want the idiot at the stoplight in front of us to turn left so we can get going. We all want to influence the behaviors of other people. This is the striving for power.

How does your product or service help your client acquire power?

If your client can see how you can help them become more influential, and power IS influence then you can virtually ensure a sale.

Look at the continuum below and see where you fall on the continuum for the desire to have power. If you find yourself to be ambitious, influential, working 60 hours per week and have a dominant personality you fall on one side of the spectrum. If you aren't particularly ambitious, tend to be people oriented and a good support person, you probably fall on the other end of the spectrum. Find yourself on the continuum first then consider where your clients tend to fall on the spectrum.

Seeking Power

Leader ←--------------------------------------→ Follower

Believe themselves to be:

Enterprising	*Simple*
Aspiring	*Humble*
Motivated	*Undemanding*
Ambitious	*Not ambitious*
Influential	*People oriented*
Hard working	*Submissive*
Dominant	

See the other half as:

Allergic to work	*Lofty*
Unmotivated	**Demanding**
Lazy	*Domineering*
Weak	*Not caring*
Unsuccessful	*Controlling*
	Workaholic

How do you use the drive of power to sell?

You sell cars.
- ✓ "Doesn't driving a Mercedes give others the impression of you that you want them to have?"
- ✓ "Doesn't owning a new car make a statement about what you can have?"

You sell real estate.
- ✓ "Some people say it's a good investment to have the least expensive house in a neighborhood. Doesn't it say something to have the nicest house in the neighborhood?"
- ✓ "When people see this house, how will they respond to you?"

You sell securities.
- ✓ "Money is power and power is freedom. Isn't that what you want?"
- ✓ "Doesn't having money mean that you can do anything you want?"

Exercise: *Write key questions and sentences that will help you enter your client's Mind Access Points. Include sentence and questions for people on both ends of the spectrum, not just one side of the instinctual drive*

Seeking Status

Everyone wants to be important to someone else. Some people want to be important to larger groups. Status and power often dovetail, but not always. The desire to be perceived as important is a driving force in human nature. In the last five years newsgroups on the Internet have become an interesting battleground for status. People who never have been well known publicly can obtain social status (good and bad) in various small groups by posting regularly to these various groups. Everyone looks the same in text so people with time on their hands can be seen as players in whatever field of interest they feel they have a right to make public comments about.

"15 minutes" is a well-known phrase in America that refers to everyone's average amount of fame they will experience at some point in their life. Many people want more than 15 minutes. Some people are motivated by their drives and desires to be seen as having "more" or become well known in certain ways. Some people will buy a mansion. Someone else might drive a ridiculously priced house or an enormous diamond. All of these are "status symbols." The people that produce status products realize this and can command a premium for these types of products.

Some of your clients may only need to be important to their family. Some may feel the need to be important to the large group. Knowing where the MAPs are is vital. Do you find yourself buying the best or the most expensive things in certain areas? Do you buy things to impress other people? If so, then you fall on one side of the spectrum. On the other hand, you may find yourself unimpressed by royalty, status, prestige and the accoutrements thereof. If you don't care what others think then you fall on the other side of the spectrum. First determine where you lie on the continuum then think of many of your clients and decide if they are driven by status.

Desire for Status

Social Climber ←---→ **Egalitarian**

See themselves as:

Moving up	*Equal to everyone else*
Prestigious	*Libertarian*
Important	*Fair minded*
Worthy of recognition	*Democratic*
Prominent	**Down to earth**

See others as:

Unknown	*Stuffed shirt*
Insignificant	*Highbrow*
Unimportant	*Snob*
Low class	*Arrogant*
Poor Taste	*Show off*

How do you use status to sell your product or service?

You sell securities.
- ✓ "Imagine how people will look at you when you are retired compared to the rest of the people who don't care about their futures."
- ✓ "When you are wealthy from all of these investments, please remember the little people who helped you get there."

You sell cars.
- ✓ "Just imagine how you are going to look driving this new car!
- ✓ "People will think you have really made it when they see you driving this!

You sell real estate.
- ✓ "There is no doubt that this house is a statement. You have arrived."
- ✓ "This house says that "you have worked hard and you deserve the best."

Exercise: Look at your product/service now and decide what phrases, sentences and questions you could ask someone on either end of the elitist/egalitarian spectrum.

Seeking Independence

The group offers protection and social contact. Those are two elements absolutely necessary for the perpetuation of your genes! Once secure in those two factors, the individual comes to an age where it is time to set out on their own. In ancient days this was necessary to find food. The group had formed. Lots of people congregating together in one place is not going to be positively correlated to having animals stop by to sacrifice themselves for the community dinner.

The desire to strike out of the collective is very important indeed. Today we find that people often need to make a change after having relied on the group for so long. In ancient days there was much more work to be done than in our 21st century society. Capturing food and preparing it was a hard days work...if not a week or months. The need for self-reliance is not only an instinctual need it is a key drive for success and achievement in life.

People who are "independent" feel they are self-reliant. They say things like, "If you want it done right, you have to do it yourself." "I just want to be free." And indeed, like a bird put in a cage, the individual struggles to become free. The birdcage becomes a prison though and over time the individual becomes reliant upon others. The need for self-reliance is conditioned out of the person and they learn a new set of behaviors. These we will call "interdependent." Interdependence serves many functions.

Interdependent people are easier to love because they are home more often! They appear to have more invested in the personal and social aspects of relationships and they are more connected with others in their home and their community. Interdependent people see themselves as loving people who are much more devoted to their spouses and families than independent people.

As you look at the continuum for independence/interdependence, where do you seem to belong? Are you more freedom seeking and autonomous or do you tend to act far more devoted to those around you than the average person?

Desire for Independence

Independent ←--→ Interdependent

Believe themselves to be:
Self-Sufficient
Reliable
Self Reliant   *Loving*
Autonomous   *Trusting*
Free   # Devoted
Resistant to the herd spirit

Believe the other half to be:
Immature   # Inflexible
Weak   *Prideful*
Dependent   *Strong Willed*
Needy   *Bullheaded*

How will we link into the MAP of your client who has a strong drive for independence?

> You sell securities. (Stocks, bonds)
> ✓ "Won't it be nice when you can rely solely on yourself when you are older?"
> ✓ "Have you ever known anyone who was wealthy who wasn't their own investor?"
> ✓ "Do you find that having money build up makes you more independent thinking?"
> ✓ "Would you say that investing for your future will give you financial freedom?"
> ✓ "Isn't it nice to not be a slave to anyone?"
>
> You sell Mary Kay distributorships. (or any face/face direct sales!)
> ✓ "Isn't nice to be able to do something on your own?"
> ✓ "Doesn't it feel good to be your own boss?"
> ✓ "What's it like being on your own?"
> ✓ "How good does it feel to know that you aren't a slave to someone else?"
>
> You sell real estate.
> ✓ "Isn't nice to not be a slave to rent any more?"
> ✓ "What's it like to have you or own home finally?"
> ✓ "Isn't it nice to live well and build your independence at the same time?"
> ✓ "How is buying this home going to help you achieve financial independence?"

Exercise: Look at your product/service now and decide what phrases, sentences and questions you could ask someone on either end of the independence/interdependence spectrum.

Desire of Curiosity

Sherlock Holmes. He searched and found the clues that pointed him to the truth. In his cases there was always a villain who left a trail of clues, albeit minute and often almost impossible to notice. Holmes was the great detective. He told fascinating stories of his travels, he was aware of every move someone would make and he was brilliant. Holmes would have made a terrible detective had he not been curious.

Richard Brodie, who you met in the last module, introduced me to a friend of his on a recent trip we all made to Las Vegas. Jeffrey Gitomer had just arrived in town. I was familiar with his book, *The Sales Bible*, and his masterpiece about client service called, *"Client Service is Worthless, Client Loyalty is Priceless."*
I had never heard Jeffrey speak but I knew from his writing style he was going to be a no nonsense kind of guy.

We met at a little restaurant just off the strip. Jeffrey and I were both exhausted from flying into town. We exchanged pleasantries and immediately he began.

"I see you wrote this book, The Psychology of Persuasion."

"I did, have you read it yet?"

"No."

"I thought your 'Worthless/Loyalty' book was great."

"Good job kid." (He called me kid. For future reference: As of the publication of this book I will be 40. Had I been much younger than this, the reference to kid would have been particularly annoying. However, the fact that Jeffrey is at least 10 years my senior, I forgave him…in less than one week…)

"How's Loyalty doing?"

"It's fine. Define selling for me in two words."

I drank my wine….or most of it at that request. Selling in two words. Geez' Jeffrey, summarize War and Peace in two words…this is what I get for being last at the table. Richard has obviously prodded you into getting inside of my head and pushing buttons instantly…OK, here we go.

"Build Rapport."

"No. Guess again."

Guess again!? Build rapport is a heckuva answer for this off the cuff, "Who Wants to Be A Millionaire" at Batista's restaurant. I look at Richard. He is restraining a smile. His girlfriend, Heather has not restrained her smile. She is clearly thrilled that I am getting tutored...

"I can't guess heads or tails on a two sided coin. You tell me, in two words Jeffrey, summarize selling."

"Ask questions."

Well duh. You have to ask questions or you're just a videotape that is constantly replayed over and over...and...why didn't I say that. It's a better answer than "build rapport." This is the kind of guy I could really be annoyed with, if I wasn't ready to learn so much...

"Good answer."

"I know."

Ask questions. Why? Because we don't know their answers. We can only imagine we know their answers until we ask. Then we know their answers. That's what selling IS all about. (By the way, lest you think the distinction had been *previously lost on me, there is an entire section in The* Psychology of Persuasion highlighting the significance of asking questions!)

Aristotle was a philosopher some two millennia ago. He wrote about curiosity and I think there is a lot to be learned from his writing. There are four things that humans are intensely curious about.

---

1) We want to know what things are made out of.
2) We are curious about the forms and shapes that things take.
3) We are curious about the beginnings and causes of things and events.
4) We are curious about the purposes or goals of people, things, and events.

We were curious about these things thousands of years ago and we still are. Begin to tap into people's curiosity!

Genuine curiosity about all that goes on around us is a survival and success mechanism. Curiosity helps individuals become capable of solving problems and that once again helps keep our genes flowing! People who are very curious consider themselves to be intelligent, thoughtful and aware. On the other side of the spectrum are people who are not interested in intellectual pursuits. They tend to lives simpler and more practical lives. They consider themselves "street smart" having learned from experience. Interestingly, people on both ends of the spectrum consider people on the opposite ends to be boring and this brings up a critical point:

The only way to avoid being boring is to ask questions!

Your only hope to not bore someone to tears is to be certain you know where they are on the Curiosity continuum! Simply communicating our wealth of knowledge and interests to another person is one of the riskiest communication behaviors there is. If you have someone on the other end of the spectrum as your listener, they won't listen for long.

Look at the continuum below. Where do you find yourself? If you are often seeking intellectual pursuits, trying to find out why you are here, are in search for the truth and general want to know "more," then you fall on the intellectual side of the spectrum. On the other hand if you find yourself to be more of the "street smart," and practical, down to earth type, you fall on the other side of the spectrum. Now, that you have "found your self," think about some of your clients. Where do they fall on the continuum?

Desire for Curiosity

Intellectual ←--→ Non-Intellectual

Believe themselves to be:

Engaging	*Sensible*
Fascinating	*Sane*
Smart	*Practical*
Interesting	*Down to earth*
Aware	**Street Smart**

Believe the other half to be:

Boring	*Boring*
Ignorant	*Nerd*
Superficial	*Arrogant*
Dull	

How do we frame our questions and statements to MAP into another person's desire of curiosity?

> You sell real estate.
> - ✓ "Are you looking for a home that is close to a church?"
> - ✓ "How many rooms will you need Internet access in?"
> - ✓ "Will you use one of the bedrooms as an office or library?"
>
> You sell securities.
> - ✓ "Would you like a complementary 90 day subscription to Investors Business Daily?"
> - ✓ "Would you like a list of the best investment websites?"
> - ✓ "Are you interested in technical analysis of these stocks?"
>
> You sell cars.
> - ✓ "Would you like to look at what Consumers Reports has to say about this car?"
> - ✓ "Would you like to see what Edmunds.com shows the value of your trade in is?"
> - ✓ "Are you interested in seeing how this car compares to our competitors?"

Exercise: *Consider your product or service. How can you MAP into the thinking of your clients with the desire of curiosity? Write down several questions, statements and themes.*

Desire for Acceptance

"You better go back to driving a truck, son." That's what the manager of the Grand Ole Opry told Elvis in 1955. The manager had determined that Elvis Presley simply didn't have what it would take to be a star. A person who lacked in self confidence never could have gone on to fought his way to the top. The non-assertive individual desiring acceptance of group norms would have immediately packed his guitar and decided to go back to driving that electrician's truck. Thankfully the need for acceptance by the group is over-ridden in cases like that of Presley's.

I spent an enormous amount of time researching and writing the book. The first draft was written in 1991. I submitted the manuscript to a publisher that in less than two years would go bankrupt and my manuscript was returned. That was 1993. Beginning in late 1993 I began submitting the manuscript to publishers all over the United States. Week after week I would receive rejection letters. Many of them said that I had no chance of being published without an agent. But I was determined that the book was an excellent piece of work that would help people sell and persuade others to their way of thinking. I was **certain** that if people read this book they would love it and more importantly that the book would help change their lives. As of 1995 I had received over 240 rejection letters for The Psychology of Persuasion. Then I wrote one letter with a personal touch...

For years I had admired Zig Ziglar. He was always one of my favorite authors and speakers. I knew Pelican Publishing in Louisiana published him. I wrote Pelican and told them that I was going to be the next Zig Ziglar. I had already begun a somewhat successful speaking career, had self published two books by this time and was ready for a hard cover. Trust me, I told them, I'll make it happen.

240 rejections...then they said "yes." Since that time I have been in a Win/Win relationship with Pelican and we're still receiving great reviews and inquiries to speak about the Psychology of Persuasion. Had I followed my "common sense," I never would have sent out any manuscripts after the first 50 and certainly none after 100. I was absolutely certain though that I was going to be a popular author. Today of course you see the Psychology of Persuasion in bookstores from Los Angeles to Warsaw and London to New Delhi. It's been published in China and Brazil. Defying the voice that said "give up" that was programmed in by the group was something I never questioned. I was certain that The Psychology of Persuasion was a great book. I've never regretted not listening to all the other people who told me I was wasting my time...and getting a real job that "paid benefits." I'm a salesman...paid benefits...geesh...

The desire for acceptance though is what keeps people in large groups though and the desire for acceptance has its benefit. People who desire acceptance tend to "go with the flow" better than people who are defiant in the storm. People who "go with the flow" tend to experience less stress and make fewer waves. There are a lot of benefits there. More calm, more relaxed. Virtually everyone would prefer that they be accepted and liked by the group. That said, not everyone **needs** to be accepted and herein lies this desire. Those people who need to be liked tend to very non-assertive by nature. They are literally needy.

As you look at the continuum below do you find yourself being more a "go with the flow" kind of person or do you see yourself as being more assertive? Which side of the continuum do you fall on?

Desire for Acceptance

Go with the Group ←---→**Assertive**

Believe themselves to be:
Insecure   *Assertive*
Lacking in Self Confidence   *Confident*
Not Assertive   **Self Assured**
Go with the flow   *Persistent*

Believe others to be:
Conceited   *Needy*
Too Confident   *Immature*
Slick   *Overly Sensitive*

How do you sell the person who needs acceptance?

You sell cars.
✓ "This is the most popular car out there."
✓ "This car will make you look and feel great."
✓ "Don't feel pressured to buy this car. Just drive it and see if it feels right."
✓ "This car is safe and reliable. You will feel comfortable owning it."

You sell securities.
✓ "I work for people who don't feel comfortable investing on their own."
✓ "I've been doing this for 15 years, why don't you let me take the pressure off you and show you what will make your future more secure."
✓ "This is a simple growth mutual fund. Nothing aggressive. Just consistent and steady."
✓ "Most people who want a solid future will have a balanced portfolio. Does that sound like you?"

You sell real estate.
- ✓ "This is a pretty conservative home that you will feel safe in."
- ✓ "This is a pretty conservative neighborhood. I think you will be comfortable here."
- ✓ "Would you like to handle getting a loan on your own or do you want me to take all the stress out of it and do it for you?

Exercise: Consider your product or service. Decide now how you will communicate with people on both sides of the acceptance spectrum. Write down sentences, questions and themes that will appeal to people on both sides of the continuum.

Desire to Have Honor

We aren't really "just" animals anymore. Consciousness is something that is experienced by just about every living person. The need to be decent to people is something that is respectable. This need certainly has its root in the evolving race we are in. If people didn't cooperate with others there would be no economic expansion, no long term relationships and eventually the groups that collect into urban areas would all turn on each other and self-destruct. That doesn't happen though because many people have honed the desire to be honorable into a key personal value.

Obviously the counterpart has its place to. There is a certain amount of checking and double-checking that takes place in honorable people. Sometimes there are so many reassurances that need to be made that things don't ever get done. Sometimes expedience is more useful than principle.

In ancient days disloyalty was severely punished. In times of war, loyalty is severely punished. You can be certain that loyalty and honor are rooted deeply in our behavior. Always remember that many have grown to make the trade-offs that disloyalty offers. A sense of individuality and freedom come with expedience. Breaking away from the group to strike out on your own becomes important to many.

As you look at the continuum below. Where do you find yourself? Are you more focused on principles, loyalty, morals and duty or are you more of an opportunist, practical minded and expedient?

The Desire of Principled Loyalty

Principled ←--→ Expedient

Believe themselves to be:

Devoted	*Resourceful*
Dedicated	*Quick Thinking*
Patriotic	*Problem Solving*
Moral	*Practical*
Have Character	*Opportune*
Dutiful	**Like everyone else**
Loyal	**Pragmatic**

Believe others to be:

Disloyal	*Self-Righteous*
Self Serving	*Holier than thou*
Lacking Character	**Sanctimonious**
	Impractical

How do you MAP into your clients mind with the instinct of loyalty?

You sell securities.
- ✓ "If I can help you begin to meet your financial goals will you work with me long term?"
- ✓ "If I help you succeed will you refer me to the rest of the people in your family and at the office?"
- ✓ "I see you've done well with Fidelity over the years. Do you want to stick with Fidelity Select Funds or would you rather switch to another company?"

You sell advertising.
- ✓ "If I can help you make money will you let me structure your marketing program as well?"
- ✓ "If I write you an ad that pulls will you refer me to your non-competing buddies?"
- ✓ "If I write you an ad that makes money will you give me a list of names I can call to help get the same results?"

Exercise*: Consider your product or service and prepare questions, statements and themes about how to specifically sell to people on both sides of the spectrum of loyalty.*

Desire for Altruism

No doubt about it, we all have our altruistic moments. Some people live a life of altruism. Mother Theresa may have been the most well known altruist of our times. People who sacrifice something of themselves for others are often living up to a higher value or spiritual level. This doesn't mean that altruism isn't rewarded many times over though. Altruism is as old as the ancients. Altruism pays off for the individual when the individual believes that their behavior is being seen or felt on another level. At this level they feel as if they are attaining their highest good and that they are truly making a difference. Self-sacrifice brings self-satisfaction and that is a very good thing indeed!

Of course many people have over-ridden the desire to be altruistic. We call these people realists. Realists tend to be more focused on the self as opposed to others. This is neither good nor bad but once again the realist is either moving away from the group or attempting to move higher up in the group. The idealistic tend to stay centered in the group.

As you look at the spectrum of behaviors below, where do you find yourself? Do you find yourself mostly caring, compassionate, self-sacrificing and altruistic? If so you fall on the left side of the spectrum. If you find yourself more pragmatic, realistic and self focused then you are on the other side of the continuum.

Desire for Idealism and Realism

Idealistic←--→Realistic

Believe themselves to be:

Caring	*Pragmatic*
Selfless	*Practical*
Humanitarian	*Real World*
Giving	*Sensible*
Compassionate	*Looking out for #1*
Visionary	**Realistic**

Believe others to be:

Self centered	*Idealistic*
Heartless	**Dreamer**
Insensitive	*Meddlesome*
Unfeeling	*Unrealistic*

How do you sell someone who has the desire for idealism?

You sell securities.
- ✓ "If you find you make a lot more money than you think would you want me to set up a giving program for you?"
- ✓ "How do you see yourself using your money if you become wealthy beyond your plans?"

You sell direct sales products or services.
- ✓ "A portion of all sales goes towards…"
- ✓ "Would you like us to donate a portion of the proceeds toward…"
- ✓ "Not only would you be purchasing your new X for yourself but you will have made a difference for me and I appreciate that.

You sell business opportunities.
- ✓ "The real nice thing about owning your own business is you can turn around and help other people help themselves."
- ✓ "The great thing about being in business for yourself is that you ultimately decide how you will help people."

Exercise: *Consider your product or service and prepare questions, statements and themes about how to specifically sell to people on both sides of the spectrum of altruism.*

Desire for Order

Once people collect things, or collect groups of people around themselves, they have a desire to be organized. People like to have "stuff" but they often want to be neat about it! Being organized is a signpost of control for a lot of people. Being organized means that the person is in charge and this is a key to motivating others. We want people's behavior to be neat and orderly as well. We tend to identify organization with intelligence although there is no evidence to support such a belief.

Some people really enjoy the ability to live without a script. Some people look at a speaker who knows all of his lines as the most boring speaker in the world. Others appreciate the organized and well-prepared individual. People who are organized like and appreciate processes and algorithms. These people taking direction and feel left off on their own all alone if they don't have the direction.

Having considered the two ends of the spectrum, do you find yourself neat, in control, socialized, orderly, organized, enjoying the process? On the other hand

114

do you enjoy spontaneity? Do you prefer being flexible instead of having to do things the same way all the time? If so you are on the other side of the continuum.

Desire for Order

Organized←---→ **Flexible**

Believe themselves to be:
Neat
Tidy
In Control
Socialized

Flexible
Natural
Spontaneous
Unrehearsed

Believe others to be:
Sloppy
Dirty
Out of control
Messy
Disorganized

Too perfect
Controlling of others
Concerned with trivia
Neat freaks
Rigid

How do you sell the organized person?

You sell real estate.
✓ "Will this house provide you with the space you need for all of your stuff?"
✓ "Where do you see all of your stuff going in this house?"
✓ "Will having the den as an office help you keep the rest of the house neater?"

You sell clothing.
✓ "How will other people see you in this new coat and tie?"
✓ "Does this suit present the image you are looking to project?"
✓ "Does this outfit give you that 'take charge and in control' appearance?"

Exercise: Consider your product or service and prepare questions, statements and themes about how to specifically sell to people on both sides of the spectrum of order.

Desire to Save

Nature has always favored that which saves and prepares for the future. The squirrel collects and stores nuts so that it will not go without in the winter. People who save their money are doing the same thing. They simply are using the currency of the 21st century, their money. The individual who saves is fulfilling the drive to preserve their self and their family...and of course that means their genes.

It is rare that a person can go through life without saving and live a fruitful "second half" (the last 30-50 years of life). If this is true what benefits are there of being a "spender" or a "consumer?" The consumer of products and services is someone who lives in the moment. They fear not for tomorrow and they probably live with more instant gratification. They believe they should enjoy life and they feel they are deserving of the fruits of life.

Very few people can live this lifestyle and have anything left over but it does make the early years of life more enjoyable. Unfortunately, like the animals that don't save, there will be no quality of life later.

Americans save less than 5% of their annual income. The Japanese save 27% of their annual income. That tells us that saving money can be done and that some societies are wisely preparing for their future. On the other hand, people who live in the United States are having a better life today, if not sacrificing their future for the pleasures of today.

Look at the continuum below. Are you the kind of a person who is storing money for the future when you may be less able to earn it? Do you regularly say "no" to consuming and spending and "yes" to investing and saving? If so, you fall on one side of the continuum. On the other hand, do you live for today? Do you find yourself living more richly today than others? If so then you are on this side of the spectrum. Now, think about where most of your clients are.

Desire to Save

Saver ←--→ Spender

Believe themselves to be:
Conserving
Frugal   *Enjoying Life*
Thrifty   *Deserving*
Planning Ahead

Believe others to be:
Irresponsible   *Miser*
Imprudent   *Money Grubber*
Living for only today   *Cheap*
Wasteful   Self Denying
Extravagant   *Penny Pincher*

How do you sell the saver?

You sell securities.
- ✓ "Would you like me to show you how to have an even richer tomorrow?"
- ✓ "Would you like to really have a retirement that is filled with fun and time for what you really want to do?"
- ✓ "How far ahead do you want to prepare for?"

You sell real estate.

- ✓ "You know what the best investment there is don't you? Your home."
- ✓ "Can you invest too much money in your own home?" "With your own home, every dollar works for you. Either you pay off principal or you get a tax write off."

Exercise: Consider your product or service and prepare questions, statements and themes about how to specifically sell to people on both sides of the spectrum of saving.

Desire for Physical Activity

In ancient times, the inactive and lazy were punished with starvation and attack by animals and enemies. It is a normal drive for people to want to be active. Not too many years ago humans spent their entire day hunting and gathering. The all day search for food was critical to survival. No activity ultimately meant death.

Today the United States is the land of the couch potato. The majority of Americans are overweight. Not only is that not attractive it is a harbinger of early demise. Within America there is a physical fitness movement. Many cities actually have become known as physically fit. These include cities like Seattle and Minneapolis. People in these cities, among others seem to have figured it out. If we keep sitting on the couch, we can have all the money we want, but it won't matter. We won't be around to spend it!

Do you find yourself to be full of energy? Do you enjoy vigorous activity? Are you a fitness nut? Would you call yourself athletic? If so, you fall on this side of the spectrum. On the other hand, maybe you find yourself easy going and low key. If so, you are on the other side of the spectrum.

What about your clients? Where do they tend to cluster on the spectrum of the desire for activity?

Desire for Physical Activity

Active ←---→ **Inactive**

Believe themselves to be:

Energetic	*Self-paced*
Vigorous	*Easy Going*
Fit	*Low Key*
Athletic	**Laid Back**

Believe others to be:

Lazy	*Jocks*
Slow	*Physical*
Sedentary	*Exhausting*
Couch Potato	*Fast Paced*

How do you sell the person who desires activity?

You sell securities.
✓ "When you have more money what will you do with your free time?"

✓ "Will you find yourself participating in more fun activities when you see your portfolio build?"

You sell real estate.
✓ "Are you going to want a room that we can put a Nordic Track or Stairmaster into?"

Exercise: Consider your product or service and prepare questions, statements and themes about how to specifically sell to people on both sides of the spectrum of activity.

The sixteen desires are all rooted in our instinctual evolutionary drives. These are the drives that shape human behavior. Some of the drives are obviously more important to tap into, on average than others, in the sales process.

Review these two modules regularly so you can be certain that your sales and marketing messages are feeding into not only the drives but the reaction to the drives (the other side of the spectrum) as well. Are you MAPping into the right drives with the right people? That's ultimately one of the keys to scientifically using covert hypnosis and the master key to success.

Module Seven

Unconscious Nonverbal Communication
Success Without Words:
Mastering Body Language

It was early in the morning on a cold winters day. The phone rang. I was still in bed after a hard day's night of writing a module in a book. I rolled over and grabbed for the phone.

"Kevin Hogan." Trying to sound like I was awake.

"Is this Doctuh Hogan?" New Jersey accent. No doubt going to sell me something.

"Yes, I am very busy." Almost ready to hang up the phone.

"This is Rita Delfiner with the New Yoke Post." I bet she means New York. Isn't that the tabloid? The National Enquirer of newspapers? I live in Minnesota. She's not trying to sell me something. I sit up.

"Doctuh Hogan, we understand you are a body language exput." Why don't they have "r's in New Jersey?

"Yes, that's right. How can I help you Rita?"

"The President of the United States is going to give a press briefing in a few minutes saying that he didn't have an affair with an office intern. We'd like you to watch it and give us your point of view as to whether he is lying or telling the truth."
"O.K. Call me when it's over. I'll turn on CNN now."

Why the heck would Bill Clinton deny an affair? Kennedy had Monroe. That's something you can write home about. If I were married to Hillary Clinton, I mean, the man is only human...but the New York Post...yeah, yeah, yeah...where is my robe. Ah, there it is. CNN. There is Bernie Shaw. Doesn't he ever sleep?

President Clinton appears on the TV screen.

He raises the index finger on his right hand. He is visibly shaken. I would be too if I had to deny an affair. It's one of those things that don't matter if you did it or not. You're guilty because some moron says you did.

"...I did not have sexual relations with that woman Monica Lewinsky."

He rested his hands on the front of the podium, fingers placed over the front. There's Gore in the background. He could be President but who knows if he can even talk. Hillary is over there on the other side. She looks annoyed but supportive. Why did he put those fingers on the front of the podium? He's never done that before. He looks like he has seen a ghost.

RING.

"This is Kevin Hogan."

"Hi Doctuh Hogan, this is Rita Delfiner with the New Yoke Post. Did he do it?"

Did he do it? I just watched the same thing you did for goodness sake. How the heck do I know? I can't read the guys mind for heaven's sake.

"Rita, I'd like to watch it a few more times and then get back to you." Click.

I rewind my tape in the VCR and push play.

"I did not have sexual relations with that woman Monica Lewinksy." Rewind. Play.

"I did not have sexual relations with that woman Monica Lewinsky." Rewind. Play. Rewind. Play. Rewind. Play.

I stand up and I raise my right index finger into the air. I say out loud. "I did not have sex with Monica Lewinsky." Who is Monica Lewinsky anyway? I stand in the exact same position as Clinton. I am denying that I had sex with Monica.

Then it hit me.

I switch hands. I raise my LEFT index finger and wag it at my TV. "I did not have relations with Monica Lewinsky." Oh my! I did. Holy smokes, I did have sex with Monica. Whoa! Mr. President, you little dickens you. Tell no one, but I couldn't be happier for you.

RING

"City of Bloomington." (It's my wife's voice.)

"Hey, did you just watch the President?"

"No, I'm working." (That's what all government employees are instructed to say when approached about working.)

I want you to raise your left hand, wag your finger at the camera and say, "I did not have sexual relations with that woman Monica Lewinsky."

"What?"

"Just like Clinton just did."

"I told you I haven't been watching TV."

"Oh." (I explain the events of the morning.)

"...so now, raise your left hand, wag your finger at the camera and say, 'I didn't have sexual relations with that woman Monica Lewinsky.'"

She does so as I listen.

"Now switch to your right hand. Do the same thing."

She does so as I listen.

"Which hand do you believe?"

"Huh?"

"Which hand is certain it didn't have sex?"

"My right hand."

"Me too."

"But you said Clinton used is his right hand, so he didn't do it, right?"

"Clinton is a southpaw."

Click.

OK. Let's think about this. I rewind the VCR again and push play. I stand and do everything Clinton does. He did it. No wonder he's always smiling. You rascal, Mr. President.

RING.

"Hello this is Rita Delfiner with the New Yoke Post again. What do you think Doctuh Hogan?"

"Rita, you can say, that Kevin Hogan, author of The Psychology of Persuasion, says that the President of the United States had some kind of sexual relationship with Monica Lewinsky."

"How did you determine that Doctuh?"

I explain the whole process to her. She asks a few more questions but she has her headline. I'm the first person in the United States to say that Bill Clinton had sexual relations with Monica Lewinsky.

Boy, I hope I'm right....

By the end of the week, I was interviewed by dozens of radio stations all over the United States. Over and over and over. The same questions, the same analysis of the body language and the dead giveaway in impotent denial.

Worst part was I like the President. Best part, this is going to sell some books. Clinton will understand. That's how you become President.

As a rule a person's body language should be similar to or congruent with their verbal communication. You should know that I could have been wrong about the President. I've analyzed the former President's body for his entire term in office. I have hours of the President speaking on video. (He happens to be the finest speaker as President we have ever had and that includes Reagan who was also a brilliant speaker.)

Had Clinton denied his indiscretion with his left hand I would have been less inclined to authoritatively state that he "did it." You can never be absolutely certain about what another person is thinking based upon their body language but there are definitely clues in the cues that you see. This was a big one. Now, before we go on, I want you to take your right hand (or your left hand if you are left handed) and say, "I did not have sexual relations with Monica Lewinsky." Now take your other hand/finger and do the same. Do you feel the difference? Now that you have one specific behavior understood let's look at some of the critical body language events in meeting with your client.

It's not fair but it's true: Your Physical Appearance Matters

Your body language and your physical appearance will boost you to the top or keep you among the majority of people in the middle and bottom. You have less than 10 seconds and realistically closer to four seconds to make a good first impression on those you come into contact with. There is a world of research that clearly indicates that you will be judged professionally and personally in the first few seconds of your meeting someone for the first time. In fact your first impression is recorded and is used as a yardstick for all future communication by those whom you meet. Whatever that first impression is going to be on your part, you want it to be intentional and on purpose.

Before going any further in discussing verbal communication we better take a look at how to really be perceived as attractive with your body language. Most people are completely unaware of just how much their body says and how it often contradicts what the words are saying! There are numerous elements of what we call body language. They include your physical features both changeable and unchangeable, your gestures and signals that you send to others at the conscious and unconscious level and the space that you use when communicating with others. In this module we will touch on all of these important areas of body language.

What You Look Like Really Talks

Let's begin with our physical appearance. Here are some astounding facts that will give you pause for thought when you consider how important appearance is in attraction.

Your perceived level of attractiveness by other people will be a significant benefit or detriment in your sales career and your life. It isn't fair but it is true. People who are attractive learn how to deal with less than perfect physical features and work with what they can. Before we consider just how to increase your face value in the next module, look at the results of some fascinating studies about physical appearance.

The Power of Physical Appearance

Did you know that in university settings, professors who are considered physically attractive by students are considered to be better teachers on the whole than unattractive professors? Attractive professors are also more likely to be asked for help on problems. These same attractive professors also tend to receive positive recommendations from other students to take their classes and also are less likely to receive the blame when a student receives a failing grade! (Romano and Bordieri 1989)

Did you know that marriage and dating decisions are often made with great weight placed on physical attractiveness? A wide variety of research indicates that men will often reject women who are lacking (in their opinion) in positive physical features. Women on the other hand place less significance on a man's physical attractiveness in considering him for a date or marriage. (studies by R.E. Baber)

Did you know that in studies done on college campuses, it has been proven that attractive females (attraction as perceived by the professors) receive significantly higher grades than male students or relatively unattractive females? (studies by J.E. Singer)

There is more evidence that shows you must make the most of what you have physically.

Among strangers, individuals perceived as unattractive in physical appearance are generally undesirable for any interpersonal relationship! (studies by D. Byrne, O. London, K. Reeves)

In one significant study of 58 unacquainted men and women in a social setting we learned that after a first date, 89% of the people who wanted a second date decided to do so because of attractiveness of the partner! (Brislin and Lewis)

In the persuasion process, attractive females are far more convincing than females perceived as unattractive. (Mills and Aronson)

Among American women, the size of a woman's bust is significant to how both American men and women perceive the woman. Women with a "medium" sized bust are considered to be more likable and have greater personal appeal than women with a large or small bust. Women with a small bust are perceived as more intelligent, competent, and moral. Women with a large bust are generally perceived as less intelligent and less competent. (Kleinke, Staneski, 1980)

In yet another study, we find that young men who are obese are generally considered to be slothful and lazy. Both men and women who are obese are generally perceived to have personality characteristics that place them at a disadvantage in social and business settings. (Worsley, 1981)

Can You Change Your Appearance?

Study after study reveals that how you look is critical to someone's first impression of you. So what can you do to change how you look? You can't change everything about your physical appearance but you can definitely make changes that will give you a booster shot.

Research studies tell us that the "exposure principle" increases our "face value." Specifically, the exposure principle says that the more often someone sees you, the more attractive and intelligent you appear to them. If you weren't gifted with a Cindy Crawford or Tom Cruise face then it's time for you to take advantage of the exposure principle.

If you don't have the advantage of being "seen" time after time by a person or a group, then you must make the most of what you have. In other words you want to look as good as you possibly can on every given day. Because of the significance of body image and weight you must do what you can to keep your body weight down and your body in shape for your overall image to be as good as it can be.

Your teeth will tell a tale as well. If your teeth are yellow and look like you just ate, your face value is obviously greatly reduced. Do everything you can to keep your teeth pearly white and you will be perceived as more attractive. (You've already seen the benefits of the perception of attractiveness.) When you watch the news tonight on TV, look at the teeth of every news anchor, weather person and sports announcer. They all have beautiful white teeth. There's a reason for that and that is positive impression management.

Where You Sit Can Change How People Look at You!

Standing in someone's office is a problem that will need an immediate solution. As soon as pleasantries are exchanged you and your client should be seated. If you are both standing for an extended period of time and your client doesn't have the forethought to offer you a chair, then you can ask, "Should we sit down and be comfortable?" Unless you are in a retail environment, sales are not made and deals are not negotiated standing up.

You may have an option of considering where to sit. If so, you are in luck. Scientific research is on your side in telling you exactly where to sit. Seating options normally occur on lunch or dinner dates at a restaurant and in meeting rooms. If you are in a restaurant, quickly search out (with your eyes) a location that allows you to sit facing the majority of the people in the restaurant so your client is obligated to sit facing you, away from the clientele and staff of the restaurant. This is ideal for booth seating.

Your client's attention should be on you, not the waitress, bus boy and the dozens of other people in the restaurant. Your seat selection will assure you his attention. Once you have the attention of your client only you can make your presentation or engage in conversation.

How Do You Select Seating?

Ideally you can create a seating arrangement that is most likely to facilitate the communication process. Here are the key rules in seating selection.

1) As a rule, if you have already met your client once and you know they are right handed, attempt to sit to his right. If she is left-handed sit to her left.

2) If you are a woman attempting to communicate effectively with another woman, sitting opposite of each other is as good or better than sitting at a right angle.

3) If you are a woman attempting to persuade a man to your way of thinking, the best option is to be at a right angle if at all possible.

4) If you are a man attempting to persuade a man, you should be seated across from each other in the booth setting if possible.

5) If you are a man attempting to communicate well with a female in business or in a social setting, you should be seated across from her at a smaller more intimate table.

What Do You Do Once You are Seated?

Waiting for the waitress to come in a restaurant can be awkward if you do not know your client very well. If you are meeting your client in her office, you will immediately get down to business after brief pleasantries. (It should be noted that sometimes pleasantries do NOT have to be brief. Many of my biggest and best presentations were made in the last two minutes of meetings that would extend to two hours discussing everything from baseball, to sex to religion. The level of rapport and quality of mutual interests will ultimately be your guide.)

Once seated, keep your hands away from your face and hair. There is nothing good that your fingers can do above your neck while you are meeting with a client. The best people in the world have wonderful and intentional control of their gestures. They know, for example that when their hands are further from their body than their elbows that they are going to be perceived in a more flamboyant manner.

While you are seated, if you are unfamiliar with your client, it is best that you keep both feet on the floor. This helps you maintain control and good body posture. People that are constantly crossing and un-crossing their feet and legs are perceived as less credible and people who keep one foot on their other knee when talking have a tendency to shake the free foot, creating a silly looking distraction. Feet belong on the floor.

Meanwhile, your hands will say a great deal about your comfort level. If you are picking at the fingers of one hand with the other you are pulling negative mindstrings that show fear or discomfort. This is picked up by the unconscious mind of the client and makes her feel uncomfortable. If you don't know what to do with your hands and you are female, cup your right hand face down into your left hand, which is face up. Don't squeeze your hands, simply let them lay together on your lap.

For men, the best thing to do is to keep your hands separate unless you begin to fidget at which point you will follow the advice of your female counterpart, noted above.

How Close is *TOO* Close?

Every four years the two (or three) presidential candidates square off in three debates so American's can get a clear view of the issues that face the nation. American's get to see the candidates in a up close and personal way. I've watched for years. Last year, the BBC asked me to analyze the body language of then Vice President Al Gore and Governor of Texas George Bush. Specifically they wanted to know what the candidates' bodies were saying, then as part of a suspenseful ploy, they asked me to predict the election, but we would wait until after the third debate to do so.

The nonverbal communication of the debate revealed a somewhat uncomfortable George Bush. He was usually ill at ease and appeared to be guarding his responses. Al Gore appeared overly confident, arrogant and even a bit "cocky." Gore was completely comfortable, at ease and felt in total control of the first debate. After the first debate, Gore was so overwhelming that his handlers coached Gore to be kinder and gentler in the second debate. After getting "beaten" in the second debate Gore took off the gloves and came out forceful in the final debate which was a stand up debate in a town meeting type forum.

At the beginning of the first debate, Gore walked toward Bush and into his personal space as Bush was speaking. This through Bush completely off and Gore appeared to be a lion ready to eat his prey. Unfortunately for Gore, his behavior came off as being rude, arrogant, and too aggressive for someone who was going to be the President of the entire United States and not just those who watch the World Wrestling Federation.

I told the BBC that this ploy on the part of Al Gore, would backfire. American's don't like jerks and the people on "the fence" would swing to Bush and away from Gore just because of this one 10 second incident on television. It was now apparent to me that George Bush would win the election, though I told the BBC, "Jason, George Bush will win but this election is going to be very, very close." I had no idea how prophetic that would be.

Had I been advising and coaching Al Gore, I never would have let him approach George Bush in any way other than a friendly warm manner. People like friendliness and feel comfortable around people who are kind. Almost all people feel threatened when their space is entered, especially when the perpetrator is physically larger than they are. When you look at the tape of the debate, Bush clearly felt threatened and the viewer feels queasy as we see Bush approached. Gore's intention is uncertain and because of this moment, he lost thousands of votes.

What is the lesson?

Whether seated or standing, you should stay out of your client's "intimate space." Intimate space is normally defined as an 18-inch bubble around the entire body of your client. Entering this space is done so at your own risk. This doesn't mean that you can't share a secret with your client. This doesn't mean you can't touch your client. It does mean that if you enter into "intimate space," you are doing so strategically and with a specific intention. There can be great rewards when entering intimate space but there are also great risks so be thoughtful about your client's "space."

Similarly, if you leave the "casual-personal" space of a client, which is 19 inches to 4 feet, you also stand at risk of losing the focus of attention of the client. Ideally most of your communication with a new client should be at the two to four feet distance, measuring nose to nose. This is appropriate and generally you begin communication at the 4' perimeter of space and slowly move closer as you build rapport with your client.

What is Effective Eye Contact?

Eye contact is critical in any face-to-face meeting. As a rule of thumb you should maintain eye contact with your client 2/3 of the time. This doesn't mean that you look at her eyes for 20 minutes then away for 10 minutes. It does mean that you keep in touch for about seven seconds then away for about three seconds, or in touch for about 14 seconds and away for about six seconds. Eye contact doesn't mean just gazing into the eyes. Eye contact is considered any contact in the "eye-nose" triangle. If you create a triangle from the two eyes to the nose of the client you create the "eye-nose" triangle. This is the area that you want 65-70% of eye contact.

Should you sense that your client is uncomfortable at this level reduce your eye contact content. Many American's who were born and raised in the eastern countries (Japan, for example) are not accustomed to the eye contact that American's are.

Eyes are a fascinating part of the human body. When a person finds someone or something very appealing to them their pupil size (the black part of the eyes) grow significantly larger. This is one of the few parts of body language that is absolutely uncontrollable by the conscious mind. You simply cannot control your pupil size. If you are interested in someone else your pupil size will grow dramatically. If someone else is interested in you, their pupils will grow larger when looking at you and there is nothing they can do about it. This is one of the powerful predictors of liking in nonverbal communication.

It should be noted that pupil size will also get larger in situations of extreme fear and when a setting is dark. Pupils expand to let more light in and like a camera, when the setting is very well lit the pupils will contract to the size of a very tiny little dot.

If you follow the tips in this module for improving your appearance, being careful about appropriate dress and are careful with your use of space you will be perceived as more attractive in personal relationships and in business.

There are two other telling behaviors relating to the eyes.

First, if someone is blinking far more rapidly than they normally do, that is usually an indicator of annoying lighting in the setting you are in or that of anxiety and/or lying on the part of the person. In 1998 President Clinton gave a short speech offering his reasons for having an illicit affair with Monica Lewinsky. During this speech his eyes blinked a momentous 120 times per minute. Two days later he gave a speech about a U.S. bombing raid on a terrorist group overseas. In this speech his eye blinks per minute were about 35 per minute. The difference is extremely important in evaluating the comfort level and honesty of the President in each situation. If someone is blinking far more often than normal (and you do have to know what normal is for each person you meet and adjust for lighting) you know they are very probably extremely anxious and very possibly lying.

When your client's eyes blink rapidly, he may be anxious or deceiving you.

Second, if you are in conversation with someone and their eyes are easily distracted by the goings on in the environment, this is usually a good indicator that you haven't earned the interest of your listener. In general it is a very wise strategy for you to keep your eyes well trained on your client in distracting environments. To constantly look around at the environment when you are with someone else is perceived as rude. To keep eye contact with another person instead of being distracted by extraneous activity is considered flattering and complimentary, especially by women.

Always sit at a table so your client is not distracted. Your client should see you and only you.

So, there you have it! You don't have to look perfect and own Trump Towers to be incredibly attractive to the multitudes! However, you want to take advantage of every aspect of your attractiveness that you can and later in this book you will discover specifically what to do to really bring your best you forward!

The Eyes Have It

Did you know that you are able to get a pretty good idea of how someone feels about you by looking at their eyes? You get even more information about how someone feels about you when you put that "look" into the context of their facial expression and their body language.

How you look at someone can be perceived as seductive, frightening, caring, loving, bored, secretive or even condescending. The eyes reveal a great deal about what is going on inside of us. If you can learn how to look and send the right message at the right time with your eyes you will be perceived as more attractive by more people.

There are six basic emotions in the human experience and the eyes capture them all. There are many more than six different emotions, but most of the emotions we experience are a combination of the six basic emotions. By simply looking at a person's eyes we can tell whether they are experiencing.

Six Basic Human Emotions

Happiness
Surprise
Disgust
Fear
Anger
Sadness

Think about that. Across the world people are the same in this respect. We all show the six basic emotions in the same fashion. The eyes are amazing windows to the emotions we all experience. By paying close attention to the eyes we can learn a great deal about our clients and, in particular, those we wish to sell to today.

It is a true statement that most people will judge other people in the first two or three seconds after their first meeting. Therefore, doesn't it make sense to have them hypnotized by your eyes and your understanding of their wants and needs? How do you do this? You use your eyes in simple yet powerful ways to build rapport and create feelings of arousal in the person you are attempting to attract. To do this you need only to apply the key ideas you will learn in this module.

I recently had laser surgery on my eyes to improve my vision without glasses. In the screening process, I learned that some people shouldn't have the surgery because their pupils dilate (get bigger and blacker!) to a size that is abnormally large. Everyone's pupils dilate when it is darker in the environment and they contract when it is lighter. When the sun is shining brightly in your eyes your pupils will be at their smallest. When you walk into a dark room, your pupils will be at their largest. The pupils get larger to gather more light. This helps the eyes see more of what is in the environment.

Your pupils will also get larger when you are terrified. There is an evolutionary response in your body that helps you collect more information about an experience that is frightening. The senses all sharpen in moments of great fear. Your hearing becomes more acute, your sense of touch is enhanced, and you can even taste fear. The pupils in your eyes get larger. This helps bring more light in even if the environment is already well lit. Your brain needs that information to help you escape and to protect you from danger.

Everyone's pupils dilate to a different maximum size and everyone's pupils have a slightly different normal state. However, there is one amazing fact about those eyes: When someone looks at you and their pupils get big and black, they are either scared to death of you, or they like you!

It's almost impossible to control the increase in pupil size that occurs when we see something we like. This expansion is also an evolutionary process that happens to take in more of something that is very dear to the person. Unfortunately for the observing person, it is an uncontrollable response.

Look at your client's eyes and you will know whether they like you or not.

Recent research into pupil dilation has proven quite interesting to attraction. A researcher showing pictures of a baby to women, results in pupil dilation of the majority of women. Women viewing pictures of a baby with the mother elicits an even greater pupil dilation response. These same women viewing a beautiful landscape experience an enlarging pupil size as well. Interestingly, women viewing a picture of an attractive man, on average, don't experience quite the size of pupil dilation noted in the above scenarios! Women can be impressed by a man's appearance but at least at an evolutionary or biological level, physical appearance isn't going to turn on every woman who passes. (Just what does turn women "on" will be discussed later in this book!)

These same researchers took the picture of that same beautiful baby and showed it to men. The men's response was a non-event. Their pupils, on average, didn't dilate. When viewing the baby with the mother there was again, a non-event. Generally speaking, nothing happened. When the men were shown pictures of a beautiful landscape, again, nothing happened. As soon as a man was shown a photo of a beautiful woman, the pupils, on average dilated to a big and black orb. A man, it would appear is very much turned "on" by the sight of the beautiful woman, even a picture of one.

Pupil dilation by women, when in the presence of real-live men, is another matter. Women typically are not visually aroused by photographs in the same way that men are. Women are very stimulated by some men in some contexts. When women are sitting across from men who arouse them, their pupils do dilate. To the observant witness, it is obvious. Most people are oblivious to the enhanced pupil size and yet it is one of the most telling signals of attraction.

As a public speaker, I have talked to hundreds and hundreds of audiences all over the world. As I speak, I am aware of the women whose eyes are big and black and I always address my presentation to them, making eye contact with those who appear to be aroused or attracted to me. They don't know this is why I selected them to make eye contact with (at least they didn't until now). Part of my job is to excite and inspire an audience when I speak. Therefore I need to gain as much rapport with the audience as I can. By making contact with the people who like me the most, I am able to gain agreement from those people. They nod their heads, lean forward, show interest, smile, and everyone in the audience sees how much fun they are having. In groups, head nods are like a virus. Once one person nods his head almost everyone does!

I receive all of this positive feedback, in part, because I don't just look at faces in an audience. It is because I look at the eyes of dozens of people in the audience and find the biggest pupils I can locate! These searches are like a treasure hunt that always has a pot of gold at the end. If I can do this with an audience of 50 or 100, can you imagine how easy this is to do in a smaller group at a party or in a public place? Start paying attention to the eyes that are looking at you.

You may wonder, "What if you are wrong? What if those eyes are just big because they are among the women whose eyes are normally large? Then aren't you just fooling yourself into believing that all of those women are attracted to you? My response is, "Of course." When you hallucinate, it should always be something that increases your self-esteem and self-confidence! We'll talk about how your beliefs and self-confidence effect your attractiveness elsewhere in this book!

A little while back there was a fascinating study, which revealed that when you show two pictures of the same woman to a man, the man will perceive the picture of the woman with the biggest pupils to be significantly more attractive. Many magazine cover editors know this and actually touch up the cover picture. Obviously in the bright light of a photographer's studio the subject's pupils would be very small. Because of the importance of pupil size and attraction, the models pupils are enlarged to be much larger than they possibly could be. This makes the final picture irresistible to the magazine purchaser. We simply love people with big eyes!

Men desperately want eye contact with women. Men gauge the interest of a woman by her eye contact. Men are very competitive and territorial when it comes to women looking at other men. They see this as a sign that the woman is no longer interested in them, or that the interest is fading. Therefore, if a woman wants to continue to make a good impression with her male client, the woman needs to maintain steadfast eye contact. A man's self esteem will crumble if a woman begins to observe all the other males in the environment.

On the other hand, we can safely predict that if we have the full attention of the one we are with, they hold us in esteem to some degree. There is no other indicator that is as powerful as eye contact that can show interest in another person. Our eyes unconsciously and automatically move toward that which interests or arouses us. We all know that and we all judge our value in some part by the response we receive from other people. The eye contact we give and receive is just the beginning of the sales process.

It's interesting to note that people with blue eyes are more demanding of eye contact than people with brown eyes. It is quite easy for us to look at a person with blue eyes and see the size of their pupils. When they expand and contract it is evident. The person with blue eyes is used to people looking at them for an extended amount of time, in part, because of the contrast between their blue eyes and black pupils. The contrast can be striking at an unconscious level.

People with brown eyes on the other hand are used to other people looking away more rapidly because at the unconscious level it appears that the person with brown eyes is not as interested in them! The brown eyes present a weaker contrast to the black pupils. It often appears at the unconscious level that those brown eyes are not interested in us! Therefore we tend to look away from the person with brown eyes when in fact they may have been very interested in us!

When the person you are attracted to has brown eyes you must pay more attention to their eyes to see the contrast between the black and the brown. What seemed to be an uninterested person may be someone who is actually quite excited about you!

Confirming our beliefs about the value of eye contact in selling yourself is an attraction study that was done some years ago. People watched films of a couple that communicated with each other in two distinct ways. The first film showed a couple that had eye contact during 80% of their communication. The second film showed a couple that had eye contact 15% of the time. The observers of the films rated the couples that had eye contact 15% of the time as cold, cautious, submissive, evasive, defensive and immature (among others). The observers of the films whose couples had eye contact 80% of the time described the people in the film as mature, friendly, self confident, sincere and natural.

Gazing into someone's eyes is much more than just something special for the two engaging in the eye behavior. It is a clear signal to the rest of the world. These people like each other!

The Eyes Don't Lie

Whenever you are in a situation where attraction takes place there is plenty of room for deception! People have been known to stretch the truth about their age and income, their intentions and even their degree of love for another. The eyes act as a leading indicator of truth and deception.

In 1997 and 1998 I was heard on hundreds of radio shows talking about the body language of President Clinton, Monica Lewinsky, Kathleen Wiley, Hillary Clinton and numerous other key players in the White House scandal that led to the President's impeachment. The interviewers wanted to know who was telling the truth, who was lying and what the facts were based on the body language cues I was reading.

Having carefully watched the President for almost 7 years, I was familiar with his every facial expression and body posture. President Clinton certainly was the most charismatic president since John Kennedy. His ability to excite an audience and win over people who disagreed with him is legendary. He is an outstanding speaker who thrives on being in the limelight. There were however two speeches and the famous grand jury testimony where the President was not his usual charismatic self. On these three occasions he was uncomfortable about the deception he needed to partake in. The first was when he shook his right finger at the world and said, "I did not have sex with that woman, Monica Lewinsky." The next was during the grand jury testimony where he was videotaped from the White House. The third was the speech he gave that very evening, after the grand jury testimony, when he offered his regret for being involved in the situation. On these three occasions his eyes gave him away as being deceptive. The one speech that I want to share information with you about is the speech where he apologized for his behavior.

For 7 years I have watched the President communicate with the country and even though has been called "Slick Willie," his body language has rarely indicated any internal discomfort with what he communicated to the public. In this particular "apology speech" however, his anxiety, fear and deception cures were very high.

When I watch someone to see if they are being deceptive, I look to the eyes for important cues. I want to especially know how many "eye blinks" per minute a person experiences in contrast to when they are telling the truth. For 7 years President Clinton's "eye blink" pattern is that of about 7-12 blinks per minute. That is very normal. During the "apology speech" however his eye blinking was recorded at 70 per minute! What that means is that on some level, the President was being deceptive in his communication.

Once eye irritants like contact lenses and allergies are ruled out, the only internal experience that will cause eyes to blink at that pace is the experience of anxiety normally associated with deception.

You should know that some people have eyes that never blink and a small number of people have eye tics that just won't stop blinking. On average though, a person will blink from 7-15 times per minute. When a person is being deceptive their eyes will blink 5-12 times that pace. Like pupil dilation, controlling eye blinks is very difficult if not impossible. Take a moment right here and now. Simply try and keep your eyes open for 30 seconds without blinking. It's not easy is it? Now here's another experiment for you to do. Stare at a friend for 30 seconds. No blinking is allowed.

It is very difficult to stop your eyes from blinking! If you are in conversation where someone is telling you about something, and suddenly you notice a big jump in the number of eye blinks per minute, you can safely bet there is some deceptive behavior going on somewhere in what they are saying!

The eyes may or may not be the windows to the soul but they certainly are strongly linked to the emotions and the entire make up of the brains responses to other people.

Sound Bytes from Scientific Research

- ✓ Generally speaking, the longer the eye contact between two people, the greater the intimacy that is felt inside.
- ✓ Attraction increases as mutual gazing increases.
- ✓ Others rarely interrupt two people engaged in a conversation if they have consistent eye contact.
- ✓ Pupils also enlarge when people are talking about things that bring them joy or happiness. They often contract when discussing issues that bring them sadness.
- ✓ Women are better non-verbal communicators than men. Men can improve though. One reason men aren't as good in reading body language is that

men often communicate sitting or standing side by side and don't see as much non-verbal communication as women do.

- ✓ Women engage in more eye contact than men do.
- ✓ Eye contact has been shown to be a significant factor in the persuasion process.
- ✓ When women are engaged in a great degree of eye contact, they tend to be more self-disclosing about personal subjects.
- ✓ When eye contact decreases men tend to disclose more and women tend to disclose less!
- ✓ The longer your eye contact, the more self-esteem you are perceived to have.
- ✓ The more eye contact you can maintain, the higher self-esteem you actually rate your self on!

Simply Irresistible Eyes

Given what we know about the eyes and attraction we can summarize the experiences of millions of people into a few key ideas for irresistible attraction.

- ✓ Start with your eyes. Are they clear or are they bloodshot? People who look at you will notice and the clearer your eyes the more attractive people will perceive you to be.
- ✓ If you wear sunglasses, get ready to take them off. People want to see what they are getting. They want to see your eyes.
- ✓ If you wear glasses, consider contacts or other alternatives. People need to be able to see your eyes!
- ✓ If you want to be attractive to someone, look at them. Look at them again and again. And smile!
- ✓ Look at a man from head to toe on the initial contact. He will be flattered. Look at the woman from the shoulders up and she will think you have depth and possibilities.
- ✓ Look at the person you are attracted to about 70% of the time when you are communicating with them.
- ✓ Avoid looking at others for any length of time when you are with someone who may be special. Make the person feel as if they are the only one in the room that could possibly catch your eye.

Scary Fact: The Client Often Says "Yes" or "No"
Before You Shake Hands and Say Hello

What you wear, your makeup, your jewelry, your watch, your socks, your shoes, your coat, your glasses and everything else about how you look can make or break a sale before you ever open your mouth. Have you ever heard of "love at first sight?" Two sales were made before two people ever spoke. Both people decided that they wanted what they saw, heard, smelled and felt inside. Sales are made and broken every day in the same manner. In this module you will learn how to help your client fall in love with you *and* your products and services, before you even say a word. Nonverbal communication is almost always unconscious communication. Most people have no idea what is going on at the sub-language level of communication. This module will help you master this most critical process of communication.

Many self-proclaimed experts of influence have mis-quoted a brilliant study by Albert Mehrabian to the effect that 93% of all communication is non-verbal. That wasn't what Mehrabian concluded at all. However, Mehrabian and most of the best psychological researchers do agree that non-verbal communication is between 50 and 80 percent of the impact of a communication. The same is true for the selling climate.

The first element of non-verbal communication you want to learn about is that of space. The space you occupy while in the sales process makes a great deal of difference as to the result of the process. Imagine that you are making your sale at a kitchen table. Would it matter if it were yours or your client's kitchen? Imagine that you were closing a deal in a restaurant and then contrast that with closing the same deal in a nightclub. Different?

Now imagine that you are in an office setting and that your client is sitting directly across from you. Next, imagine that your client is sitting to the right of you. Imagine you are standing in a retail store next to your client. Now, imagine that you are seated and your client is seated. How are each of these different to you? Each of these images creates different feelings and probabilities of selling your client.

Is Your Scent Making A Statement About You?

If you are going to be spending most of your day meeting with men and you are wearing a cologne or perfume you have already lost valuable percentage points on your selling probabilities for the day. If you are a woman and are going to be selling to women, you can be lightly scented. Whether you are a man or a woman, if you are seeing men, have no scent but that of a clean body. If you are a man selling to women you should have no scent.

> *In general, all of our studies show that colognes and perfumes are a biological turn off to the opposite sex. There are minor exceptions, but there are no scents that you can wear to enhance sales compliance.*

Scents are powerful in the selling process and if you have clients coming to your office you should contact the authors for a special consultation. The science of aromachology has revealed that certain scents cause people to spend more money, take more time in stores, relax, feel more erotic and a plethora of behavioral changes from arousal to helping attitudes. In the sales process, outside of your home office, you, the sales professional need to be scentless. If you wear deodorant, buy one that is scentless.

20 Tips to Look Perfect for Your Client

Both female and male sales professionals make many mistakes that cost some people far more than ten thousand dollars in income per year. It is interesting that our research indicates that women will far outsell men of the same skill and knowledge level IF your appearance is perceptually correct. Women make far more mistakes with their appearance than men do for selling.

Physical attractiveness is important to how many sales you make and how much those sales are for. We know that in personal relationships people tend to choose their spouses based on two factors: One is money or potential income and physical attractiveness. Women value money as the number one characteristic in a spouse and physical attractiveness as second. For men, it is the opposite. Both find physical attractiveness as very important. In selling the same holds true. Physical attractiveness matters.

In order to begin to understand how important physical appearance is, let's look at some research that has been done in the area of interpersonal relationships. Study after study show that physical attractiveness is very important in one person's perception of another person. 89% of all people on their first date decided "yes" or "no" to a second date based on the physical attractiveness of the other person.

> *People judge others positively or negatively, in large part on their physical attractiveness. Enhance your attractiveness to increase sales..*

Numerous studies show that men will reject women based on what they perceive as deficiencies in the woman's appearance. (In the realm of interpersonal relations, women are more interested in money than men, showing some practicality but continuing the thread of superficiality in this Mind Access Point!)

Many elements of your physical appearance are genetic and are not going to change. You can't grow two more inches and you can't change the shape of your face. There is much you can do to enhance your perceived physical attractiveness. Here are the keys to your appearance for both men and women. Follow these 20 tips and you won't be pulling the negative response Mind Access strings in your client's mind.

1) Women: Never dress suggestively. Research shows that you will get a longer interview but you will make fewer sales. Dressing suggestively pulls out an entirely different set of Mind Access strings to be pulled. Low cut blouses and shirts are out. Mini-skirts are out.

2) Women: If your wedding ring is large and you are going to be seeing women, take it off and put your band on instead. A large wedding ring reduces sales. Women outwardly express their excitement about a large wedding ring but it is perceived as a negative for numerous reasons. Your sales will go down if your wedding ring is significantly larger than that of your client's.

3) Women: If your fingernails are more than 1/2" long cut them and you will increase your sales. Men and women perceive long fingernails negatively in the sales process.

4) Men and Women: If your fingernails look like anything but clean and well rounded fingernails, get a manicure. Your fingers are the one area that both men and women can be turned off at. A sales professional has nice looking hands.

5) Men and Women: If you wear glasses, normally smaller glasses are appropriate. You are normally better off making sales presentations wearing contact lenses if they do not irritate your eyes too much. Glasses rarely make sales and often break them.

6) Men and Women: Your weight will make or break sales. If you are more than 20% over normal, you lose credibility in the sales process. Begin a program of eating right and activity to reduce your waistline. Thinner people sell more. Period.

7) Men: Facial hair reduces sales in almost all cases. If you are a man and have a beard you should cut it now. There are no men with beards in the top 100 sales professionals. If you have a mustache, ask men and women for their opinion. Some men appear to look better with a mustache, but in general, all facial hair reduces sales.

8) Men and Women: Ear and nose hair can create feelings of disgust in many of your clients. If you look in the mirror and you see ear or nose hair, cut it and keep it cut.

9) Women: Makeup that is lightly applied is not distracting. If your make up is heavy, you will lose sales. The closer to "natural" you appear, the better.

10) Men and Women: Teeth. Teeth should be white, flossed and clean before you meet any client. If your teeth are stained, get them cleaned. Yellowed teeth lose sales.

11) Men: Hair Length. If your hair length goes beyond covering the back of your neck you will lose sales. Long hair can feel good and even look good, but, it isn't taken seriously. Decide whether you want to make all the sales you want to or whether you need your hair long.

12) Men and Women: Dress like your clients dress... plus 10%. If you see conservative clients, dress very conservatively. If you are selling to casual clients you will dress "dressy casual."

13) Men and Women: When wearing suit coats, nothing goes in the outer pocket except a spotless and perfectly fitted handkerchief. No pens, no calculators. Nothing else goes in the suit coat outer pocket.

14) Men and Women: Your shoes should be shiny and looking new.

15) Men and Women: Jewelry. Men should wear nothing other than a watch and a wedding band. Women should wear nothing more than a watch, a wedding ring or band, a thin necklace and a pin. Earrings that are small for women are acceptable but they should not distract. Earrings for men are always out. No earrings are permissible for men. You will lose sales.

16) Men and Women: You should be showered every morning and have your hair conservatively and neatly in place before every sales call.

17) Men: Unless you absolutely must, your briefcase should be no larger than a case that will hold two copies of the Encyclopedia Britannica.

18) Women: A large purse is out. Never bring a large purse on a sales call with you. If you do, you will look disorganized. Bring a trim purse with whatever essentials you need during the day. Everything else can stay in the car or your desk at the office.

19) Men: Your suit should fit properly. With your coat buttoned, take your fist and place it between your belly button and the coat. It should comfortably touch both. If you can't squeeze your fist comfortably between your stomach and your coat, your coat is too small.

20) Men: Your pants should touch the "bridge" on your shoes. They should not run on the ground or be raised high up on your socks. They need to touch your shoes or get them altered. Anything unusual costs you sales and that means you lose money.

Saying Hello and Shaking Hands

What should be the most natural thing in the world has become one of the most difficult. How do you say hello to your client?

Walk into the office with excellent posture taking medium length strides and say, "Hi, I'm Kevin Hogan, the author of the *Psychology of Persuasion*, you're John, right? Nice to meet you."

On the word John, you shake hands. If you walk into the office and your client takes the lead by introducing himself, simply follow his lead and shake hands as he extends his.

Hold his hands for two or three beats and gently release it. Assuming you shake hands with your right hands, your left hand should NOT take part in this ritual. Here are the ten keys of shaking hands properly.

Ten Do's and Don'ts of Shaking Hands

- ✓ Always maintain eye contact when shaking hands.
- ✓ Do not use the infamous two hand, handshake.
- ✓ Do not grab his elbow with your left hand.
- ✓ Do not hold their hand for more than two seconds.
- ✓ Do not squeeze to crush their hand.
- ✓ Do not try to get a better grip than your client.
- ✓ Do not have a limp handshake.
- ✓ Your hand should be firm but under control.
- ✓ Your hands should be dry and warm.

Do I Walk Funny?

Many people do. When I moved from the Chicago area to a small rural town in Minnesota in my senior year of high school, I learned this lesson the hard way. I had won a role in a play called, "The Crucible" as the Reverend Hale. It was a wonderful role for the young person that I was. Unfortunately, I didn't walk "normally" and my posture was terrible. I had a bit of a "swagger" and my shoulders bounced as I walked. It was cute, to some, but it was a sign of bad posture and needed correcting.

The drama's director, John Fogarty, needed his Reverend to walk with an air of confidence and not a "Chicago shuffle." He decided he would tie five-pound weights to each of my ankles. Now that may not seem like a lot of weight but imagine a half of a gallon of milk tied to each of your ankles. It slows you down and straightens you up. I had to wear these weights all day for six weeks. At the end of the six weeks I walked upright and not like the Cro-Magnon man I had become accustomed to.

In life we all play roles. We play the roles of parents and spouses. We play the roles of volunteers and business people. As a salesperson, you play the most important role of all. You play the role of a person who literally helps the world go around.

When you are walking, you should be walking as if a big hand was scooting you along by putting pressure on your butt to go forward. This is an important first step to improved posture. Practice walking around the house as if a big hand was pushing you gently and slowly forward by scooting your butt forward. That will help you with your walk and your posture. The alternative is the weights...and that is a lot of work.

How Do I Make Presentations to Groups?

Everything you have read up until this point still applies of course. Presentations simply offer a few more challenges and a few greater rewards.

If you are presenting to a group you already know that you have something important enough to say to get the attention of the group. No one in the group showed up by accident.

Know what you are going to say in advance. You don't have to write out your presentation. In fact, unless you are the President of the United States, no one will listen if you do.

There are a few keys to speaking before groups. One is seat selection. If you are the key speaker and will be speaking from the one and only table you want to sit on an end or in the middle of one of the two sides.

If you have any known detractors of your product or service, you should have them sit to your immediate left or immediate right. These are the least powerful positions on the table. Notice that in presidential press conferences where members of both parties are present at a seated table, President Clinton always had the house Republican leaders seated immediately next to him. These positions have no focal attention and rarely speak with any credibility.

If you have to speak before a group and you have a podium you have an opportunity to make or break a sale by a strategy that I discovered by watching television evangelists. This strategy takes some time to master but is remarkably effective.

Strategic Movement?

The most powerful nonverbal process you can use with an audience that must determine as a group to "buy" or "not buy" your products or services is that of strategic movement. Other sales trainers call similar strategies spatial anchoring. Both are applicable and here is what strategic movement is all about.

Do you remember Johnny Carson? He was the host of the Tonight Show for almost 30 years before Jay Leno took over in the 1990's. Each night that Johnny came out he stood on a small star, which marked exactly where he was supposed to stand. It was the best spot on the entire stage for camera angles, connecting with the audience and because of the curtain back drop, we knew without seeing Johnny's face that he was there and not a guest host, who would stand on a different star.

The only thing Johnny ever did from this specific location was make people laugh. He didn't wander around the stage and tell his jokes. He stood right there and made people laugh. There were many nights when Johnny literally could just stand on his star and people would laugh. That is spatial anchoring. Audience laughter was anchored (conditioned to) Johnny's standing on his star.

When I first visited NBC in 1984, I thought it was fascinating that only Johnny stood on that star. At the time I thought it was an ego trip or some bit of arrogance on the part of Carson. How wrong I was. I knew nothing at that time of spatial anchoring and strategic movement.

When you are called on to make your sales presentation in front of a group, you are on stage. You are the star. You will want to select three specific points on the stage, or in the meeting room from which to speak. Each of these points is a specific location and not an approximate area. Point "A" is your podium. Teachers and preachers use podiums and lecterns. Therefore, *the podium (point "A") will always be used only to relay factual information to your audience.*

You will choose a point to your left about four feet from your podium that you will deliver all of the bad news discussed in your presentation. (You can't make many sales without painting a vivid picture about how bad things will get if the corporation doesn't hire you.) The bad news point, is point "B" and you will only talk about problems and anything that is going to be perceived as "bad" by your audience. *Point "B" will be approximately four feet to the left of the podium.*

Point "C" will be approximately two and one half feet to the right of the podium and you will always paint uplifting, positive, exciting, motivating pictures from this location. Everything we want the audience to agree with will be discussed from this point after we establish this as the "good news point."

Imagine that you are giving your presentation for this group and you need to be very persuasive. My favorite example here is that of fund raising for a charity. Your job? Get a big check for your favorite charity.

You place your folder or notes on the podium and immediately walk to "B" point. You tell a story about a hurting child or a suffering individual. You then explain how this one incidence is far from isolated. You move to the podium. You expound the facts and figures about the devastation of the problem that you are asking the group to help solve by making a big donation.

Now you move to point "C," where you will become excited about how the charitable organization is currently solving the problems and helping the suffering you talked about at "B." Everything that is good and wonderful you will "anchor" into point "C."

As you conclude your speech you will have a path that you have laid. You have moved from A to B to C to B to A, several times. ***You conclude on point "C" because it is the good news and offers each person to participate in healing the wounds you opened at "B."***

The truly unique tactic in strategic movement is the ability to subtly answer questions at the unconscious level without saying anything significant on the conscious level. Imagine that the audience is given the opportunity for questions and answers with you. An individual in the audience asks you about the group's considerations of donating to a competing charitable organization.

"Well, of course, you know that charity is a good charity and there would be nothing wrong with that...of course...(walking to point "C") by taking advantage of the plan that we have, we can accomplish all of the goals that you want to have accomplished in the community. I'm sure you realize it is up to you to make it happen. We can only help those who need it if you make a decision tonight."

Discussing the other charity in a neutral or slightly positive manner from point "B", allows you to unconsciously associate all of the negative feelings to your "competitor" and you solve the problem as you move to the "C" point. *If you find this manipulative then you are working for the wrong charity. If anyone else is more qualified to help a group, sells a better product or offers a better service, you should be working for them!*

There is no more powerful manner of utilizing space than that of spatial anchoring and then using strategic movement. The next time you watch a great speaker, notice how he or she utilizes strategic movement. If they stay at the podium, notice how all the good news is given while gesturing with hand "A" and all the bad news is discussed when gesturing with the other hand. The greatest speakers are masters of spatial anchoring and strategic movement.

Body Language:
29 Points to Make Sales Soar

- ✓ The right side is where you make the best impression.
- ✓ Pupils dilate when they are interested in what they see.
- ✓ Rapid eye blinks often mean anxiety and deception.
- ✓ Forward leaning is a sign of liking.
- ✓ Eye contact when it isn't necessary is almost always a good sign.
- ✓ 70% eye contact is just about right in the USA.
- ✓ Your body weight sends a message.
- ✓ Your hairstyle speaks volumes.
- ✓ Hairpieces usually indicate insecurity.
- ✓ Rapport begins by matching physiology.
- ✓ Women feel comfortable when men are just a bit below eye level.
- ✓ Women feel comfortable when you are straight across from them.
- ✓ Men feel comfortable when you are at a 90-degree angle from them.
- ✓ Touch is a sign of liking.
- ✓ Nod your head. It unconsciously affirms your client.
- ✓ Look out for leakage: A sure sign of nervousness.
- ✓ The nose usually engorges when the person is deceptive.
- ✓ Dress to the situation is appropriate.
- ✓ Radical dress means the person is making a statement. What?
- ✓ Spatial anchoring is a powerful non-verbal communication tool.
- ✓ The people who sit in "Mom and Dad's chairs are looked to for assurance.
- ✓ The person sitting next to the person standing up has no power.
- ✓ People in rapport tend to synchronize together.
- ✓ Physical attractiveness means more than we wish it would.
- ✓ Blue-eyed people expect to be looked at more than others.
- ✓ Scents of vanilla are considered positive in the USA.
- ✓ Our face value goes up with each exposure!
- ✓ Negative emotions are usually triggered on the right side of the brain.
- ✓ Smile. It's tough to resist a sincere smile.

Module Eight
The Psychology of Covert Hypnosis

The Ten Unconscious
Laws of Unconscious Communication

You drive down the street. You have to stop at stop signs, yield to oncoming traffic and even slow to 55 (at least when you see a highway patrolmen!). These are all simple laws. Laws created by society for the safety and betterment of the masses aren't necessarily perfect nor are the absolutes. Laws of society don't always work.

On the other hand, universal laws like the law of gravity always work. If you drop 10,000 baseballs off the top of the Sears Tower in Chicago, the balls will all drop to the street below, probably doing major damage. None of the balls will rise up toward the atmosphere as you drop them off the Sears Tower. These are universal laws that never change. If you try to break a universal law...normally you won't get a second chance to make things right!

Legislated laws are different. If you follow them, you will probably live longer and pay fewer traffic tickets. The laws of persuasion aren't quite like the laws of society or the laws of the universe. In fact, most people aren't even aware of the laws of persuasion...they simply tend to act in accordance with the laws at a completely unconscious level. There are major prices to pay when the laws of persuasion are broken. The problem is that most people aren't aware of the laws in the first place. If people unconsciously follow the rules, they will be happier and communicate well with others. If people don't follow the rules, they will run into lots of problems, broken relationships, less income, be more readily downsized in corporations that are cutting back and well...you get the idea.

There is nothing that you do that is more important than communication with others. There are very specific laws that govern not only the communication process but also the sales process. It's interesting because, sometimes when you drive past the highway patrolmen at 75 you don't get a ticket. Sometimes you

147

don't yield to oncoming traffic and you don't get in a car accident. Every now and then you run the stop sign and you don't hit a pedestrian. The laws exist, though, and when they are followed they tend to work in the favor of the law-abiding citizens. When they are broken, the chances that something will go wrong are dramatically increased. The same is true of the laws of selling, which are only slightly different from the laws of persuasion.

How can there be laws of selling? How can something like sales or communication have laws?

As our species has evolved for millions of years we have discovered that we tend to need the cooperation of others to succeed. Gaining the cooperation and compliance of other people is absolutely critical to the persuasion process and the continuance of society as we know it.

The remainder of this module will deal with the 10 Unconscious Laws of Persuasion. Following each of these laws is important in gaining compliance from others. In most situations on most days of your sales career, if you follow each law you will find selling to be a fairly simple experience. What's better? If you utilize these 10 laws in all of your communication you will find that your sales career is fun, sometimes challenging and always rewarding.

Law of Reciprocity- *When someone gives you something of perceived value, you immediately respond with the desire to give something back.*

It's December 24 and the mail has just arrived. You open a Christmas card from someone who you had taken off of your Christmas list! This is a crisis! "Honey, are there any more Christmas cards left?"

"Yeah, in the drawer."

"Thank god." You go to the drawer and sure enough there is a card there but there are no envelopes to fit the card into! You search and search, finally deciding to use an envelope that isn't quite large enough…but you have to use something!

You sign the card and yes, you personalize it! (You write something special just for the sender!) You stuff the card into the envelope that is still too small…you slide a picture of the family in and you even find a left over "family newsletter" that tells everyone what your family has been up to all year.

"I'll be back in awhile, I have to go to the post office and mail this letter."

Why do you have to go to the post office?

You have to go because the letter must be mailed with a postmark before

Christmas! December 24 will show that you cared. December 26 will show that these people were an after thought in your mind...not worthy of sending before Christmas. You race off to the post office and you have just discovered...the power of reciprocity.

You were taught to share your toys and your snacks and your space and your time with you all those around you. You were scolded when you were selfish and you were rewarded with kind smiles and pats on the head when you shared. The law of reciprocity was installed at a very early age.

The world's greatest people and marketing mavens give something to their clients and I don't mean a business card.

- ✓ Have you ever received a bar of soap in the mail?
- ✓ Have you ever received a box of cereal in the mail?
- ✓ Have you ever received return address labels from a charity, in the mail?
- ✓ Have you ever received a handful of greeting cards from a charity, in the mail?
- ✓ Have you ever received a sample size shampoo bottle in the mail?

These are all examples of what we call "inducing reciprocity." The practice is very simple, yet absolutely brilliant. If your product is top quality and it is something that everyone can use, send everyone a small sample of it and they will be more likely to buy it the next time they go to the store for two reasons.

1) We will recognize it as something we have used. The brain picks up on what is familiar. (Have you ever noticed how many cars there are like yours on the road? What happened to all the rest?!)

2) Reciprocity has been induced when someone gives you something and you give them something back. Reciprocity has also been induced when someone gives you something and you feel compelled to give something back. Kellogg's was nice enough to send us their free box of cereal and because it tasted good we should at least buy their cereal this one time. We return the favor.

Reciprocity, based on scientific research, appears to be the single most powerful law of selling persuasion there is, but is there a problem?

- ✓ If you sell life insurance, you can't give away $10,000 of free coverage.
- ✓ If you sell real estate, you can't give away bathrooms.
- ✓ If you sell speaking services you can't give away free speeches.
- ✓ If you are a stockbroker you can't give away 100 shares of Microsoft.

What do you do if you don't have sample size products and services? How do you take advantage of this powerful law of share and share alike?

149

> **Give away something of perceived value to someone and others will feel compelled to do likewise.**

You do not have to give away free samples to utilize reciprocity. You MUST give away something that has perceived value. My favorite method of inducing reciprocity is taking someone to lunch or sharing a valuable tip related to building their business or income in some way. (I like these approaches because they are measurable and the person knows that you really helped them when they follow through on your suggestion.) Taking someone to lunch is usually an inexpensive way to induce reciprocity and you have the added benefit of meeting one of your clients 16 basic desires. (The desire to eat.) Sharing helpful secrets that are truly specialized knowledge is also an elegant way to induce reciprocity. One simple idea can often help someone earn hundreds or thousands of dollars per year more in income.

Can I share a secret with you?

I keep some of my money in the Strong Funds Money Market account. It pays a lot more interest than a bank does and the money is safe. You can write checks on your account just like a checking account and if you just knew that secret to make more money, I'd be happy that I shared that with you.

Can I share another secret with you? The Strong Advantage Fund is even better! It pays about 1-3% more interest than the Strong Money Market Fund and you can write checks on that account to. If you only took $10,000 out of the bank or CD and put it into the Strong Advantage Fund you would earn 2-3% more per year on that money than you do in the bank or CD. Now, granted that only comes to about $300 per year, but how many free copies of this book can you give away to your friends in return for that one $300 gift? How will your friends feel about you when you give them a gift that gives them the most cutting edge selling power ever put into one book?

Here are a few creative ideas for people to use as inexpensive give away items to your persons.

Life Insurance and Financial Product people:

Give away a free report that lists all of the top performing investments for the last three years. (Even if it contains information that is positive about your competitors!) Give away a handy chart that people can place on the refrigerator that shows the ten questions to ask telemarketers to determine the legitimacy of investment opportunities and charitable donations.

Real Estate people:

Estimate the dollar of the loan the client will take out and run several amortization tables showing how small extra payments each month will cut years off the life of the loan, save the client tens of thousands of dollars and create long term financial freedom. If the client is already putting every penny toward the 30 year mortgage, give away a handy booklet that shows how to do simple maintenance on the house, how to find good service people to work on the home in the future, and also tips on keeping the home in top dollar condition should they decide to sell.

Automobile people:

If you sell a great car, give away a recent Consumer Reports article to all of your persons comparing your car with others in its class. If you sell a car that is a good car, but not listed as one of the best, give away a list of the top ten strategies to keep the car running cheaply and it's re-sale value high.

The message to you is that everyone can give something away for free with nothing expected in return. It is a scientific fact that reciprocity is effective. The key is that what you give away must have perceived value by the part of the client. Traditional promotional items like personalized pens and date books may be useful or they may not be. You can test them to see if they assist in making sales. It doesn't matter what you give away actually cost you. What matters is the value the client places on the item, report or product.

Law of Time- *Changing someone's time perspective helps them to make different decisions. When people change their time perspective they change how they feel about something and the decisions they make in regard to it.*

Time is the subtle equalizer in life. No matter how rich or poor you are, time is the one commodity that is the same for everyone. Everyone has this moment of experience only. What happens in this moment is normally not a matter of conscious choice or thought.

Quite often when you walk into a clients office or you contact them in some other way they will immediately equate you, at the unconscious level, with all of the other people they have ever met. In all probability they probably have more negative experiences than positive experiences with people.

Two things need to happen. You must distinguish yourself from all the other people they've known and you need to move their time filter from the past to the present or future. People have emotional responses that are attached to various stimuli. You are a stimulus. You trigger positive and negative experiences in all of your clients' minds whether or not each client knows it. What's more interesting is that this response isn't necessarily linked to YOU! Most people see you as a SALESMAN and they have a negative emotional response to ALL people. Therefore, in most cases, you are a BAD SALESMAN when you walk in the door. You haven't opened your mouth or asked any questions and you are already a BAD SALESMAN. Ready for more?

When you walk out the door your client is going to think differently of you but by the next time you talk with your client his brain will be back in BAD SALESMAN mode for two reasons. First, he will confront many other IDIOTS posing as people between now and then. Second, his past emotional memories are not going to be wiped away by a fun one hour meeting with you!

Therefore, you must become an expert at altering time. You MUST become a master of moving people through time so that they are not effected by their past programming and emotions. You must be able to get them to look at your product and service from a completely different perspective! And you can.

Time plays a big role in people's decision-making process. There are three fundamental ways that people experience time. Past, present and future.

Past: Some people live in the past or use the past as their guidepost for all decisions they will make in the present and future. These people are often cynical and depressed. They also make fewer bad decisions than other people. Their guard is up and they will make fewer errors because of this. They will also miss out on opportunities because of their experiences. You will need to remember this!

- ✓ I was ripped off once before doing this.
- ✓ I ate at a place like this once and it was terrible.
- ✓ I got conned the last time I bought a car.
- ✓ I never get a good deal.
- ✓ The stock market always goes down when I invest.

These are all common experiences for people who process all information through "filters" of the past.

Present: Some people live in the present moment. These people tend to have much less stress and tend to give little thought to the past or future. They tend to be lousy planners and seek instant gratification. Usually their credit cards are maxed out because they have sacrificed a future they cannot see for the pleasure of the moment. They think like this:

- ✓ I know it's right when I feel it.
- ✓ I do what feels good.

- ✓ I just wanted to have fun.
- ✓ It looks fun so I'm going to do it.
- ✓ I never thought I'd get pregnant.
- ✓ Who'd have thought I'd lose all money?

Future: Some people filter most of their thoughts by the future. They tend to live in the future, delay instant gratification and have determined that the past, for better or worse, isn't that relevant for them. People who live in the future are constantly planning, organizing, preparing and sacrificing. They sacrifice the moment for a brighter tomorrow. They think like this:

- ✓ I could buy a car now but that money is better off invested.
- ✓ I'll wait for retirement.
- ✓ I could buy that now but I'd like to watch that money build up over time.
- ✓ I better not do that because I might get pregnant.

Once you know how a person generally filters their information you can have them look at different events in the past, present or future OR you can change their perspective from which they are looking.

You can change someone's time perspective with some linguistic maneuvers that rival the martial arts.

To get your client out of the mistakes of the past, get him to see things from a future perspective.

Client: "Look what happened to the market this last year. It went to hell. Dropped by 50%. Why would I want to invest in your mutual funds?"

Salesperson: "You might *not* want to. But the next time the market doubles or triples wouldn't you want just a little piece of that for your future?

Client: "My experience is that I listen to a salesperson and I get ripped off."

Salesperson: "When you go out 10 years into the future and look back, what do you do right to correct that?"

Client: "Last time three times I bought a big yellow page ad I lost my butt."

Salesperson: "Understand. If we can create an ad that will pull in the future will you be up for that?"

Client: "I tried hypnosis before and it doesn't work."

Salesperson: "So you had someone who didn't know what they were doing. If you were to work with someone who was adept at his art that knew how to help you would you be willing to do that?

Law of Contrast- *When two things, people or places that are relatively different from each other, are placed near to each other in time, space or in thought, we will see them as more different and easier to distinguish which one we want most.*

There is a wonderful piece of television history from the archives of the Tonight Show with Johnny Carson. Carson hosted the Tonight Show for almost 30 years before Jay Leno became the host. One night, Johnny had the number one Girl Scout cookie salesman in the country on. He asked her the secret of her success. She said, "I just went to everyone's house and said, 'Can I have a $30,000 donation for the girl scouts?' When they said "no," I said, 'Would you at least buy a box of girl scout cookies?'" The audience couldn't stop laughing and neither could Johnny. The little girl had mastered the contrast principle, at age eight

Have you ever walked through a grocery store and watched people, especially women, take two competing products and put one of them in each hand then look at them side by side, literally weighing which one they should buy? The principle that guides people in this product choice is called the Law of Contrast.

Psychological studies have shown that people can use the Law of Contrast in a very specific and pre-designed fashion. If you can show your expensive product or service first then show what you would like to sell (what you think creates the best win-win with your client) second, the client is very likely to purchase the second item.

When you were a child you would go into a store with one of your parents and as Mom shopped, so did you. You may have picked up two or three items to propose to your mother for possible purchase. Time after time your Mom programmed into you either one of two themes:

    1) It's too expensive, you can't have either of them.
    2) You can have the little (cheapest) one.

You soon learned that the best method of selling Mom was to note how little the item cost. "Mom, it's only a dollar," your voice would resonate in a pleading fashion. With the proper eye contact and pitiful face the strategy regularly worked.

The Law Of Contrast doesn't say that you will always sell the least expensive of two products. It does say that if you put two products or services close together in space, in time or in a person's mind, the person will begin to clearly see the differences and their programming will help them choose "which" instead of "whether or not to." Price was the most common programming installed into children as a child, but there definitely were many parents who programmed the theme, "it's junk, don't buy garbage," into their children. These adult clients now buy higher quality items when possible. The Law of Contrast acts within each of us to help us choose which of a number of items to buy.

> *Show your client the product you believe is their best option and/or least expensive last. The client is compelled to own something and normally will take the last or least expensive item if it is shown last.*

Real Estate people: Show your client a home that they will dislike first then show them a home that meets all of their buying criteria second. People tend to buy what they are shown or experience second.

Financial Product people: Tell your client you have two products to show her. The best financial fit for your client is to own is a diversified portfolio of mutual funds. You first show them an expensive annuity product and then follow that by a brief explanation of another option, that of owning mutual funds that require a smaller investment and easier "out" should they need their money. The better product and lower price both come second in this case, creating a compelling unconscious urge to invest in the funds.

Clothing people: Once the client has agreed on buying the suit or dress, now present a tie, a scarf, a new pair of shoes or a nice necklace as an absolute must. If the client has purchased a $400 suit, isn't a $37 tie a necessary purchase?

Electronics people: Your client has said, "Yes," to the computer, now you can show them the extended service plan, a piece of useful or fun software or an extra battery for emergencies. These $100 items contrast nicely to the $2,000 they just spent on the computer and almost seem irrelevant, in contrast.

> *Let your person buy one of several necessary items first, then let them buy the add-ons or accessories second. In contrast to the large investment they seem small and a good value for the price.*

A useful rule to remember in any sales situation is that when someone mentions that your product or service is "too expensive," or "costs too much" you respond with a gentle, *"Compared to what?"* "Compared to What"? is a question that puts your clients thoughts into perspective and allows them to re-think their apparent, "no" response. If your client was heading toward a "no" response, "compared to what?" may often bring them back to the "yes" response.

Law of Friends- *When someone asks you to do something and you perceive that the person has your best interests in mind, and/or you would like him/her to have your best interests in mind, you are strongly motivated to fulfill the request.*

How many times have you experienced someone knocking on your front door asking you to donate money for some cause? Compare the number of times you donated to the cause when you knew the person who asked you to donate in contrast to how often you donated when you didn't know the person who asked you to donate.

If you are like most people you donated more often when your neighbor came to the door asking you to donate. You felt empathy for the person you know who is possibly being put "out" by this charitable requesting. The people who solicited from you less regularly received donations because they didn't have that same empathy or trust. We tend to say "yes" when we know someone or perceive they are your friend.

In a similar context, most people would never go to a meeting for multi-level marketing if their friend or acquaintance didn't ask them to look at this business opportunity. The greatest strategy a multi-level marketing corporation can utilize is the "listing of friends and family" strategy as the first contacts in the MLM'ers early days in his new business. These friends and family are the most likely to say, "yes" to actually going to a meeting.

As people develop relationships with their clients they become friends. Friendships grow and become special and future sales are all but assured with the ongoing relationship.

Help people see you as their friend and someone who cares about them and you will dramatically increase the probability of their compliance.

An extremely powerful persuasion tool that few if any people ever use is that of *pointing out the negative aspects of your products and services*. Psychological research backs up our assertion. One of the most effective ways to influence people is to argue against your own point of view or argue against your own self-interest so that it appears that you are being unbiased in your proposals.

One group of researchers had a heroin addict tell people that there should be stricter courts and more severe sentences. The researchers found the heroin addict to be more credible than others presenting similar points of view. This was one of the few instances when people believed someone who was not perceived as physically attractive. When the message conflicts with the expectations of your buyer you'll be perceived as more serious. This is a powerful Mind Access Point and when you utilize it with a careful skill you will regularly bring out any minor negative aspects of your products and services.

Be eager to point out any negative aspects of your proposal. This accomplishes two important things. First it makes you appear far more trustworthy and second it allows your client to be set at ease as you are doing his job of finding the drawbacks of the proposal.

Financial Product people: Tell your client a story of how you recently helped your family members with their finances in the same manner that you are going to help your client. When they understand that they are going to be treated exactly like family, they perceive you also have their best interests in mind.

Real Estate people: Share with your client why you would NOT buy a specific house. If it is clear that your client is NOT interested in the house, and you don't like it either, explain why this house is not something you would recommend your friends buy and then explain in detail why. This strengthens your bond between you and your clients.

Law of Expectancy- *When someone you respect and/or believe in expects you to perform a task or produce a certain result, you will tend to fulfill his expectation whether positive or negative.*

There is a famous study from the 1970's by psychologist, Dr. Rosenthal that reveals that the expectation of one person can radically alter, both positively and negatively, the actual results of how people will perform. The study dealt with dividing students into what teachers were told were bright and dull groups of students. The students were told nothing. In the group that was made up of supposed high IQ students, they performed at an average of an "A" level after 8 months. The group that was made up of supposed low IQ students, performed at an average of a "D" level after 8 months in their school work. In reality, there was no difference in the IQ's of the students. They were randomly divided into the groups and the only variable in the study, which was immediately discontinued, was the expectation of the teachers involved.

> **The behaviors you expect of yourself and others are more likely to be manifested in reality. If you believe that your client will most certainly buy from you, they probably will.**

In psychology, the placebo effect is a well documented and scientifically measurable response on the part of the body to be healthier (or in the case of a nocebo, to be sicker) based upon expectancy, suggestion and belief. In the Korean War, there were thousands of casualties and not enough morphine to relieve the pain of the suffering soldiers. Medics and doctors were forced to give sugar pills and the suggestion that the soldiers would shortly be out of pain. Approximately 25% of all soldiers taking the placebo had their severe pain relieved.

This same level of expectancy is necessary as a belief in yourself about your abilities to be successful and also about your influential ability with your clients to win them to your products and services.

Exercise: How can you utilize the Law of Expectancy when selling your products or services?

Law of Association- *We tend to like products, services, or ideas that are endorsed by other people we like or respect.*

Tell me, what is it that Michael Jordan knows about underwear that I don't? Didn't Michael sign a $40,000,000 deal with Calvin Klein to do a few commercials about underwear? Now, it's my opinion that I know as much about underwear as Michael Jordan and I would have shot those commercials for HALF what he got! BUT Kevin Hogan is a name known in the field of selling. Michael Jordan is a name known throughout the world. Michael Jordan was really paid 2 cents for every person on earth that knew his name. If I were paid two cents for every person that knew my name, I'd get paid about $7,000. That is why Michael Jordan got paid $40,000,000.

Calvin Klein paid $40,000,000 to link one of the world's most loved and best known people to their product. Underwear. That is what the law of association is all about.

When your products and your services are linked to credible, likable, positive image people your client will tend to like the products or services.

For years authors have known that the best way to sell a book is to get people to write favorable back matter and front matter for the book. This adds credibility to the book because we respect the person who wrote the quotes.

The power of a testimonial or of someone famous using your products or services can be the key that turns the locks of the doors of the unconscious mind. If you do not have the ability to have the famous endorse your products or service, ask other people who are using your services to write you a short letter testifying to the fact that your product or service has helped them change their life, their business, or made some significant difference that they didn't have before.

The testimonial speaks volumes about you so you don't have to.

Allow people to see you and your products or services linked to the respected, the famous, the experienced and your probability of the "yes" response is heightened dramatically.

Exercise: How can you utilize the Law of Association in selling your products and services?

Law of Consistency- *When an individual announces in writing (or verbally to a lesser degree) that he is taking a position on any issue or point of view, he will strongly tend to defend that belief regardless of its accuracy even in the face of overwhelming evidence to the contrary.*

Your clients past decisions and public proclamations dramatically influence their beliefs and attitudes. Once a person has publicly said, "I'll never X," they normally never do. Many people make public statements that they have not thought out, that often turn into beliefs and permanent attitudes. The reason is simple. We are taught that our word is our bond. When we say something you can count on us.

Former President Bill Clinton has been on both sides of this law. In 1994 his continual changing of his publicly stated positions cost the house and senate seats, creating a republican majority in both houses of congress for the first time in decades. In 1998 his adamant stand against talking about the Monica Lewinsky case for ethical reasons helped him build the highest popularity rating by a president in years. By consistently stating, "I'm going to just do my job," the country began to believe in Bill Clinton again and stood behind him as their president.

Did you know that 70% of all people are the same religion they were when they were raised as children? This is the law of consistency in real life action! The following graphic will illustrate the power of various religious sects to hold members over a lifetime. Maintaining consistency is at the core of loyalty.

Percent of Current Members Raised in Same Faith

Source: Adapted from American Demographics Research.

Fundamentalists	52%
Southern Baptists	86%
Misc. Protestants	40%
Other Baptists	77%
Lutherans	75%
Methodists	72%
Inter/non-denom.	27%
Liberals	49%
Presbyterians	59%
Episcopalians	54%
Catholics	89%
Jewish	83%

All Religions	70%

Americans respect consistency and predictability.

A recent research study had subjects make decisions among various choices.

Group A was asked to "remember their decision."
Group B was asked to "write their decisions on a magic slate and then pull the sheet up 'erasing' their decision."
Group C was asked to write down their decisions on paper with ink and hand them in to the researchers.

Which group stuck with their decisions? Right. Group C stuck with their decisions over 3/4 of the time. Group B kept their decisions half the time and Group A tended to change their minds. The lesson is to get your client to write things down as he participates in the sales process. He could write down anything from goals for the coming year to what he would really like in a car, a house, a stock portfolio or a vacation time share package. The key is to get a pen in the client's hand and have him write!

> **Never ask a question which will pin the client down to a permanent "no" response.**

Exercise: How can you utilize the Law of Consistency in selling your products and services?

Law of Scarcity- *When a person perceives that something he might want is limited in quantity, he believes the value of what he might want to be greater than if it were available in abundance.*

What the public finds valuable never ceases to amaze us. Remember the Christmas season of 1996? This was when advertisers promoted Tickle Me Elmo dolls to children and then to drive the price up, simply refused to produce the dolls in quantity. The prices of the dolls grew outrageous. Stores sold out of the dolls after creating huge demand and over-pricing them. Within weeks, the Minneapolis Star Tribune printed six and seven *columns of classified ads* offering to sell their Tickle Me Elmo's for anywhere from $300 all the way up to $695!

Imagine this: A child goes into the store when the dolls first come out and Mom buys her child a doll for $30. Eventually the media promotes these dolls to the point where stores and shopping centers are flooded with people trying to find Tickle Me Elmo's being forced to settle for all the other products in the store for their children's Christmas presents. The marketing campaign was a bonanza for Tickle Me Elmo, radio station giveaways, retailers and it was all induced by intentional marketing scarcity.

Which of the following should you use as an indication of scarcity?

1. Act now!
2. Limited Supplies!
3. One Day Only!

All of those are common themes in advertising and marketing. Which works best? Act now is third most effective. One Day Only!, is an effective theme but doesn't even compare to Limited Supplies. If you can show that there are only a few of your products or services available that is going to increase your products perceived value!

The limited supply frame almost always goes back to your client's childhood. There was one or two pieces of cake left and when your client was four years old, he knew that if someone else got that piece of cake there would be none for her. It was imperative to attempt to get one of the last pieces of cake. Scarcity was installed at an early age and has been reinforced throughout our adult life. The strings wound into scarcity are very powerful indeed and you should begin to devise methods to use the principle of scarcity in your daily sales meetings.

> **Your client must be made aware that something about you or your services, or your product is scarce. (Scarcity can include quantity of product, the time you have to spend with someone or a number of specific products at a special low price.)**

Real Estate people: In the state of Minnesota, in the year 2000, many homes are selling in literally days. It is completely ethical to tell your clients that, "The average house in Minnesota is selling in 11 days. If you want this house, put an offer on paper, now."

Automobile people: There are only three cars like this on the lot. I suspect they will sell out by Monday. That doesn't mean you can't get this car again, but it does mean you could wait weeks or months to get a factory delivered car with all of these options. It's up to you.

Financial Product people: You can never predict the future, but, what happens if this January is like most Januarys and the market goes up 4% while you are deciding whether this is the time to open your IRA?

What is it that your client loses if he doesn't buy from you? That is your scarcity point.

Law of Conformity- *Most people tend to agree to proposals, products, or services that will be perceived as acceptable by the majority other people or a majority of the individual's peer groups.*

Everyone wants to be accepted. "What will people think," is something that we all think about at the unconscious level. We all want to be liked and we all want people to look at what we buy and do with respect and admiration. When your client thinks about how his peers will view his purchase, the sale can be made or broken without going any further. *Therefore it is important to assure your client, at the unconscious level that his buying your product and service is an outstanding idea.*

Conformity is related to consistency in some ways. Conformity is being consistent with your peer group's acceptance. Consistency is being perceived as predictable and ethical within your peer group and even within yourself.

Non-Conformists and "rebels" even tend to conform to their groups that are known to be rebellious against society. Consider that Greenpeace activists are very much non-conformists in the eyes of the public, but among their own group they conform to the non-conformist standard.

Jehovah's Witnesses and Latter Day Saints are both Christian sects who are considered apart from Christianity by other denominations. They are non-conformists and are proud and honored to be. However, within their own groups, they have clear-cut and definite standards that must be conformed to. Your understanding of your client's conforming standards can make or break your sales.

> **Allow your client to see his future after purchasing your product and services as one where his peers and family not only approve but are excited about his purchase.**

"Imagine how your wife will respond when she sees that you have gone out and bought her, and really your whole family a brand new car..."

"Imagine how your husband will feel when you show him that you took the initiative to invest in your retirement so his life will be easier...essentially not having to work until he is 77."

Law of Power- *People have power over other people to the degree that they are perceived as having greater authority, strength, or expertise in contrast to others.*

Power comes with authority and charisma. Power is the ability to change. Power is both real and a perception. Your clients will perceive you as more powerful if you act with confidence but not conceit, comfort but not disregard, and certainty but not knowing it all. Power is something that exists within you and must be brought out. Once people perceive you as competent, caring, knowledgeable, confident and certain, then their confidence level in you goes up.

If you attempt to use power *over* other people, instead of with other people, then you will lose sales and lose friends. Power with people is perceived by most as strength and is often called "charisma." Power over others is normally resented and people are less likely to conform if they think you are trying to control them.

One recent study that discussed power and authority revealed that 95% of all nurses were willing to dispense drugs to patients, after being authorized by physicians, that they knew would indeed likely kill the patient. That's power.

> **When you are selling a product, it is assumed you are the expert. If you know everything there is to know about your product you become the go-to guy. Subtly make sure your client knows you are the best or among the best in your company. People like to deal with the guy at the top.**

Auto mechanics may not have a high recognition value for power, but when your car breaks down, they become the most powerful people in the world don't they? They have the solution to your problem. If they made the solution appear easy they would have no power. The simple fact that most people are ignorant of how to utilize power is why most people are perceived as beggars or nuisances.

Exercise: What are three subtle ways you can let your client know you are among the top people as far as knowledge, client service and/or sales in the company? How can you show your client that you are not "just another salesman?"

Module Nine
The Secret Ingredients of Covert Hypnosis

"It's only words…"

The following conversation happened so often to all of us in childhood that we all recognize it immediately before coming to the "punch line."

Child: "Mom can I go to the neighbors?"

Mom: "No, honey."

Child: "C'mon, Mom, can I go to the neighbors to play?"

Mom: "I said, NO."

Child: "But why?"

Mom: "**Because**, I said so.

The word *"because"* is the first "Word MAP" you can use every day with every client you meet. This simple word is the perfect example of a MAP (a stimulus/response mechanism) that was installed early in your client's life. Early in childhood, the word "because" was conditioned as the absolute answer and reason for questions that we asked Mom and Dad. Today we respond the same way to the word "because" as we did when we were children. "Because" is typical of a MAP easily entered. Like magic, you utter the word and people comply.

Use the word "because" as part of your verbal reasoning, for almost any question asked of you and you will find your clients begging to comply with your requests.

Does this sound too amazing to be true? Is unconscious communication really this simple? Does just uttering the word "because" in a sentence really cause an instant reaction for compliance in your clients? What evidence exists for such a claim?

Dr. Ellen Langer, a Harvard social psychologist, and editor of Psychology Today magazine wanted to know the answer as well. In a study where Dr. Langer was considering the impact of asking for "favors", she contrasted the use of inquiries with the word "because" (a reason for having something done) and without the word "because." The study, which is now almost a part of persuasion folklore, went like this:

People were waiting in line to use a copy machine in the school library. Someone would ask one of three questions.

A) "Excuse me, I have five pages. May I use the Xerox machine because I have to make some copies."

B) "Excuse me, I have five pages. May I use the Xerox machine because I'm in a rush."

C) "Excuse me, I have five pages. May I use the Xerox machine?"

Before going any further, take a moment and imagine the scenarios and predict what the results were.

Ready?

When option (C) was used an amazing 60% of people agreed to let the person make copies, just for asking.

When option (B) was used an astounding 94% of people agreed to let the person make the copies.

Finally, option (A) which was used as a control to contrast with option (B), found that 93% of the people complied with the requests.

At least one and maybe two MAPs are immediately displayed in this simple but brilliant study:

> **Asking for a favor can be an effective tool in gaining compliance**.

The second point is to remember that the word "because" is a MAP. It is a stimulus-response mechanism in most people.

> *Use the word, "because" in response to "why?" questions because it triggers compliance at over 50% the normal response rate in many situations.*

There are a number of words and phrases that are MAPs that are easy to enter. You will learn how to utilize words that are MAPs later in this book. For now, you can easily understand how simply and innocently word-strings are programmed into our thinking.

In the *Psychology of Persuasion*, I wrote about seven of the most powerful words in the English language and how to use them in communication. Through some prodding from my partner we have decided to publish the complete master list of magic words. These are the words we use when we sell and write. In the next few pages you will find the magical building blocks of selling: The words you use. First, we have listed the magic words of selling. These are 150 of the most attention commanding words in the English language. When you prepare your message for your clients, make sure that these words are peppered throughout! These words seem to have equal effectiveness in interpersonal communication and in text.

Later in the module you will read phrases and sentences that have a proven track record of selling in face-to-face communication. Begin practicing today so you develop the nuts and bolts skills of selling. Nothing you read here can take the place of actually writing out sentences and headlines for your services. Nothing you read here can take the place of adopting these words into your vocabulary.

Acclaimed
Advancement
Amazing
Announcing
Appealing
At last
Attention
Authentic
Aware
Bargain
Because
Boosts
Breakthrough
Challenge
Change

Choice
Classic
Comfortable
Compare
Complete
Convenient
Delivers
Deserve
Discount
Discover
Discovery
Distinguished
Easy (ily)
Effective
Energy
Exceptional
Exciting
Exclusive
Experience (d)
Expert
Extraordinary
Fast
Free
Fresh
Fun
Guarantee
Heal
Help
Honest
How to
Hurry
Imagine
Important
Improved
Indispensable
Incredible
Informative
Instantly
Intimate
Introducing

Irresistible
Last chance
Love
Luxurious
Magic
Miracle
Money
Money-making
Money saving
Natural (ly)
New
Now
Offer
Original
Overcome
Peace of mind
Perfect
Please
Pleasure
Plus
Popular
Power (ful)
Practical
Prevents
Price Reduction
Profitable
Promise
Proven
Quickly
Realize
Recommended
Refreshing
Relax
Reliable
Relief (ve)
Remarkable
Research
Results
Risk free
Revolutionary

Romantic
Safety
Sale
Satisfaction
Save
Scientific
Secret
Security
Sensational
Service
Simplifies
Soothe
Special offer
Status
Stop
Stimulating
Striking
Stylish
Superior
Sure fire
Surprising
Thank You
Timely
The truth about
Traditional
Trusted
Ultimate
Unlimited
Unusual
Useful
Valuable
Wanted
Warning
You
Yours

Exercise: Create at least 25 sentences using this instruction: Utilize two or more of the magic words in sentences that pertain to your product or service. If possible create several possible uses for the magic words and weave them into phrases and sentences that will help you sell. **Reading this book will help you sell. Utilizing the tools in this book will ensure you success.**

(Example: This scientifically **proven** program includes three **easy** to use techniques that will **change** your life forever.)

Hypnotic Language Patterns

People who study hypnosis learn that there are many ways to get a person into a specific frame of mind and then get them to think about anything the hypnotists desires. Without digressing too much, our goal in hypnosis is to get people to imagine something or a specific outcome. Imaging something is often the first step to getting it, or avoiding it. In the case of selling, we want people to put their attention on our products and services. Then we want them to tell us how they will go about buying our products and services. People will not give you these secret codes to their thinking just because you ask however. You need to use the scientifically proven techniques in a very artful manner. There are specific words and phrases that yield amazing results in gaining compliance. Below are some of the phrases that have been show to get a person to come to a conclusion that is all but predetermined.

You will notice that the hypnotic language patterns are in bold face and we assume that whatever follows the pattern will be acted upon. In other words, in the first example, the hypnotic command is to ***"buy this car, that's your decision."*** It follows the hypnotic sentence fragment, **"I wouldn't tell you to…"** All of the commands are written in small type below and the hypnotic language is in bold. A command is the specific action we want the client to take. Most of these patterns are not what would be considered "good English" or "grammatically correct." ***However, these patterns are very powerful and we recommend caution when using them. Some brief but important comments follow in parentheses.)***

I wouldn't tell you to buy this car, that's your decision.
I wouldn't tell you to invest more money in stocks, you need to figure that out on your own.

(I wouldn't tell you, but notice that the command is still coming!)

How do you go about deciding to buy a new car?
How do you go about deciding how much you are going to invest?

> **When you ask how they go about deciding you learn specifically how they decide and then they give you the specific instructions on how to sell them!**

You might want to... now, join the club for only one year then renew.
You might want to... now, buy this beautiful or car.

(You don't **have** to, you just might!)

What is it that helps you know whether you should buy an X or a Y?
What is it that helps you know whether you want to upgrade **now** or wait awhile?

(Again, you are really asking for their specific decision strategy.)

You don't have to decide **now**.
You don't have to invest in several funds, one or two is just fine.

("I will if I want to!")

Why is it that some people just don't see the value of owning a quality car?
Why is it that some people just see greatness and others it eludes them?

(Not you Mr. Client, but some people...)

I don't know if signing up **now** is what you want to do.
I don't know if deciding **now** is absolutely necessary so you don't lose out.

(Actually I do know but I'm being very gentle.)

Would you like to see a bigger house?
Would you like to see this in blue?
Would you like to see our client service people call you regularly?

(You are asking for specific features and benefits that they might want...or not.)

Some people are investing a great deal of money right **now**.
Some people are snapping up houses like they are going out of style.
(Some people...are your client(s).)

If you could have a perfect car, what would it be like?
If you could have the perfect speaker for your function what would he be like?

> **"If you could have…" = "imagine"**
> It goes straight to the unconscious mind and goes to work like a mind virus.

If you could choose any mutual fund what qualities would you want it to have?
If you could choose a better insurance company what would be most important to you?

(He can choose and his brain will tell him so, now!)

Have you ever seen a truly amazing sales trainer?
Have you ever seen a speaker that motivates the day AFTER they leave?

(Again, this is the same as "imagine." It's a no-pressure question that darts through the brain at high speeds causing a "yes, I want it" response.")

Would you be surprised if I told you that most people aren't as astute as you are?
Would you be surprised if I told you that this car gets 30 mpg?

("Would you be surprised if I told you," implies you have the shocking truth.)

Imagine what would happen if your portfolio averaged 12% per year!
Imagine what would happen if you lived in a house that you could really be proud of!

(Once again, we have "imagine" lighting up the brain like a Christmas tree.)

Are you interested in making more money short term or long term?
Are you interested in making the online experience for your clients easy and fun?

(He knows he should be interested and now he has to say yes or pick which is best for him.)

If I could show you a way to make more money **would you** hire our firm?
If I could show you a way to literally look 10 years younger would you do it?

(This is a perfect, pre-closing question. You wouldn't ask it unless you COULD show him, so now you get the "yes" response and then you close after you show him.)

What would it be like if you had an extra $25,000 per year in income?

What would it be like if you had a body that people would be magnetized to?

(Imagine that....)

You may not know that this is going to be fun.
You may not know that we are going to be working together for a long time!

(He'll know right after you say, "You may not know...")

Can I show you seven ways to increase your personal sales?
Can I show you how to work out in such a way that you will be stronger and look better?

(Getting permission to sell your client is kind and effective.)

I'm wondering if deciding today will make you feel comfortable inside.
I'm wondering if investing today is going to make you the most money long term.

(I'm wondering while you imagine.)

Don't you think that it's time for a new President to lead our country?
Don't you think that a mutual fund that has a proven track record is better than...?

(It's hard to say no to anything that follows, "don't you think that.")

Don't you feel that you are happier when you have someone do your taxes for you?
Don't you feel that you are better off with a new car than an old one?

(Same as previous comment.)

Exercise: Use each of the language patterns above and fill in commands for your clients to respond how you want them to respond to you. Do this exercise before going on!

Sometimes, hypnotic language patterns don't translate particularly well from language to language (English to Polish for example) or from real life to the textual environment of a book. Words and phrases need to be stressed and articulated in very specific ways to be most effective. In the resource section in the back of the book is an NLP (neurolinguistic psychology) home study course listed that will teach you the formula for creating thousands of mesmerizing sentences that will directly relate to your product or service. If this area of selling is particularly interesting to you that is your next step in evolving the scientific use of hypnotic language.

The Masters Formula to Find Your Magic Words

What are the most powerful phrases in your specific industry? Is there a way to know what words are changing minds for your competitors? Here's the formula that will allow you to finally get the inside information.

1) Find the most successful products in your category. If you sell aspirin to retail stores you will select Advil, Tylenol, Bayer, etc.

2) Rank the products first by total gross sales. Assign the best selling a product value of 10. The next best a value of 9 and so on. You will weigh each word based upon the value assigned to it. A company's advertising that sold 10 bottles of aspirin doesn't receive as much weight as a company that sold 1,000,000 bottles.

3) Write out each word that appears on the label of the product on a sheet of paper. (Ignore ingredients and consumer warnings in this specific case.) In the case of Tylenol, there are several hundred words on the label of the box I'm holding. Here are some of the words that are in the biggest and boldest fonts.

   A) Easy
   B) Swallow
   C) Extra
   D) Strength
   E) Pain
   F) Reliever
   G) Fever
   H) Reducer
   I) Geltabs
   J) Exclusive
   K) Gelkote
   L) Process

   (Of course no one cares about the "Gelkote process" but the marketing big shots at Johnson and Johnson will figure this out and replace those words at a later date. Aside from this error, the people who make Tylenol are using the magic words and hitting all the hot buttons.)

4) After all of the words have been cataloged move to your next competitor and write down all of the words on their packaging.

5) Put a check mark on a master sheet that lists all the words on all the packages of all of your competitors by each word so you can count the

frequency of the word in all of your top competitors. For example: If Gelkote is listed on all of your top competitors packaging, you know that it belongs on yours. However, it's not there, so don't put it on yours! Instead, I bet you will be using PAIN, RELIEVER, FEVER, REDUCER, EXTRA, PRESCRIPTION, and STRENGTH. These are the words that are going to be on all the top products in the analgesic group.

6) Therefore you will model the success of the 10, 9, 8 and 7's in your industry! It would have taken you MILLIONS of dollars to find out this information in test marketing, however you are getting it for the price of two hours work.

But what if you don't sell a product? What if you sell a service or own a restaurant or you sell mutual funds? Find the advertising from all of your top competitors, the boys at the top of the totem pole and do the exact same process. Find out the frequency of words and phrases that all the companies at the top are using. These then become the words and phrases you want to model for your written communication with your clients. Of course knowing that these are the words that got your clients to buy your competitors products gives you some pretty amazing advanced intelligence doesn't it?!

Module Ten
How Your Client Decides
and
How to Know In Advance

Buying Profiles for You and Your Clients

If the "highest values exercise," earlier in this book   was the only exercise of self discovery you have ever partaken in, then you learned a great deal about yourself...but there is much more. You learned how to create a hierarchy for your values and how to elicit the most important values from your customers. Now it is time to focus your laser beam and uncover your buying profile.

Discover your buying profile by answering just a couple of quick questions in this section. Buying profiles are based on the VALS2 research developed at SRI Consulting. Buying profiles are critical to the salesperson because they help us understand why people buy what they buy. Learning your buying profile assists you in gaining personal insights into your own personality and buying "programs."

Learning how to easily decode other people's profiles is one of the keys to making more sales per contact. In addition to the greater short-term profits this brings you, you build relationships, which create long-term success in the selling business.

Once you know why people buy, pulling Mind Access strings is quick and easy.

SRI Consulting's brilliant work has helped the field of psychographics explode. This book cannot hope to reproduce the powerful survey methods of VALS2 to so we will simplify the process from 40 questions to 2 questions. For the face-to-face salesperson, a 40-question survey is not practical. Two questions don't offer us the precision we would need for market analysis, but it does offer us a predictable and useful model for understanding what causes people to buy from you. The two key elements are why people buy things and what means they have to buy them with. First consider the "why."

Principle oriented people do things because taking action meets with their code of ethics, their values and beliefs. A fundamentalist Christian and fundamentalist Muslim are both likely to be principle oriented. Both have very different evidence for what is right or wrong but both are principle oriented. Principle-oriented people are guided by ideas that in their mind appear to be etched in stone. They see little gray and view the world in terms of "right" and "wrong."

Principle-oriented people may invest in socially responsible mutual funds because they don't buy tobacco stocks. They tend to buy things because it is the right thing to do. They tend to buy products and services that make a statement about their beliefs. They will buy to rebel against what is wrong. The principle-oriented person will buy to destroy evil. They may be interested in ecology and the environment. They are likely to find education as very important.

Status-oriented people do things to impress others. They buy things that make it obvious to others that they have a certain status with their peers. Adults that are status oriented will buy to impress their peers. Teenagers will do the same thing but it may not appear that way to adults. Young people may dress in a particular style of dress or have a specific kind of appearance, which may not be typical of what might be considered "high status," but they are status oriented regardless.

Status-oriented people want to look better or worse in society. They want to fit into a group by appearance if not reality. (Clubs, gangs, churches)

Experience-oriented people do things because they are fun, adventurous, exciting, enticing, challenging, etc. They want to take part in something. They are interested in physical or social activity.

They will do something for the pleasure of doing or the avoidance of pain.

When you buy most of the things you buy, is it for the status it brings you, the experience you get from buying/using it or the principle behind buying it? Before you answer the question below, a few more examples will help you know which of the three categories most applies to you.

Example: If you buy an automobile to impress others because, "it looks good," write down status. If you bought it because it is American made, write down "principle."

If you bought it because it is fun to drive regardless of what it looks like write down, "experience."

Example: If you bought your house or a certain type of house to impress others, write down status. If you bought a home because it is the right thing to do for your family, write down "principle." If you bought your home because you wanted a space for you to really dwell in and love as part of yourself, write down, "experience."

Example: Is most of your expendable money (not bills and payments, but "fun money" spent on things that will be visually impressive to others (status), functional for you or your family (experience), or things that are in the best interests or beliefs of yourself and/or your family (principle).

Write down what you sincerely believe your major buying value to be in the space below. (status, experience or principle)

_____   _____

What are Your Means?

The second key element in determining your customers (or your own) buying profile is to identify what your "means" are. Your means include your income, your education, your potential, your credit line, and your willingness to spend money now regardless of when you have to pay for what you buy.

Most people will buy if they perceive some benefit of pleasure or some reduction in pain as long as they value the benefit more than money.

Because we do not have the ability to judge all the means of any one individual without a survey we are obligated to predict based upon environmental clues as to what another person's means are. For you, we will utilize your household gross income, which is a predictor, but not the only element of your means, as we have just noted.

In the space below write down your household's gross income for the previous year. This is an *approximate* **measure of your "means."** It doesn't include your future potential, your education, your credit, your net worth, your ability to leverage and other estimates of your "means," but it does give a rough estimation in helping create a psychographic profile of yourself.

_____

If you wrote a number higher than $75,000 write the letter, "A" by your income figure. If you wrote a number between $40,000 and $75,000 write the letter, "B" by your income figure. If you wrote a number between $18,000 and $40,000, write the letter, "C" by your income figure. If you wrote a number below $18,000, write the letter, "D" by your income figure. If your figure was within $7,000 of a higher or lower income figure, write both letters.

We will now use this information to create a basic profile of your buying typology.

There are eight categories of buying profiles that SRI Consulting has identified.

Our categories, while given the same names are not identical to those noted by SRI simply because our typologies are more predictive in nature as we have far less data about each person we meet to determine specifically which category an individual will most represent his type.

By combining your means measure with your buying value, you can see for yourself which profile fits most closely to you. There are eight profiles including Actualizer, Fulfilled, Achiever, Experiencer, Believer, Striver, Maker, and Struggler. Each of these profiles will now be discussed along with typical questions that help open the keys to the mind of the person of each profile.

Select your profile category from below and then read about yourself to determine if you have accurately predicted your buying profile.

The high means profiles are Actualizers, Achievers, Fulfilleds and Experiencers. The low means profiles are the Strivers, Makers, Believers and lastly the Strugglers.

The experience profiles are the Experiencers and the Makers. The status profiles are the Achievers and the Strivers. The principle profiles are the Fulfilleds and the Believers.

The Eight Buyer Profiles and How To Pull Their Mind Access Strings

Actualizers, according to SRI, make up approximately 10% of the population. This group makes up the smallest percentage of the population. Actualizers are set apart from the rest of the population by the fact that *neither status, principle or experience seems to be a driving force in their buying profile. It is their means, their resources that allow Actualizers to express themselves by taking advantage of their resources.* Actualizers tend to have many assets, greater education and knowledge and even greater health, all resources that they use as "means" for self-expression.

Actualizers have certain experiences and habits that are far different than the normal American.

They are five times more likely to read publications like Conde Naste Traveler and Scientific American. They are four times more likely to read Audubon, Tennis, Sky Magazine, Barron's, New Yorker, Travel and Leisure and the NY Times Daily Edition than the normal American.

The Actualizer is three times as likely to listen to Traditional Jazz, Folk and Broadway Soundtracks. They are twice as likely to listen to Beautiful Music, Contemporary Jazz, and Pop from the 40's, 50's and 60's.

The Actualizer is four times as likely to have membership in an Arts Association.

They are three times as likely to be a cross-country skier and three times as likely to visit an art museum.

The Actualizer is twice as likely to own a cappuccino maker, give dinner parties once each month, travel abroad, vacation on a cruise ship, swim 20 days per year and own a foreign car when compared to the average American.

Actualizers tend *not to* own a motorcycle or watch wrestling on TV. They are less likely to use cinnamon toothpaste!

The most common zip code for Actualizers is interestingly enough, 90210!

Given this detailed information about Actualizers we now have enough raw data to know specifically how to pull their Mind Access strings .

Appeal to the Actualizer's sense of independence, taste and character. Show the Actualizer how they can express themselves by utilizing their resources.

The Actualizer is an independent and take charge type of person. When dealing with an Actualizer, utilize that sense of independence and power to facilitate communication. You learned a great deal about the power of a few well-designed questions earlier in this book when we discussed values.

Here are some examples of questions that will help you pull the strings of the Actualizer.

(Business Machine Sales) "Doesn't it make sense for you to *own the finest equipment available*?"

(Travel Agent) "Isn't a trip to Eastern Europe metaphorical of the freedom *you have found in life*?

(Multi-Level Marketers) "Owning your own business is the final *expression of your independence*, don't you think?"

(Life Insurance) "By allowing your family to be *financially independent* after you are gone is really the icing on the cake for your ability to *control the destiny and security* of their life."

Key Points for pulling Actualizer Mind Access strings : Appeal to independence, character, self-reliance, and taste by utilizing their resources.

Fulfilleds, according to SRI, make up about 11% of the population. The Fulfilled, like the Actualizer, tends to have a higher income and more resources and assets than the norm. They differ from the Actualizer in that they buy not to live through their assets and resources but to express their principles.

The Fulfilled personality does things because they believe it is the right thing to do. You may find the fulfilled person to be a literalist or a fundamentalist whether Christian, Jew or Muslim. They tend to be responsible, mature and family oriented. They tend to be satisfied with life and seem to be pleased with the level of success they have achieved. Fulfilleds are homebodies. They don't need to travel a great deal to find fulfillment. Trend analyst and futurist, Faith Popcorn, might call these people "Cocooners." These people appear calm, self-assured and have self-confidence.

They have some respect for authority but are open to social change for improvement of society or self. The sensible Fulfilled tends to shop for value and not lean toward the extravagant. They buy quality and products that will last. In contradiction to the "cocooning," they will tend to travel internationally more than the norm. Interestingly this person of great means is also much more likely to own a station wagon than the norm. The Fulfilled is twice as likely to have a swimming pool in their backyard than the norm. Fulfilleds are much more likely to have a piano in the house, than the norm.

The Fulfilled isn't likely to wear cowboy boots and probably doesn't enjoy drag racing.

> *Appeal to the Fulfilled's sense of what is right, the right thing to do, principles and their sense of what is right and wrong.*

The Fulfilled is probably a happy and content person. They have found the right religion, are happy with their family and content with life. Appeal to their values and beliefs, which they know, are right.

Here are some examples of questions and statements that will assist you in pulling the strings of the Fulfilled.

(Satellite Dish Sales) "The best aspect of the new satellite dish system is that it offers *something for everyone in the family."*

(Car Sales) "What is great about the Saturn is that it *maintains 61% of its value* after five years."

(Real Estate) "This home will allow you and your *family to live together* in the way that will bring you the most *happiness.*

(Life Insurance) "Do you already see how taking care of your family's future after you are gone is *the right thing to do?*

Key Points: Focus on their rules of right and wrong. These rules could be the Ten Commandments or the principles that have guided their lives. The rules will be different for everyone, of course. Focus on their happiness and continued happiness. Remember that family is normally a driving factor for the Fulfilled.

<u>Achievers,</u> according to SRI, make up about 16% of the population. They are status-oriented people with means. In general they like to be in control and they are proud of the fact that they are in control of their work and lives. They pride themselves in their work. Many are workaholics. They seek and like consensus, predictability, agreement and stability. They shy away from risk, intimacy and self-discovery. The new age movement is not something that interests the Achiever.

Work provides the achiever his prestige. They tend to be committed and dedicated to their work and families. Their social lives include church, family and business relationships. They are conservatives, respect authority and accept the status quo.

"Image is everything?" Not quite, but *achievers like to look good to their peers.*

The Achiever reads magazines like Parenting and Entertainment Weekly almost twice as much as the average person. Achievers about 50% more often than the norm read golf Magazine, Country Home and the Wall Street Journal.

Here are some examples of questions and statements that allow you to pull the strings of the Acheiver.

To access the strings of the Acheiver, appeal to the low risk, tried, true, and tested. Appeal to the Achiever's need to look good to his peers.

(Financial Products) "What is best about this mutual fund is that it has a *proven track record* and a *very low risk* compared to the S&P."

(Real Estate) "This home shows the world that you have made it."

(Auto Sales) "Is this the car that is going to make you look good?"

(Seminar Sales) "You won't be subjected to a lot of that self-improvement-*new-age nonsense*. This is a *nuts and bolts program that is tried and true in the real world."*

Key Points: Focus on the fact that your product or service will make you look good. Remember the key themes of tried, tested, and true.

Experiencers, according to SRI make up about 12% of the population.

The action packed person with means to take action is the Experiencer. This often younger, rebellious person is the person who is vital, enthusiastic, risk taking and impulsive in nature. They like variety as the spice of life. They like what is new, different, bizarre, offbeat.

They are quick to take on new start up projects and just as quick to let them fall apart. The good starter and often-poor finisher makes them easy to involve in new things. Their politics and beliefs are not extremely important to them. They tend to be "uncommitted." Experiencers do not like to conform.

They are covetous of the wealth of others and also want prestige and power. Experiencers spend a lot of money on consumer goods like fast food, music, movies and videos.

The Experiencer is three times as likely to read GQ as the average person. Hot Rod, Rolling Stone, Inside Sports, Seventeen, EW, Mademoiselle, Glamour, Vogue and Penthouse are also read over two times more often than the normal person.

Rap, Heavy Rock, New Wave Rock, Contemporary Rock and Contemporary Black music genres are popular with Experiencers. So is dance music.

The Experiencer will play pool once per month at least two times more often than the norm. They go to concerts more often than the norm. They are twice as likely to own a speakerphone and go horseback riding than the norm. They often buy weight-training equipment and are 77% more likely to own a foreign sports car than the norm.

Experiencers do NOT buy small dogs, rarely own pianos or radial saws compared to the norm. They won't see the ophthalmologist much compared to the norm. They will almost never own bonds.

Appeal to the Experiencer's right and desire to have more than they do. Appeal to the Experiencer's need to participate, have fun, and rebelliousness.

Here are some examples of questions and statements that will allow you to pull the Experiencer's strings.

(In general) "If you're sick of doing things the way everyone wants you to do them, then you should really sign on with our company..."

(Selling Clothes) "If you really want to be on the cutting edge of fashion, this dress/suit/outfit is for you..."

(Insurance Sales) "If you're sick of the government stealing your money, then you can fight back by owning a tax free annuity..."

(Auto Sales) "Do you want a car that you can easily work on and make a statement with?"

Key Points: Remember to appeal to the fact that Experiencers tend to be on the rebellious side. How is your product or service going to help them rebel? Appeal to their spontaneous nature.

<u>Believers,</u> make up about 17% of the population according to SRI Consulting.

The Believers tend to be principle-oriented people without the means of the Fulfilled. The Believers tend to be conventional and conservative people who often have church as a focal point in their life. The believer is a person who has certain and specific beliefs. What they believe is traditional, family, church, patriotic, etc. Many believers have moral codes that are deeply rooted and literally interpreted.

The Believers follow routines and rituals and are organized around the home, family, social and/or religious institutions. Believers buy American made products, may be conservative democrats, and prefer established brands. Their income, education and means are moderate but sufficient to meet the needs of life.

Believers read Organic Gardening, Weight Watchers, and the National Examiner about 50% more than the norm. Prevention, Readers Digest, Woman's Day and the Ladies Home Journal are read about 30% more than the norm.

Appeal to the Believer's specific beliefs by revealing a knowledge and appreciation for their beliefs. Appeal to family, tradition and moral behavior.

Here are some questions and statements that allow you to open the doors to the Believer's minds.

(Product Sales) "There is nothing more important than supporting our own people and that is why we want you to consider our American made products..."

(In General) "How important are your religious beliefs in deciding whether to....?"

(Real Estate) "How close do you want to be to your church when you decide what home to buy?"

(Financial Products) "Do you want to invest in funds that are primarily invested in socially responsible stocks?"

(In General) "Are values important to you in making decisions about...?"

Key Points: Remember to appeal to their beliefs, their specific beliefs. Remember that Believers make up the largest buying profile in the USA and Canada.

Strivers, make up about 14% of the population, according to SRI.

Strivers want to, and feel they deserve to, "make it." They want motivation and incentive. The Striver's life often revolves around planting roots and finding security. They are low on the economic totem pole and often have social and psychological difficulties.

Strivers need and appreciate a pat on the back and a great deal of positive feedback.

The Striver will buy something if they think it will help them make more money. Money is a central and revolving theme in the Striver's life. They feel they have been ripped off and have had bad luck in life. Strivers are impulsive and get bored rather easily. Strivers may dress beyond their means. They probably buy more products per person on credit than most other people. They want to have nice things and probably don't think about the long-term consequences of their actions when they plunk down their credit card.

Strivers read Jet, Penthouse and Essence more than 50% more than the rest of the population. Other magazines that are read by Strivers almost half again as often as the rest of the population: Playboy, Ebony, Mademoiselle, Motor Trend, Rolling Stone, Sporting News, Inside Sports, Muscle and Fitness. Strivers listen to Contemporary Black and Rap about 25% more often than the norm.

Strivers are 31% more likely to buy a lottery ticket than the norm. They are 74%

more likely to visit a CircleK Store and 60% more likely than the norm to buy an Instant Developing Camera.

Strivers are very unlikely to work for a political party, contribute to public TV, or be enrolled in Frequent Flyer programs. They are half as likely as the norm to attend adult ed classes as the norm. They are only 2/3 as likely to buy golf irons, and PC's as the norm.

***

Appeal to the Striver by noting how he has been given a raw deal in life and deserves better. This is an active theme in his life. Appeal to his beaten down ego by giving positive ego strokes.

***

Here are some examples of statements and questions that open the mind of the Striver so you can pull their strings.

(In General) "You deserve to have the things that everyone else does don't you?"

(In General) "Up until now, life has truly given you a bad deal. Now you have a chance to take back control..."

(Financial Products) "If you really want to be like (name a wealthy or famous person), do what they did and invest your money now so you have what you deserve when you retire."

(Real Estate) "Is this the kind of home that your friends and family will like?"

Key Points: The Strivers have little income and low self esteem. They will buy on credit and extended payment plans. Appeal to the fact that life has given them a bad hand of cards and that you are going to do what you can to change that!

Makers, according to SRI, make up about 11% of the population.

Makers work with their hands. They may be construction workers, homebuilders or work in any field where they can use their building skills. They place a high value on being self-sufficient. What they can't afford to buy they make or fix. Their lives are family, work and physical activity. (See the magazines they read below.) Though certainly in the lower half of the income earners, they make the most of what they do have with their handyman like skills.

The Maker tends to be politically conservative, sometimes conservative democrats. They are skeptical of what is new, whether products, services or ideas. They respect the government but take personally government intrusion into their personal lives. They are un-moved by the possessions and appearances of wealth by others.

Makers read Hunting, Field & Stream, Guns and Ammo, Outdoor Life, Hot Rod, Sports Afield, Popular Mechanics more than twice as often as the norm.

Appeal to the Maker's skill at working hard and his practical points of view. If your product or service can help him do his work better or allow him time for physical recreation, you have found his Mind Access string.

Questions and statements that allow you to pull their Mind Access strings more effectively are noted below. Notice the common themes.

(In general) "You want to have this X because it will help you do Y in a more efficient manner."

(In general) "Sensible people with a practical bent appreciate owning X because it is useful...."

(Financial Products) "With your ability to do so many things that others have to buy or pay for in services, the opportunity for you is that you can secure your future by investing in a good mutual fund portfolio..."

(Automobile Sales) "This car is easy to fix and is big enough for your entire family and all of your camping gear."

(Retail Sales) "Sure, you may not have enough for a huge down payment, but you can fix it up, and re-finance at a lower interest rate, later, which will save you money. Even adding a bathroom will up the value of the house to where you will quickly build equity."

Strugglers, according to SRI, make up almost 11% of the population.

The Struggler is living in poverty or is surviving on a very close to poverty level income. He or she, probably has a poor education and very few marketable skills. They are most concerned with issues of security and stability. They probably aren't even living paycheck to paycheck. They are likely to be behind on their bills and have difficulty in all related areas of finance.

Strugglers read True Story, Soap Opera Digest, The National Examiner, Star, Jet, and the National Enquirer more than the norm, but not much. Lack of money simply prohibits this category of people from being anyone can sell to other than products that Ed McMahon represents....

Key Points: The Struggler only needs to buy products that are going to solve short term problems and should not be the focus of marketing and sales campaigns.

The Changing Face of America

Current research is showing that people born in the 1977-1994 are less rebellious and more likely to be computer literate. This group, which we call "the echo boomers," is ethnically more diverse than the baby boomers. They have a tendency to believe that education is a life long endeavor. They have no problem looking to women as leaders.

The echo boomers are familiar with family break-ups, tragedies of drugs, gun, violence and gangs. For the most part, they really have not rebelled against their parents.

The echo boomers in general are likely to be comfortable with the technology all around them and lead America and the world into the rapid changing techno-world. As your customers change as people and we change as a society, we will need to know more than the two basic components of a buying profile that we examined in this module. We will need to learn more about the unconscious basis of personality and how to pull all of the right strings all of the time. In this module we looked at how a customer's means will effect his buying profile and who he is as a person. Then we looked at how a person's reason for buying whether it is status, principle or activity and experience effected the buying profile. Those are two unconscious filters that everyone has but we rarely think about. They effect whether your customers are buying or not buying every day.

In the next module, you will learn about many more of these unconscious filters of our experience called metaprograms. The ability to see a client's metaprograms, the unconscious filters of experience, is almost like being able to read his mind.

Once you know a person's metaprograms, you don't need to be able to read a person's mind, because you can easily change it, if you want.

Module Eleven
Taking the Veil Off of The Unconscious Mind

Understanding Metaprograms: The Software that is installed in Your Client's Mind

Inside the Mind: How Your Client Decides

Your customer buys what she wants and not necessarily what she needs. That is a fact. If you sell your product only to your client's apparent needs, then you are losing sales and thousands of dollars per year in income. Your customer buys all products and services based on the result of awareness, desire, opportunity and the final interaction of numerous meta-programs.

Persuasive messages that only include what people need are not as likely to be acted upon as those that focus on building wants and moving the person toward those wants.

Once the person decides they want something they merely need to justify the purchase of the product or service...or idea. How we can help them justify the purchase is where understanding and utilizing their metaprograms comes into play.

METAPROGRAMS

Meta programs are unconscious filters and directions of experience and behavior. (We often alter this definition slightly for the convenience of utilizing similar software like programs that are running in your customer's head but are as yet uncategorized.)

A metaprogram is a personality trait that a person is unaware of in most communications, at the conscious level. Each personality trait is so powerful that if you could alter it even modestly it would change the future of your customer (or even yourself!).

Carl Jung discovered metaprograms in the 20th century and called them temperaments. He believed that people were different from each other in fundamental ways. He used terms like "function types" or "personality types" to describe these differences. While noting the differences Jung also agreed that within each person is the same multitude of instincts that drive them that we all have.

In the 1950's Isabel and Kathryn Myers (daughter and mother) synthesized Jung's typing themes into the famous Myers-Briggs Type Indicator. (Their book, *The Myers-Briggs Type Indicator Manual*, along with Keirsey and Bates', *Please Understand Me* are required reading if you are going to be working with customers. The MBTI helps you analyze where your customer fits into each of the temperaments discovered much earlier by Hippocrates, Adickes, Kretshmer, Spranger and Adler.)

It is believed by many that the four metaprograms (or temperaments) measured by the MBTI are inborn, genetic and are only relatively changeable throughout a person's life. There do appear to be some context related differences within some people. (Some people are very extroverted in work and introverted at home for example.)

Here are the four metaprograms that have been utilized in developing the 16 type MBTI, and how to utilize them to pull Mind Access strings. *The key words that pull Mind Access strings for each person's sorting pattern are listed below that trait. These are the words that pull the strings of the people viewing life through each specific program. Utilize these words and the themes behind the words in your sales presentations.* Refer to *Please Understand Me,* by Keirsey and Bates for far greater detail into the four Jungian metaprograms.

World Experience Program

1. Extrovert...Introvert

sociable	territorial
breadth	depth
external	internal
interaction	concentration
many relationships	limited relationships

The **extrovert** is a person who is more likely to be outgoing and socially adept. They like to go out to places and mingle. They are focused on what is going on in the outside world. The **introvert** is more interested with intrapersonal communication. They are interested in what lies within. The introvert is interested in ideas. Introverts tend to be territorial. Notice that the .... above indicate that these traits or characteristics lie on a continuum and that the continuum can be context dependent. A person who is 51% introverted will act and experience life much differently than a person who is 99% introverted won't they?

About 75% of the English speaking population describe themselves as extroverted.

Judgment Program

2. Thinking...Feeling

objective	subjective
principles	values
policy	social values
laws	circumstances
criteria	intimacy
firmness	persuasion
justice	humane
categories	harmony
standards	good or bad
critique	appreciate
analysis	sympathy
allocation	devotion

The thinker is someone who analyzes information in the decision making process. The thinker aims toward the objective and "real" result. The feeler is someone who is more inclined to go with his gut level instincts. The feeler is someone who is likely to move toward the subjective result. Both groups seem to have the same emotional intensity but the feelers are more likely to let their emotions "show."

About 60% of men are thinkers and about 60% of women are feelers.

Closure Program

3. Judgment..Perceiving

settled	pending
decided	gather more data
fixed	flexible
plan ahead	adapt as you go
run one's life	let life happen
closure	keep options open
decision-making	"treasure hunting"
planned	open-ended
completed	emergent
decisive	tentative
"wrap it up"	something will turn up

The judger is someone who deals with the outer world in a more black or white fashion. The perceiver sees the outer world and accepts it, more or less, for what it is. When judging begins, perception ends. The two attitudes do not occur simultaneously as in some other metaprograms. A person will perceive discussion or debate until a specific point and then a judgment is made. Similarly, a person will suspend judgment until he has enough perceived information. The distinction in this continuum is what is the person more comfortable with. Do they prefer to come to judgment or do they prefer to consider and perceive. Judgers put order into their lives, perceivers simply live their lives.

The English speaking population seems to be divided into about a 50-50 split as to which tendency each person is likely to fall into.

Perception Program

4. Intuition...Sensation

hunches	perspiration
future	past
speculative	realistic
inspiration	actual
fantasy	down to earth
possible	no-nonsense
fiction	fact
ingenious	practical
imaginative	sensible

How does your customer perceive the world? His life? You? That will depend upon his perception program. This program helps us see that some people are exploring what is possible while others are more interested in what "is." The intuitive person is directed by the unconscious mind to a far greater degree than the person who is a sensor. The sensor is guided by his five senses and his specific and verifiable experiences.

The intuitive person may have difficulty putting their hunches into words but they are just as certain about the veracity of their knowledge as the sensor is.

The sensors tend not to worry about the past or the future. The intuitive may often seem unaware of all that is going on around him. Intuitive people love metaphors and imagery and are excellent prospects when you have a wonderful story to tell.

Approximately 75% of the English speaking population are sensors.

The New Metaprograms

There is a definite quality of overlapping programs within each of us. If you watch the NBC news and flip to the CBS news, some of the stories are the same and some are unique to each channel. Metaprograms are similar to this experience. In this section, you will learn some of the "new metaprograms" that are critical to pulling Mind Access strings in the sales process. You may feel that there are relationships between two metaprograms and that is a sign that you are becoming consciously aware of the programs that are running your mind, and a good sign of understanding this method of understanding and utilizing personality traits in Mind Access strings .

Metaprograms are among the deepest filters of perception. These internal sorting patterns unconsciously help us decide what we pay attention to.

Metaprograms are, generally speaking, "content free but context dependent."

Like a computer software program, the sum of your client's metaprograms do not actually store information but determine what drives him. His state (of mind) is affected by his metaprograms and they play a significant role in creating his internal representations (his pictures of how he views the world at the conscious and unconscious level).

In order to use a computer program effectively you must understand how use it. In order to communicate with and sell your products and services to your customers in an efficient manner you must understand what metaprograms they use. Because metaprograms are deletion and distortion filters that adjust our generalizations (beliefs), we can predict the states of mind of our customers if we know their metaprograms. If you can predict your client's internal states, you can easily influence your customer's decisions and actions.

There are about 50 metaprograms that have been identified as sorting patterns, types, traits and functions for individuals. You will now learn the "new" metaprograms that most affect the sales process. Remember that all metaprograms exist on a continual and are not either/or representations of personality! As previously noted some people are *very* extroverted and other people may be just a little extroverted. The behavioral distinctions between someone who is extroverted and someone who is *very* extroverted can be described as analogical to a good conversationalist compared to someone who never stops talking to listen.

We have already discussed the four core metaprograms that Jung, Myers, Briggs, Keirsey, and Bates have so brilliantly educated us about. The first of the new metaprograms we want to examine is that of the pain /pleasure sorting pattern. This metaprogram is probably the most important metaprogram in making or losing sales.

Pleasure/Pain Program

A. Experience Pleasure......................................Avoid Pain

bright future	sick of the way things are
feel great	stop getting hurt
move toward	away from
make new friends	stop being lonely
obtain	get rid of

Decades of scientific research clearly show that people are more motivated by pain than by pleasure.

What this means is that you not only will paint a picture of a vivid wonderful

195

future for your customer but you must also find their current wounds (pain) and heal them. In fact, this one Mind Access Point drives over a hundred other Mind Access Points the foundational string is that people will do almost anything to avoid significant pain.

People are motivated to move toward pleasure and away from pain. Of the two drivers, most people are programmed to move away from pain more than moving toward pleasure.

When your customer was a child he was regularly threatened with pain (a spanking, a slap in the face, loss of privileges) when he behaved in a bad way. This developed very thick and powerful Mind Access Points, which many other Mind Access strings are attached to. A smaller number of your customer's parents regularly motivated them as children by offering rewards for good behavior. Most parents use threats of punishment in order to gain compliance. Your customer continues to want to do anything he can to avoid pain. If that means complying with you, that is what he will do.

The Amway Corporation has built one of the largest privately held corporations in the world by pulling the Mind Access Points of those with an entrepreneurial spirit and focusing on the pleasure end of the pain pleasure metaprogram. They help their distributors build dreams and create vivid and lush futures. They move their distributors toward pleasure, as a rule of thumb.

In contrast, hundreds of the world's largest corporations have built their fortunes by pulling the Mind Access Points of the populace on the pain side of the pain/pleasure metaprogram. History and scientific research has shown that people are very averse to pain. As mentioned above, most people will do far more to avoid pain than experience pleasure. The experience of pain is the driving force of billions of dollars in the advertising industry. How many of these slogans and commercial themes sound familiar to you?

> "Aren't you hungry for Burger King, now?"
> "Do you suffer from headache pain?"
> "Do you feel achy?"
> "Can't sleep at night?"

When you are talking with your client, your job, in part, is to show how your product or service will create great pleasure if they buy from you and also act as a way to avoid pain. If they fail to hire you, you show them how their wound will grow and create pain for them in the future. If they hire you, you will help them heal their wound.

Anthony Robbins, the world's most powerful motivational speaker, got to that apex by being able to clearly create vivid pictures of what would happen to people if they didn't allow him to help them. You can utilize the power of the pain/pleasure metaprogram just like Robbins has done.

If you have elicited your client's metaprograms then you can focus on the context specific information you have elicited instead of relying on the general rules we have discussed here. In marketing we must rely on the norms. In the direct sales situation we have a marked advantage of knowing exactly what motivates each specific client.

One effective language pattern that helps the client experience the pain of not working with you, is for you to say a variation of the wound opening, "If you don't act on this now, then won't things simply get worse?"

The more the customer fears and moves away from pain, the more likely she is to act now. It is our job to paint a picture of the consequences of failing to hire you. Experiencing pain must be more than an idea, it must be real to the customer.

If we fail to sell our customer the services that they need, then they still associate too much pain to change and you have not done your job. No amount of "closing techniques" will get a person to change their point of view or buy a product if they are still unconvinced. You must help the person see the obvious and clear benefits, emotional and logical to accepting your products and services.

Your job is often to paint the status quo as miserable. Most people have a fear of change. It is pre-programmed within them. Therefore, when painting the status quo, it must hurt to experience it. You must bring out the pain of not changing and make it vivid. Someone who associates no drawbacks or very little pain in the status quo will not accept your proposal. They will say, "no."

The more someone moves away from pain and experiences fear, the more likely they are to act on a decision, now.

The Amway Corporation has utilized a wonderful tool for helping potential distributors feel the pain of failing to become Amway entrepreneurs. For just a moment, remember when you were first presented with the opportunity to become involved as a distributor. One of the dark pictures the speaker painted for your future was this: If you don't become a distributor, how else are you going to become, financially independent? Do you really want to work at that the same job and forever? Are you really going to be happy with $35,000 per year, every year for the rest of your life?

Does Amway or *any company or salesperson,* have a right to pull at these Mind Access strings? You bet they do, because they are making the world go around. Multilevel marketing may or may not be an outstanding entrepreneurial opportunity for any individual, but just for a moment, realize how Amway has become so vast: *Amway utilizes the pain/pleasure metaprogram better than any private organization in the world.*

This Exercise Is Worth $100,000, Do It Now.

Use the space below to write down 20 painful futures that your customers could experience if they don't own your product or use your service. Then write down 20 bright futures that your customers will experience if they do use your product or service. The next time you meet with a client you will have a vast array of futures to offer your customer. It is the quality of the images that you help your customer see that will make you thousands of dollars per year in additional sales.

Cost/Convenience Program

B. Cost... Convenience

At some point in the sales interview, you will need to determine whether your client is more concerned and with speed and convenience or cost.

Many people will take a quick trip to the local convenience store to pick up a few items even though they cost far more than the grocery store charges, for the simple reason that the convenience store is right on the corner and it only takes a minute to get there. It is convenient. The convenience of the store's proximity is considered by most to be more important than the increased cost of the goods at the store.

If you are selling financial products then you'll need to find out whether your client really has the time to closely follow the daily stock reports and make day-to-day decisions about his investments. Would he be happier if you took care of this for him? Is it worth the small cost involved for you to handle his finances in exchange for the incredible burden it lightens within him?

If you sell real estate, does your buyer really want to commute an extra 30 minutes per day to save ten thousand dollars on the price of a house? You need to find out whether the person is more motivated by cost or convenience before the buying process begins.

Relationship Program

C. Match...Match/Mismatch...Mismatch/Match...Polarity

same as	same except	completely different
in common	more	totally changed
like before	progress	one of a kind

Take three coins and place them on the table in front of you. Describe the relationship between those three coins.

If you said that the three coins are *all money* or that they are *all coins* or that they are *all heads* off or *all* made of metal, then you are what is known as "a matcher."

If you said that they are all somehow similar but there are also differences in some way, then you would be typed as "a matcher with a mismatch."

If you said something to the effect of "they're all different but they do have this in common," then you are a "mis-matcher with a match."

If you found that all three coins were *distinctly different from each other with nothing in common* then you are what is known as a "polarity responder."

In the real world, you may or may not be able to utilize such a tool. In your sales interview, if you needed to instantly know your clients relationship program, you would ask, "What is the relationship between your job (or something similar) this year and last year?"

Convincer Program

D. Internal...External

I think	She thinks
I feel	They tell me
My instincts tell me	Research shows

How does your customer know if he should buy your products or services? You can ask him how he was convinced the last time he *successfully* made a major purchase like yours. You don't want to know how he was convinced of making a big mistake, you want to know how he was convinced of making a good decision.

"Are you glad you bought your current home?"
"Sure it's been great."
"What convinced you to buy this home?"

Your client will now tell you a story. That story will largely revolve around people and data helping him make his decision or around his gut level intuition, his feelings. Once you know whether your client is convinced of good decisions by either Internal or External sources of information, you can then pace and match that source of information.

"I just had a feeling that it was the right place."
"I want you to tell me if you get that feeling again when we look at the next home we are going to visit."

or

"It matched all of the criteria we set up. It had three bedrooms upstairs, an office and a swimming pool."
"You mentioned that you are now looking for a larger home earlier with a fireplace and the same nice qualities of your current home. When we come across your next home, let me know right away."

Convincer-# of Times Program

E. Assumed....Once....Many Times.....Regularly....Always

Some customers won't buy from you the first time you propose something to them. Some people will need to look at your program numerous times before they decide to buy. This being the case, we can elicit their metaprogram for how many times it takes them to see something of quality before they actually purchase it.

"I'm curious, the last time you bought your life insurance, how many times did your agent have to come and show you the benefits of insurance before you actually said, OK?"

"We talked about it after the first time he came out, then he called back and we told him to stop back out the next week. He did and we signed up then."

"Gotcha, so you and Mrs. Johnson appreciate someone who gives you the night to make sure you are doing what is in your best interest then have me come back out tomorrow, is that right?"
or

"...well frankly we had a pretty hard time deciding whether or not to buy insurance from our guy or not. It was such a great expenditure. I think he was out here three or four times..."

"Makes sense to me. I can easily see how difficult it is to make important decisions carefully. What I'd like to do is leave you with several print outs (proposals), you look them over and I'll stop back tomorrow. Then if you feel you still want to move carefully, I'll stop back next week. OK?"

Picture Size Program

F. General/Big...**Specific/Detail**

Overall	Exactly
The important thing is	precisely
Generally speaking	to be exact

Have you ever noticed that many customers you have get bored to tears when you start going over the details and nuances of your products and services? These people are what we call "big picture" people. Other people will feel that you are trying to cheat them if you just give them a few broad strokes of information. They want all the details. Anything short of a full disclaimer and a detailed future amortization puts you in their doghouse and they won't buy from you. These people are "detail buyers."

People who are rushed for time generally need you to put your proposal into a four-minute sound byte commercial. If they want more information they will ask for it as you then become a priority in their day. This may or may not mean that you literally talk faster. It does mean that regardless of what you sell, you should be able to discuss your product intelligently for 20 seconds, 20 minutes or two hours. You will meet people who will buy a car in 20 seconds and a house in 20 minutes. You will also meet people who won't buy anything until they have had hours, days, weeks, or months to consider it. Be aware of their Picture Size Program and you will enhance your probability of making the sale.

"When you bought your last car, how long did you actually have to think about it before you told the salesman, yes? Did he give you all the specs on the vehicle or did you just see it and say, 'Hey, that's a nice car, I'll take it.'"

Possibility/Necessity Program

G. Possibility...**Necessity**

Opportunity	Must
Chance	If need be
Could happen	only if

Does your client buy your financial products because he *needs* a nest egg at retirement or because it expands the *possibilities* of how he can live his retirement years? The distinction can be very important.

You must propose your products and services through the same filters as your client's metaprograms for instant compliance. If your client invests in mutual funds because it will afford him the *opportunity* to travel abroad and have freedom, then he is a possibility investment buyer. Another salesperson attempting to sell him because he'll need the money to replace social security will fail to make the sale because he has not utilized the filter.

A useful question to find out whether the person tends to be possibility or necessity thinking is,

"Why are you in the business you are in?"

Your client either had to get the job they have or start the business they own, or, they saw this job or business and opportunity or possibility for some brighter future. Once you know which end of the spectrum your client is on, you operate through that filter as well. As with all metaprograms, if you pace the client's metaprogram and work within their filters you will gain rapid compliance.

What are the similarities and differences between the Possibility/Necessity metaprogram and the Pleasure/Pain metaprogram? What differences do you notice?

Change/Status Quo Program

H. Change...Status Quo

Change	Status Quo
Different	Consistent
Evolve	Stable
Alter	Steady
Switch	Same

Does your client like things to stay the way they are? Does he like to see his business or himself evolve? Grow? Does he like to change? Does he need to keep things status quo?

If you know the buyer's Change/Status Metaprogram you have a grand opportunity to create security in the status quo or excitement in change.

People who like change rarely keep jobs for a long period of time. They tend to get bored easily and they are constantly trying new things. People who like the status quo will tend to stay in the same jobs and do the same things day after day, month after month, year after year.

Accept Readily/Skeptical-Closed Program

I. Accepting.................Cautious........Skeptical.........Closed

Accepting	Cautious	Skeptical	Closed
understand	careful	beware	never
unconditional	consider	can't	
always	sometimes	makes no sense	
friendly	nervous	afraid not	

You will discover that your customers fall on a continuum from open acceptance to critical skepticism of new ideas, products and services. The program has some similarities to that of Change/Status Quo. However, they are not the same. People who are accepting are willing to listen. Those who are closed are usually closed because of some event(s) that have transpired in his life. Interestingly, people who are closed to opinions often got that way because they were once vulnerable and got hurt or taken advantage of. These are the people that put up "No Soliciting" signs. As every salesperson knows, they are among the easiest people to gain compliance with.

Module Twelve
The Psychobiology of Covert Hypnosis

Easy to Understand Mind Access Points that Tap Your Clients DNA

Covert Hypnosis for the Genes

There are a few multi-billion dollar corporations that know how to reach the inborn genetic programming within each of us so we will be inclined to purchase their products. You are going to now learn a few of the secrets of these multi-billion dollar international successes. The world's best advertising is not geared at just our behavior but at something that is next to impossible to change: our DNA. We aren't going to take you through a scientific explanation of how each of these Mind Access Points work. That would take a set of encyclopedias. What you are going to learn is how to apply the research that we have done in the sales situation so that it is easy for you to utilize.

All people need food, clothing and shelter in our society. Those are inborn programs. We must eat to survive. We must have clothing to survive the cold winters. We must have some kind of shelter for inborn needs of security and territorial ownership. Beyond this, there are very few inborn needs, but there are many inborn tendencies that drive human behavior as your customer grows and becomes an adult.

Your Appeal Should be to the Many, not Just the One

Our genes do not simply generate the tendency for us to survive and care for the self, but they virtually command and carry out a powerful compulsion to care for the larger groups that we are part of. In fact, almost all of our genetic make-ups are so designed that we will help the larger groups we are part of survive before they will save themselves.

Have you ever seen a news story where a man raced into a burning building to save a young child? Not only is that an altruistic act, it is part of most people's genetic programming. The compulsion to care for others in our group is very powerful.

Almost all people are pre-programmed to act in the best interests of the following:

- Themselves
- The Family
- The Group
- Society
- God

The big mistake that salespeople make is that they only appeal to the customer's best interest when they should be appealing to the customer's interest in how your product will help his family, his employees, his civic groups and church organization, society as a whole and even God. It was only in 1998 that there was discovered a portion of the brain that is activated when communicating with the divine. This will be discussed in greater detail in other Mind Access books.

There is an old McDonald's commercial that illustrates how to appeal to the greater genetic needs. The theme song, "You deserve a break today, so get up and get away, to Mc Donalds..." plays in the background. The image is that of a man who has had a long day at work and the theme initially plays to his deserving a break. The genetic motivator however is not self-satisfaction. The motivator is when you see Dad and Mom and the kids all driving off to Mc Donald's together.

> *What a person may not be able to justify for himself can often be justified if it becomes obvious that it benefits our family, or society, or the group with which we belong.*

Exercise:
We learned that in order to motivate a person you often must widen the context for the emotional reasoning to engage. Describe how you can you do this for your product(s) and/or services?

Competition is a Driving Genetic Force of Survival

The field of evolutionary psychology has taught us that competition between individuals and groups is what naturally selects winners and losers in society.

When you are appealing to your customer to purchase your products and services appeal, subtly, to the fact that owning your products or services will give him an advantage in society, within the group or against his competitors. The make up of the individual is to survive competitively. The world's greatest competitors are those who become the wealthiest individuals. Bill Gates, Ted Turner, Warren Buffet. All of these men are very good people yet brilliant competitors. Bill Gates doesn't seek to own a share of the market with Microsoft, he seeks to dominate the market with Microsoft and does so by providing outstanding products at reasonable prices. Microsoft seeks to dominate with great products and services. You can do the same by appealing to the competitive nature in your customers. Do so quietly and with careful subtlety. *It is a genetic fact that those who opt out of competition reduce their level of prestige on the societal ladder.*

> ***Success, survival and failure in all levels of animal and human society are wrapped up in the ability to compete and dominate***.

Exercise:
Realizing that competition is one genetic component of what creates success and failure in society, take your time and carefully answer the following three questions.

How can competing to dominate your market with great service and great products help you and your family ascend the ladder of success?

How can you sell more of your products and services by appealing to the need in our customers to be at or near the top of the success ladder?

How does being competitive enhance the quality of your life?

Persuading Groups is Far Easier Than Individuals

It is a known fact that madness is the exception in individuals and far more common in groups. Most normal humans would never throw ice balls at un-protected innocent people walking down the street. Watching a football game in season would never convince you of this truth as referees are constantly on the look out for spectators who they know can generate great harm. Fans watching soccer games have been seen on numerous occasions to literally kill people at soccer games because of the intensity generated during the competitiveness of the game.

Every public speaker knows that persuading most of the people in a large group of people is far easier than persuading one individual in a one on one setting. There is an almost evident IQ deficiency in groups. Groupthink takes over and people will follow the vocal proponents of a proposition. Most people are like sheep waiting for the shepherds.

Scientific research clearly shows that the more people are in a group the more likely that the vast majority of the group will comply with whatever the leader is proposing. The fascinating caveat is that there is a very common fear of speaking and presenting before groups. This gives the master salesperson that is adept in Mind Access, a powerful edge against all others in the selling process.

People act like animals in groups and are easily herded. Even the master of Mind Access cannot expect or even consider having 100% assenting opinions in group settings. In all groups there are individuals who rise above group think. When facing their objections always honor and respect their point of view and continue on with your presentation. The vast majority will always rule and you will nearly always succeed in group selling situations if you follow all the key elements and pull all the right Mind Access strings .

Remember the truism from the 19th century: The larger the lynch mob the more brutal the lynching. Those in an emotional frenzy lose all sense of ethics. Think of experiences that you have had that make this fact clear to you.
Those in group settings tend to be led by the unconscious minds of the rest of the group. The average intelligence of the unconscious mind is about that of a six year old. This doesn't mean that there isn't a vast array of information stored in the unconscious mind, indeed there is. It does mean that the unconscious mind is far more reactive and emotional than the analytical conscious mind. The conscious mind rests in group settings making an easy target for the ethical salesperson or the unethical swindler.

It is encoded in people's genetic make up to find safety in groups. Once in a group, the normal person's defenses are dropped as there is a feeling of safety in almost all of the group.

Appealing to the Genetic Quest for Affiliation

All humans need to feel wanted. Science and medical research clearly reveals that feeling un-wanted stunts all forms of human growth and development. Physical, psychological, and emotional growth all are influenced by a person's perception of feeling wanted. In fact, people who say they don't need to feel wanted are literally lying or psychotic. The need is pre-programmed.

You need to make it clear to your customers that you are interested in them as more than a customer. People can literally sense a true sense of interest and when they do, they are likely to develop the long-term relationships with you that will create win-win selling situations.

One recent medical study concluded that, "a lack of warmth and meaningful relationships" is a significant cause of heart attacks in many people. What does this tell us about needs pre-programmed into our behavior? We are physically influenced by love, compassion and relationships.

> *It is imperative that your customer perceives you as someone who truly cares about him. He must feel a sense of compassion and interest in him by you before you can predictably make sales at will.*

Dr. Dean Ornish published a wealth of material in 1998 about the fact that closeness can literally heal people and separation from loved ones can kill. Understanding this biological fact helps us influence others in a powerful way, doesn't it?

Exercise:
Name and explain how numerous products and services are utilizing and/or exploiting this information. (Dating services, 900 lines, Psychic Friends, Chat Rooms, etc. etc.)

Is Your Customer Happy in Her Work?

Did you discover that your client doesn't like her current job? Does she think that her work is important? (This would likely have come up during the values elicitation in the selling process.)

> *If people do not believe their work is important, use this fact as leverage for them to buy your product or service, saving them from physical illness.*

Did you know that if a person doesn't think what they are doing is important, that they are extremely likely to become ill and experience numerous and lengthy illnesses? With the knowledge that this has been pre-programmed into our thinking, this allows the persuader powerful control in any process.

Exercise:
Explain how you can utilize the fact that perceived importance of a person's work is directly linked to illness as a Mind Access Point.

He Seems So Confident

There are no self confident and supremely confident people. In fact, research shows that although we may feel secure, we do not feel extremely self-confident.

Exercise:
How do the world's leading corporate marketers utilize this absolutely critical to sales, Mind Access Point? List numerous examples. Include examples of selling cosmetics, clothing, and automobiles. Isolate the buttons that they push.

Positive Attitude? Here's the Truth for Salespeople

Projecting a positive attitude is not nearly as helpful to the self when contrasted with the great degree that it encourages others. When your customer sees your positive attitude, it gives them optimism and encouragement that you are a good person to be with and buy from. Generating a "positive attitude" is very important to sales success, because it improves the relationship you have with others.

Your Customer Likes some People...
...But not as many as You Might Think

Your customer doesn't like many others in his group. He tolerates them. If your customer is a franchise owner, he probably has a few friends in the same franchise, but not many. Remember this as you are pacing your customer. Just because he owns a McDonald's doesn't mean he likes all the other franchise owners. He probably will be hard pressed to admit this, but just knowing this genetic pre-disposition on your part is enough to save sales for you. Within the group there are various cliques of people. The fact that everyone is in the same high school doesn't mean they will like each other. It means they will all be happy to be rivals against another school but it doesn't in any way imply there will be friendliness within the school.

People tend to form cliques within their own larger groups. They tend to like the people in their clique. They are less interested in other people in the larger whole and they are likely to strongly dislike those in competing groups.

What is even more interesting is how much your customer doesn't like those outside his group. If you are selling insurance to the First Church of God, you will not build rapport by noting how well the First Church of Christ liked you. In fact, you are likely to lose the sale. They are not in the same group. The more intricately they play a role within their own group, the less likely they are to like or even tolerate those in another competing group.

Exercise:
For your product or service, specifically list marketing and sales strategies using only the Mind Access Point listed in this section. How would you sell to a political or religious group? How would you sell to an individual with strong group affiliation?

How the Enemy Makes A Sale for You

When it seems that there is no competitive edge to your product or service, you can utilize a genetic predisposition that was alluded to in the Mind Access Point discussed above. You can assist in creating an enemy to bind people together. The Internal Revenue Service is an enemy that has been able to bind the thoughts of the public together. Our elected officials have done this so we will vote for them. The enemy can be "good" or "evil." Appearances of good and evil are in the eyes of the beholder, of course. McDonald's doesn't like Burger King. Microsoft doesn't like Netscape.

> ***Create or identify an enemy that needs to be fought and then define how you, or, your product or service will help in the fight against the common enemy. An enemy can be a person, a group, a nation, or a non-living thing, like drugs, cigarettes, associations, churches, newspapers, etc.***

How do you utilize this principle of genetics in your favor? President Clinton, in the wake of the Paula Jones/Monica Lewinsky hearings was able to take focus off of himself by finding a common enemy of almost all Americans, Saddam Hussein. The strategy of "talking war" was brilliant as it bound the nation as it did seven years earlier in the Bush administration. The real threat of biological weapons in the hands of Iraq was enough to take Clinton/Lewinsky off of the front page of the newspaper and put Hussein, UN Inspectors and talk of war on the front pages. This created a new perspective in the public's thinking about the significance of the Jones/Lewinsky scandals.

Creating or identifying a common enemy is an excellent tool for building rapport and increasing compliance. If you can assist your customer to become frustrated with the status quo, his likely future, the success of his competitors, he is more likely to act in a positive manner on your request for his compliance.

The concept of using anger, disgust, fear, hatred and negative emotions in effective selling and marketing is as old as monetary exchange. For years we have seen commercials about how disgusting roaches are to have in the house.

We spend billions on security systems every year in America, but only once the customer has experienced through future pacing or in actual case history of his security being violated. People will purchase products to relieve pain, reduce anxiety, be less depressed...and these products go far beyond medications! Some people buy magazines, books, CD's, computer games, Internet services, cars, houses, groceries, all to reduce negative emotions.

Exercise:
Discuss numerous examples of how you can utilize this powerful Mind Access Point with your sales campaigning.

The Have's and The Have Not's

"Money doesn't bring you happiness."
"People care too much about money."
"Money isn't important."
"I don't need things."
"I don't like being around all those control freaks."
"All I need to be happy is..."

When you are selling, you pace the client's actions and beliefs, but, also realize that he is only human and therefore programmed like most other humans. Your customer will often state something that he really doesn't believe, because, he wishes that what he was saying was true.

What are the facts about control, having, and happiness? How do these biological truths relate to your selling your products and services?

> *Control: The more you have, the healthier you are. Control is what keeps you focused and aware. People who experience a great deal of control in their lives tend to be healthier. When people feel in control or they feel your product or service will put them in control they are likely to buy from you now.*

If your customer is to succeed in life and move up the ladder of success and survival, he needs problems, the ability to solve them and the victories that come from defeating his problems. Control is analogous to personal power. Personal power is the ability to take action and achieve. The ability to meet life's challenges head on and win is not only useful in raising self-esteem and self-efficacy but also the general health of your client!

If your product or service will give your customer more control in his life and she realizes it, then she will buy your product. PERIOD. Without control people become hopeless. When people become hopeless you are once again able to help your customer. If your product or service can generate hope, you give new life to your customer...literally. If your customer sincerely believes that your product or service can help him, then you can literally help him change his life.

We need a significant amount of control for happiness. If you can paint a clear picture of how you can help the other person regain control in some area of his life or business, he will buy anything from you.

Exercise:
Hope and control are necessary to the immune system. Assuming the mind/body "knows" this, explain the utter usefulness of this information to the salesperson, the husband, father, and friend...

Who Your Customer Wants to Be Like

In all species, including humankind, the masses are compelled to be like the leader of the group(s). Your appeal to your customer therefore, should in part be one of installing the desire to be like the leaders in his or her field. This could mean being a better parent, a better employee, and a better supervisor. Your job is to show how your products and services help your customer be more like the leader(s) of the group(s) he is most intimately linked to. In general, we imitate our leader's behavior. As a sales person, we therefore want to show how using our products will make the customer more like the leaders.

A Key Male Mind Access Point

Men who are rich in testosterone often find themselves in great trouble or achieving great success. Testosterone inspires confidence and aggression. Most entrepreneurial types tend to be high in testosterone and tend to be confident of their ability to achieve in business and life. Knowing this allows you to pull a useful Mind Access Point. Appealing to the core urges of a man in some manner is useful in awakening his confidence and "go for it" attitudes.

> *Help your client re-experience past victories in any aspect of life and you will probably succeed in creating a "testosterone rush." Linking your product to this rush, will enhance the probability of compliance.*

Testosterone is tied to "winning" in men. An excellent manner of instilling a testosterone rush into men is to have them recount a story of a time when they overcame the odds and "won." This normally creates a testosterone surge in men and builds confidence. By successfully linking this internal state to your product or service you almost assure yourself of making a sale.

Exercise:
Describe at least five methods of subtly linking your products or services to a man's past successes to enhance your probability of making the sale.

See You at the Top

One of my all time favorite self-development books is See You at the Top by Zig Ziglar. When Zig wrote this book he had little if any idea that the book would go on to sell 1.5 million copies. Zig could have predicted such an outcome had he known the genetic draw of humans to gravitate toward leaders in a group. Not only do we want to be like the leader in a group, we want to be *liked* by the leader in a group.

The higher up the ladder a person climbs, the more "friends" a person has. Now, it should be noted that these friends may be "fair weather friends," but clearly those who wish to consider themselves friends of the leaders in groups are far greater than those who dwell near the bottom of the societal ladders.

Therefore you have an opportunity to appeal to an individual's pre-programmed desire to first be at the top of the ladder and second, to be friends of the person at the top of the (or "a") ladder.

You may have the opportunity to share with your customer that if he moves up the ladder in his group that his health will improve. Recent research shows that those who are higher up the "ladder" have less hypertension. Health benefits are going to be a good justification for any action in the 21st century and this is one that is truly worth noting when it ties in with your products and services.

> *People want to either be at the top, be seen with the people on top or be given hope that they may be able to make it to the top. Your product or service should somehow be able to help your client up the ladder.*

Genuinely "Nice"

There are a great number of truly nice people in this world. We have all met a true altruist. This person is willing to give you the shirt off his back and he would literally feel blessed to do so. However, you may be surprised to know that gestures of compassion are not always the result of altruism. In fact, such is not the case, in the majority of situations.

Compassionate gestures help us feel superior, often causing people to look down on benefactors. In fact, not only are those who give doing so for a heightened sense of importance but those on the receiving end rarely gain long term appreciation of those who helped them. Resentment, oddly is often the result.

The greatest example of this Mind Access Point occurs on a macro level. Over the last several decades America has given or loaned numerous countries billions upon billions of dollars. What is the normal attitude of the countries that have been the beneficiaries of these loans and donations? They hate America passionately.

> *When appropriate you may find it useful to appeal to the feelings of strength a person gets from doing "a good thing" in addition to the feeling of "goodness" a person experiences upon helping others.*

The Best of Times...The Worst of Times

When times are relatively good, on average, we are biologically programmed to venture out and increase risk and adventure in our lives. When times are bad, on average, we are likely to play our cards closer to the vest and be much more conservative.

When participating in the sales process it is very useful to know whether your client is going through good times or bad. If she is going through good times you can appeal to her desire to experiment, her need to expand her horizons and explore. If she is going through bad times, you need show how your products will allow her to meet her conservative needs.

The emotional appeal of your product is very important in determining whether you will make the sale or not. People will justify their purchase logically, but first need to fit the product into their emotional filters.

Appeal to your customer's need to take risks and participate in adventure in good times. When experiencing bad times, appeal to your client's needs of security and safety.

The Enhanced 21st Century Covert Hypnosis Model

In Module Four you learned the basics of the 21st Century Covert Hypnosis Model. As you approach the end of this book, you realize that you have gained a greater understanding of your customer, what he needs to be happy and successful, and how he thinks. This provides you the opportunity to begin to integrate all of the Mind Access Points in this book, into your thinking. You are going to soon find the ability to facilitate change in others' thinking and sell virtually at will. In order to accomplish the ability to sell at will, you must be able to develop strategies for selling in 10 key areas of the selling process.

You must develop specific strategies (patterns of behavior) in order to achieve rapport, develop relationships, pull Mind Access strings, change "no's" into "yes's" and close sales. In the next module you will learn the eleven key areas that you will fine-tune in your skills.

Module Thirteen

Ten Powerful Persuasion Strategies...

...for the 21stCentury

These are destined to be the ten keys to persuasion success in the twenty first century.

1. Managing Your State of Mind in All Situations

Your state of mind is one element of the sales process that you have a great deal of control over. Your "state" is generally considered to be made up of three elements, two of which you can control and one of which is difficult to control.

A) *Your Internal Representations*

There is no question that the pictures, words and emotions you experience in your mind, are in large part under your control. If your internal representations are sabotaging you, then you need to take back control of your mind. You must begin to paint new pictures for yourself. Begin to see your life as more likely to succeed. Begin to see yourself as becoming competent in understanding the behavior, actions, and thinking of other people. Realize that as you become effective in understanding the workings of others you become more in control of yourself.

Your Internal Representations include what you say to yourself when you talk. These representations include the tone of voice when you talk to yourself. *If you don't like what is going on in your brain change it now.* You can change the tone of your voice when you talk to you from one that implies, "You Dummy" to one that commands, "You ARE going to Make it BIG!"

When you experience pictures that create a sense of hopelessness immediately change the picture to a struggle that ends with your success instead of failure. Taking an active role in your self-management is very important to your success as a highly effective salesperson.

B) Physiology

Managing your mind is inextricably linked to managing your body. If you are finding yourself to be obese, suffering from aches and pains that can be attended to and notice that your day to day posture and "carrying of yourself" is impotent you must take action to change now.

Overweight? Start a weight reduction program immediately. Your body image directly affects your self-esteem and that means it affects your sales. *Become active and get your body image in line so you are proud of the way you like. How you see yourself impacts your perceived attractiveness by others.*

Do you suffer from pains, aches, and other somatics that can be treated or helped with therapy? Do it! Pain and other somatics reduce your effectiveness and drain you of necessary energy that you need to give to your customers.

Is your posture lousy? Start sitting up straight and walking as if someone has a huge hand pushing your buttocks forward. This will improve your posture dramatically. The way you carry yourself will change many "no's" into "yes's" because many people perceive that a hunched over appearance is indicative of low self confidence. When people think you are not confident it drains their confidence in you as a salesperson and reduces your sales volume.

C) Genetic Factors Can Be Helped Too!

If you suffer from depression, anxiety, panic disorder, and other emotional challenges, talk to your medical doctor and find appropriate medications to help yourself. There is no shame in utilizing anti-depressants and anti-anxiety medications to make up for inefficient neuro-biology. It is very difficult to change your "brain chemistry" in a predictable manner with cognitive techniques alone. Take advantage of the laser beam like medications that are available to help you. Consult your physician. There is ALWAYS something you can do.

2. Managing Your Customer's State of Mind

You can begin to manage other people's minds once you have your own state managed. Managing your customer's states is accomplished in the same manner that you manage your states of mind. The only difference is that you must pull your customer's Mind Access strings instead of pulling your own.

A. Internal Representations

If your client needs to experience a brief dose of status quo misery to help him change to a brighter future, then you are obligated to paint a vivid picture of both what he must move away from and what he must move toward. Make the voices he is going to hear in his mind clear and loud. Help him feel the pain of stasis and the pleasure of change if he can't do it for himself.

B. Physiology

Sometimes it is necessary to get your client to move to create internal change his state of mind. Hand him something. Give him a book and have him turn the pages. Ask your client to participate in some activity with you. DO SOMETHING with your client. You are not obligated to always sit face to face, across the table from each other.

If your client is in a "stuck state," the sale is going to be lost if you don't change his state. Sometimes it is appropriate to get up and go or at least move somewhere else. Changing your client's physiology will change his internal state.

C. Appeal to You Client's Genetic Makeup

You have learned in this book dozens of genetic traits and pre-programmed tendencies. Utilize this information by practicing the strategies necessary to pull the genetic Mind Access strings that you have learned about.

3. Gather, Manage and Implement Intelligence

Eliciting values, beliefs, and feelings, is a method of gathering vital intelligence about your customer. The best salespeople gather intelligence about their customers before they meet, if possible. In this book you have learned about personality and buying types and who buys based upon what metaprograms. That is intelligence. There is more to be learned, however.

If you are selling to corporations, you can uncover everything from corporate earnings to corporate strategy by simply making phone calls to the company and asking before you go on your visit. Learn what you can about the needs, interests and wants of the company.

Secretaries are a fountain of knowledge. One of my favorite selling strategies is to not try and bypass the secretary but instead, make friends with her.

"Hi Jane, this is Kevin Hogan, the author of The Psychology of Persuasion. Does your boss decide what speakers to bring into your corporation or is that someone else I should talk to?"

"Once I get him on the phone, what does he look for in a good speaker?"

"Does he really go for motivational speakers or those who present more practical applications in sales and marketing?"

"What was your favorite speaker in the last year or two?"

"What was his favorite speaker in the last couple years?"

This gathering of intelligence is powerful. In this example you are speaking with the secretary who is indeed the gatekeeper in the corporate world. Instead of passing by the gatekeeper you have made friends by asking for her opinions and building a sense of respect for her and her knowledge about what her company likes. This is how you want to gather intelligence beyond the more general buying profiles we discussed earlier in the book.

4. Networking Your Way to Sales Success

Networking only works if you have at least one of three things. You are the best in your business, you have great products and/or you have great services. If you can meet someone's needs time and again then you can network your way to sales success.

One rule that is constructive to keep in mind is to do something to help someone else's career every day. If you can help others with their families, businesses, careers, you will eventually reap the rewards of what you have sown.

Networking is more than keeping a fat Rolodex. Networking is the ability to recommend someone who can solve someone else's problem. People appreciate you when you help them and have nothing to gain in return.

Assist people every day with random or intentional acts of kindness and you will build a network of friends and people who will help you in your future. It is almost impossible to help people every day and not experience the rewards of networking down the line.

Networking also demands that you have the courage to call the people who can make a difference in your career. Many people will not call on the right person to buy or even for advice simply because they believe the celebrity won't talk to a humble salesperson. This is nonsense. 10-20% of celebrities, CEO's, and even political leaders are attainable. If what you have to offer is useful enough, you can get your minutes with the biggest decision makers.

Be willing to be bold and occasionally embarrassed in exchange for the benefits of being known by the "right people."

5. Be a Hunter

The world's greatest salespeople don't simply sit back and wait for business to come to them. The world's greatest become adept at hunting for those who will buy your products and services. Business *is always* good for someone. Business can almost always be good *for you.*

One distinction between those who have great success in sales and those who are work-a-day salespeople is the hunter mentality. The hunter is always looking for people he can help. The hunter is relentless in the pursuit of the right groups and markets for his products and services. The hunter doesn't rely on lead sources from inside the company. The hunter is constantly developing his own contacts.

People who succeed in multi-level marketing are those who see opportunity for almost everyone they meet. This doesn't mean the hunter is pushy or involves people in a project that won't be in the individual's best interest. It does mean that a hunter will always be aware of people's needs and desires.

The hunter always goes the extra mile. When you go the extra mile you always have more opportunities for success than the average salesperson. Going the extra mile can mean asking for referrals or better, asking who else will definitely benefit from an outstanding product or service. The hunter is always bending over backwards to help others. The hunter is generally thought of as "lucky" because they seem to regularly be meeting opportunity with preparation, one definition of luck.

6. Building Credibility with Your Clients

When communicating with your clients, is it apparent that you have their best interests in mind? If you have any doubt that you are not selling a great product or a great service you must choose a product or service that is great to sell. If you are selling yourself as a consultant, then you must be the best. You must constantly go the extra mile to make yourself part of the top 20%. This is where credibility begins.

An excellent manner of establishing credibility is that of being able to bring out the key drawback of your product or service and make certain that your customer sees that one flaw. Once you have done this you have not only established credibility but you have already dealt with what is normally the only objection to your making the sale, except money issues, which may or may not be easily solved.

Remember the call letters: WII-FM. They stand for "What's in it for me?" If you can put yourself in your customer's shoes and answer that question with a laundry list of benefits, you will begin making more sales, higher volume sales and a higher percentage of sales.

How do you appear less than credible on occasion?

Sometimes we get nervous in the sales process that our product may not be the best for our client and we continue to sell anyway. It is at this point that you must ask your customer, "If this product could only help you to this certain degree at this price, is it something that would be really useful to you?"

If they say "yes," you can allow the pangs of nervousness to leave. If they say "no," then forget making the sale. You could still choose to pull all the right Mind Access strings, walk away with a check, but you will have created a Win-Lose, and that means your career will take a step backward. *Never, ever, enter into any sales transaction where one party loses.*

Creating beliefs (i.e.. levels of certainty) is critical. If you expect to fail you probably will. If you expect to succeed you probably will. What you say to yourself in private is what you become. Begin to see yourself as a provider, a helper, a caretaker, and a creator of value. If this isn't possible, you are selling the wrong product.

You will have a difficult time selling a particular make of cars if you don't believe that they are the best cars, for the money in the country. Believe it or move to a different dealership. Refuse to sell what is second best. Never compromise your integrity. People will talk about you and believe in you if you are the best, selling products that have great value. Once you are selling something you believe in, your enthusiasm will be contagious.

Your potential in selling, and that of all of your competitors is correlated to beliefs. These beliefs fall into two distinct categories. First, ethical selling demands that you believe in your idea, product, service, etc. Second, it must be evident that you KNOW that you are creating value by partaking in the sales process. If you feel tainted by selling then consider how your customers will feel if they are buying someone else's products and services. Are your customers going to be buying second best if someone else goes to see them? Don't let it happen.

Being believable is about being congruent. Remember when Kathleen Willey appeared on 60 Minutes in 1998 and clearly but emotionally told of her encounter with President Clinton at the White House? American believed her because she was congruent. She was perceived as congruent because what she said matched with how she said it. Her verbal communication matched her non-verbal communication. She was, believable.

Once you reach the point that you are congruent with what you are persuading another to, you will be unstoppable.

Exercise:
Name some congruent people? Describe specifically why you believe these people to be congruent.

Name some incongruent people? Describe specifically why you believe these people to be incongruent.

What can you do so you stay in the category of congruent people?

If you are not perceived as congruent and believable you will not make the sale. If you are perceived as believable and you sell excellent products and services, you will be on the road to success in selling. Your enthusiasm about the home you are selling, the stocks you are touting, the automobiles your customers are going to drive away in, is all going to be transferred to your customer like a mind virus. (A meme)

Your level of certainty, combined with pure rapport, and meeting their true wants and needs, allows you to sell at will.

7. Develop a Sense of Fascination

Decide that you will learn everything about your customer that she is willing to comfortably share with you. Develop a sense of fascination about the work and livelihood about others. What is grand about your customer? What is great about their job? What is fascinating about their philosophy of life? Allow yourself to become curious and excited about learning about other people and their interests. Remember that what is interesting to you is likely to be boring to most other people. What is interesting to your customer, on the other hand, is something he can talk about for hours on end. Your customer's interests become your new areas of fascination and curiosity.

8. Change the Frame

Everyone looks at "things" from their own point of view, from their own perspective. Key number eight, will help you learn how to alter the way someone is looking at something so you can alter how they feel about that self same "thing." Framing is analogous to what light you are going to place a communication in. What may seem to be a disaster for a client, can be re-framed as being an opportunity for change and growth. What may be seen as the end of a long sad marriage could be re-framed into the beginning of a new happy life.

Reframing

Reframing is taking lemons and then upon further review, you make lemonade out of the lemons you have been given. Reframing allows you to help someone see something they perceive as a problem that really may be an opportunity in disguise. Read the examples below then write out common objections to your products and services and "reframe" them so you never have to think about doing this "on the spot."

Example: If you are working with "big picture people," you will now see the value of framing (creating an areas of focus) "things" in a manner where they are small and barely worth consideration or where they are large and life changing.

"You know John, I realize that $197 per year for life insurance doesn't seem to be much to think about, but, it really is important that you do this now, because of the un-predictability of life and death."

or

"You know John, I realize that $18 per month can be seen as quite a bit of money, yet, that is why you MUST decide to do this. If anything happens to your wife will have a check for $100,000 waiting for her to take care of your kids. What greater gift can you give?"

Obviously frames help us see an issue from a different point of view than the one we just saw. Frames are used in Hypnotherapy and NLP to enhance and control the communication process. (Erickson, Rossi, Bandler, Grinder, Robbins, et. al.) Here are a few different kinds of frames and how to utilize them in putting your products and services, and, yourself in the best light possible with your clients.

The "As If" Frame

Have you ever had a client that said, "I don't know what will happen if..." It may be that you have heard something like, "I don't know what my wife would say if I..."

When you face these unknowns the most effective strategy is to utilize the "As If" Frame. You can utilize this them by asking one or more of these three pattern questions.

If you did this X, what would happen?

Imagine that we were successful at X, then what would happen?

If you did decide to do "this" (agree to "this") what was it that would have changed your mind?

These patterns are so powerful that normally the customer's objection or worry will be drained right from his mind as he answers the question.

Preframing

You will recall that pointing out a minor flaw in your product or company can be a very useful tool in the sales process. It gives you immense credibility. Always, always, handle the problem that is likely to come up, in advance of the problem (objection/perceived, argument, obvious other point of view). Deal with any challenge early in the sales meeting while the significance of any issue will be considered to be very small and seemingly irrelevant.

Persuasion and Influence is in large part an issue of controlling the frame of communication. You must realize that unless a person dismisses you out of hand, that they see something they like about your offer. Therefore control that frame, that focus of attention and key in on this area. Therefore in any disagreement, argument, objection you must change the focus of attention of the other person or people.

Example:
"Mind Access may not be the ideal weekend sales and persuasion course for you. It is possible that you will consider the price tag of $1,000 too great an investment in return for control of your life and a dramatic near term increase in income. Mind Access is about people who want to be happy, in charge of their lives and their communication. Mind Access is for people who want to be influential because they offer something unique to the world. If this isn't you, then simply don't come."

Deframing

Jim Pickens, the author of the most powerful sales book in history, "Closers," calls deframing, the "take away close." Once you are skilled in Mind Access techniques you will have the confidence and ability to prudently utilize deframing.

Deframing is a linguistic tool that can only be effectively implemented when you know a person's match/mis-match meta program, or, when you know the person definitely wants your service, product or offer. In a nutshell, you give the customer one opportunity to purchase your product or hire you. If they don't, you make it explicitly clear that you will move on and allow others to take advantage of your services.

This is the basic deframing pattern:

"It makes no difference to me whether you buy this X or not. You have until tomorrow to make a decision and reserve your X or not. If I don't hear from you by noon, I'll know you didn't want it. No pressure. Bye."

8. Uncover Conditions to Confirmation

Even the greatest product in the world may not be able to help a person with a condition. You may be able to sell a $300,000 home at half price to an owner occupant, which is a bargain anyone is unlikely to ever experience. But if your client doesn't have the money for the down payment and hasn't got the income, resources or ability to sign the loan for other reasons you have a condition and you should never ask a person to enter into an agreement where he will lose. Value is very important but it is not the only element in deciding whether to make a sale or not. If the client cannot do something, don't ask them to. A condition exists in some selling situations, which means a sale won't be made, and when they do exist, you won't let that sale happen. It's a Win-Lose.

If you sense your customer has a condition, simply ask, "Is there something I'm missing, that I should know about that is causing you to wonder about this product?" If they respond with a concern, address their concern and let them own your product. If they respond with a condition, don't let them buy your product. There will be another day for both of you.

9. Develop a Series of Logical Reasoning

People will buy your products and services based upon their desires in most cases. You need to develop a step-by-step process that will assist your client to bridge the gap between emotion and logical reasoning to purchase your product. You should have several series of thought processes that you have prepared for your client to consider.

If you are selling a home and your client has the requirements met to buy the home you have a potential sale. If your client falls in love with the home you have an emotional sale. Your job is now to move your client from emotional thought to logical justification for purchasing this home.

How can you go from logical to emotional?

First you can ask if this is a home they would really love to live in. An affirmative response leads you to your next thought, which is,

"Are you aware that every dollar you spend on your monthly house payment works for you in one way or another? Either it goes toward the principle which means the *money comes back to you* or you can use the rest of the payment as a tax deduction which means *some of the money comes back to you.* When you pay rent, all of the money goes away from you, down the toilet, flushed into the sanitation system forever. The question is, do you want to own a home or do you want to make someone else wealthy, instead of developing your own wealth, for the rest of your life?"

You move from an emotional response to a logical rationale to an integration of emotions and logic. This is ethical, it is honest and it is in the best interest of your client if no conditions exist.

10. Know When to "Close" and When to Leave

Most salespeople believe that you "close" the sale after the sales presentation is over. That is not correct. You close the sale the moment the customer wants to buy and not a second later. When the customer is ready, you let them agree to buy your product. You have them sign the papers, take ownership and shortly thereafter, you leave. If the customer asks you for a lunch date, that is one thing. If they are busy and have a schedule to keep, make the sale happen and then politely but with efficiency wrap up your business. In many cases, I have made the sale, had the client write a check, put it away in my briefcase and then had lunch with the client. In situations such as this you do not discuss your business, you continue to develop the long-term friendship by focusing on the client and his loves and interests.

In general, when your client is non-verbally or verbally telling you they want to hire you or they want your product, let them buy it now. Then, after you have taken care of business, take care of any post-closing activities and thank your new customer.

It's my hope that this massive volume on persuasion, covert hypnosis and subtle influence will be used with ethical intent. These are the secrets of unconscious communication and they will change your life.

Bibliography

Allesandra, Tony and Michael J. O'Connor. The Platinum Rule: Do Unto Others As They'd Like Done Unto Them. New York, NY: Warner Books, Inc., 1996.

Anastasi, Tom. Personality Selling, Selling the Way Clients Want to Buy. New York, NY: Sterling Publications, 1992.

Andreas, Steve and Charles Faulkner. NLP: The New Technology of Achievement. New York, NY: William Morrow and Company, 1994.

Aronson, Elliott. The Social Animal. New York, NY: W. H. Freeman and Company, 1995.

Bagley, Dan and Edward J. Reese. Beyond Selling: How To Maximize Your Personal Influence. Cupertino, CA: Meta Publications, 1988.

Bandler, Richard & John LaValle. Persuasion Engineering. Capitola, CA: Meta Publications, 1996.

Bethel, William. 10 Steps to Connecting With Your Client: Communication Skills for Selling Your Products, Services, and Ideas. Chicago, IL: The Dartnell Corporation, 1995.

Bloom, Howard. The Lucifer Principle: A Scientific Expedition Into the Forces of History. NY. Atlantic Monthly Press, 1995.

Brodie, Richard. Virus of The Mind: The New Science of the Meme. Integral Press. 1996.

Brooks, Michael. Instant Rapport: The NLP Program the Creates Intimacy, Persuasiveness, Power! New York, NY: Warner Books, Inc., 1989.

Brooks, Michael. The Power of Business Rapport: Use NLP Technology to Make More Money, Sell Yourself and Your Product, and Move Ahead in Business. New York, NY: Harper-Collins Publishers, 1991.

Buzan, Tony and Richard Israel. Brain Sell. Brookfield, VT: Gower, 1995.

Cialdini, Robert B. Influence: The New Psychology of Persuasion. New York, NY: Morrow, 1993.

Cohen, Allan R. and David L. Bradford. Influence Without Authority. New York, NY: John Wiley & Sons, 1991.

Dalet, Kevin with Emmett Wolfe. Socratic Selling: How to Ask the Questions that Get the Sale. Chicago, IL: Irwin Professional Publishing, 1996.

Dayton, Doug. Selling Microsoft, Sales Secrets from Inside the World's Most Successful Company. Holbrook, Mass. Dayton, 1997.

Dawson, Roger. Secrets of Power Persuasion: Everything You'll Ever Need to Get Anything You'll Ever Want. Englewood Cliffs, NJ: Prentice-Hall, Inc., 1992.

Decker, Bert. You've Got To Be Believed To Be Heard: Reach the First Brain to Communicate in Business and in Life. New York, NY: St. Martin's Press, 1992.

Elgin, Suzette Haden. Success with the Gentle Art of Verbal Self-Defense. Englewood Cliffs, NJ: Prentice-Hall, Inc., 1989.

Farber, Barry J. and Joyce Wycoff. Breakthrough Selling: Client-Building Strategies from the Best in the Business. Englewood Cliffs, NJ: Prentice-Hall, Inc., 1992.

Gitomer, Jeffrey. The Sales Bible: The Ultimate Sales Resource. New York, NY: William Morrow, 1994.

Grinder, John. The Structure of Magic, Vol 1. Palo Alto, CA: Science and Behavior Books, 1976.

Hamer, Dean. Living With Our Genes: Why They Matter More Than You Think. NY. Doubleday, 1998.

Hogan, Kevin. (Audio Program) Mind Access: Beyond the Psychology of Persuasion. Network 3000 Publishing, Eagan, MN: 1997.

Hogan, Kevin. (Video Program) Persuasion Mastery Course, Network 3000 Publishing, Eagan, MN: 1997

Hogan, Kevin. Life By Design: Your Handbook for Transformational Living. Network 3000 Publishing, Eagan, MN. 1995

Hogan, Kevin. The Psychology of Persuasion: How to Persuade Others to Your Way of Thinking. Gretna, LA: Pelican Publishing Company, 1996.

Hogan, Kevin. Through the Open Door: Secrets of Self Hypnosis. Gretna, LA: Pelican Publishing Company, 2000.

Johnson, Kerry L. Sales Magic: Revolutionary New Techniques That Will Double Your Sales Volume in 21 Days. New York, NY: William Morrow and Company, Inc., 1994.

Johnson, Kerry L. Subliminal Selling Skills. New York, NY: AMACOM, 1988.

Keirsey. David and Marilyn Bates. Please Understand Me: Character & Temperament Types. Del Mar, CA: Prometheus Nemesis Book Company, 1984.

Kennedy, Daniel S. The Ultimate Sales Letter. Holbrook, MA: Bob Adams, Inc., 1990.

Kent, Robert Warren. The Art of Persuasion. Surfside, FL: Lee Institute, 1963.

Knapp, Mark and Judy Hall. Nonverbal Communication in Human Interaction. 3rd Ed. Fort Worth, TX: Harcourt Brace College Publications, 1992.

Knight, Sue. NLP at Work: The Difference That Makes A Difference in Business. Sonoma, CA: Nicholas Brealey Publishing, 1995.

Kostere, Kim. Get the Results You Want: A Systematic Approach to NLP. Portland, OR: Metamorphous Press, 1989.

Lavington, Camille with Stephanie Losee. You've Only Got Three Seconds: How to Make the Right Impression in your Business and Social Life. New York, NY: Doubleday, 1997.

Lewis, David. The Secret Language of Success: Using Body Language to Get What You Want. New York, NY: Carroll & Graf, 1990.

Linden, Anne with Kathrin Perutz. Mindworks: Unlock the Promise Within — NLP Tools for Building a Better Life. Kansas City, MO: Andrews McMeel Publishing, 1997.

Mehrabian, Albert. Silent Messages: Implicit Communication of Emotions and Attitudes. Belmost, CA: Wadsworth, 1981.

Moine, Donald J. and John H. Herd. Modern Persuasion Strategies: The Hidden Advantage in Selling. Englewood Cliffs, NJ: Prentice-Hall, Inc., 1984.

Moine, Donald J. and Kenneth Lloyd. Unlimited Selling Power: How to Master Hypnotic Selling Skills. Englewood Cliffs, NJ: Prentice-Hall, Inc., 1990.

Nicholas, Ted. Magic Words That Bring You Riches. Indian Rocks Beach, FL: Nicholas Direct, 1996.

Overstreet, H. A. Influencing Human Behavior. New York, NY: Norton, 1925.

Patton, Forrest H. Force of Persuasion: Dynamic Techniques for Influencing

People. Englewood Cliffs, NJ: Prentice-Hall, Inc., 1986.

Piirto, Rebecca. Beyond Mind Games: The Marketing Power of Psychographics. Ithaca, NY: American Demographic Books, 1991.

Peoples, David. Selling To The Top.New York, NY: John Wiley & Sons, Inc., 1993.

Qubein, Nido. Professional Selling Techniques: Strategies and Tactics to Boost Your Selling Skills and Build Your Career. Rockville Centre, NY: Farnsworth Publishing Co., Inc., 1983.

Richardson, Jerry. The Magic of Rapport. Capitola, CA: Meta Publications, 1988.

Robbins, Anthony. Unlimited Power. New York, NY: Fawcett, 1987.

Robertson, James E. Sales the Mind's Eye: What They Didn't Teach You In Sales Training. Portland, OR: Metamorphous Press, 1990.

Sadovsky, Marvin C. and Jon Caswell. Selling the Way Your Client Buys: Understand Your Persons' Unspoken Needs & Close Every Sale. New York, NY: AMACOM, 1996.

Solderholm, Craig E. How 10% of the People Get 90% of the Pie: Get Your Share Using Subliminal Persuasion Techniques. New York, NY: St. Martin's Press, 1997.

Stiles, William H. Hypno-Salesmanship: The Suggestive Art That Helps People Buy. New Castle, PA: Bill Stiles Associates, 1996.

Thompson, George J. and Jerry B. Jenkins. Verbal Judo: The Gentle Art of Persuasion. New York, NY: William Morrow and Company, Inc., 1993.

Tracy, Brian. Advanced Selling Strategies: The Proven System of Sales Ideas, Methods, and Techniques Used By Top people Everywhere. New York, NY: Fireside, 1995.

Vitale, Joe. Cyber Writing: How to Promote Your Product or Service Online. New York, NY: AMACOM, 1997.

Vitale, Joe. The Seven Lost Secrets of Success. Houston: VistaTron, 1994.

Willingham, Ron. The Best Seller: The New Psychology of Selling and Persuading People. Englewood Cliffs, NJ: Prentice-Hall, Inc., 1984.

For More Information

Get your Free Copy of Kevin Hogan's 163-page e-book, **Mind Access**! Learn how to ask just two questions and know someone's buying profile! This is some of the finest material ever written about influence and persuasion!

And as a super bonus gift, get Kevin's 179 page e-book, **Breaking Through the 8 Barriers of Communication**. You'll discover the 8 ways to avoid turning people off and instead, build powerful LASTING rapport. A full length book!

And.... the gift that keeps giving, a one year subscription to *Coffee with Kevin Hogan,* the e-zine that everyone reads about influence, selling, body language and personal development every Monday morning. Go to http://www.kevinhogan.com/bonus.htm today!

Printed in the United States
58917LVS00006BB/48